T0334843

NEBRASKA'S BUCKS AND BULLS

The Greatest Stories of Hunting
Whitetail, Mule Deer, and Elk
in the Cornhusker State

Joel W. Helmer | *Foreword by Randy Stutheit*

UNIVERSITY OF NEBRASKA PRESS   LINCOLN

Chapter 23, by Dick Idol, originally appeared
as "How the No. 1 Buck by Bow was Bagged,"
North American Whitetail 10, nos. 1 and 2
(January and February 1991): Part 1, January,
52–55; Part 2, February, 52–59. Chapter 60 first
appeared in *Legendary Hunts: Short Stories
from the Boone and Crockett Awards* (Missoula
MT: Boone and Crockett Club, 2006).

Publication of this volume was
assisted by Concordia University.

Library of Congress
Cataloging-in-Publication Data
Names: Helmer, Joel W., author.
Title: Nebraska's bucks and bulls: the
greatest stories of hunting whitetail, mule
deer, and elk in the cornhusker state / Joel
W. Helmer; foreword by Randy Stutheit.
Description: Lincoln: University of
Nebraska Press, [2020] | Includes
bibliographical references and index.
Identifiers: LCCN 2020001625
ISBN 9781496212818 (paperback)
ISBN 9781496223142 (epub)
ISBN 9781496223159 (mobi)
ISBN 9781496223166 (pdf)
Subjects: LCSH: Hunting—
Nebraska—History—20th century. |
Hunting—Nebraska—History—21st century.
Classification: LCC SK101 .H45 2020 |
DDC 639/.109782—dc23 LC record available
at https://lccn.loc.gov/2020001625

Set in Sabon Next by Mikala R. Kolander.
Designed by N. Putens.

This book is for Nebraska hunters, past and present,
who have done so much to preserve and protect
wildlife, habitat, and our hunting traditions.
And especially for my beautiful daughter Hannah,
whose state-record elk was the inspiration to
write this book.

The story is as important as the hunt.

Contents

Foreword by Randy Stutheit xi

Acknowledgments xiii

Introduction xv

PART 1. TYPICAL WHITETAIL DEER

1. Barn Find: The John Harvey Buck, 1963 3

2. Hold Low: The Bob Vrbsky Buck, 1978 6

3. Next Generation: The Kyle Newcomb Buck, 2016 11

4. Platte River Giant: The Vernon Virka Buck, 1983 15

5. Deer Drive: The Greg and Mike Hansmire Bucks, 1996 and 2006 . . . 22

6. Handgun: The Jerry Lauby Buck, 1983 26

7. Back-to-Back Booners: The Adam Zutavern Bucks, 2009 and 2010 . . 30

8. Father and Son: The Frosty Adams Buck, 2000 36

9. Trifecta: The James Hamick Bucks, 2007 and 2008 40

10. Giant of the Bohemian Alps: The Kevin Petrzilka Buck, 2010 45

11. Perfect Eight: The John Woloszyn Buck, 1994 51

12. Missouri River Breaks: The Keith Fahrenholz Buck, 1966 56

13. Plane Crash: The Keith Houdersheldt Buck, 1985 61

14. High Five: The Kevin Wood Buck, 1999 64

PART 2. NON-TYPICAL WHITETAIL DEER

15. Kitchen Window: The Peggy Easterwood Buck, 2018 69

16. Twenty-Five Points: Hunter Unknown, 1990 73

17. Pocket Cover: The Jon Allen Buck, 2007 76

18. Talk of the Town: The Robert Snyder Buck, 1961 80

19. Records Are Made to Be Broken: The Wesley O'Brien Buck, 2009 . . . 84

20. Like Father, Like Son: The Gary and Adam Stohs
Bucks, 1994 and 2015 88

21. Crossbow: The Bob Malander Buck, 2017 95

22. 2 County: The Jeff Moody Buck, 2003 99

23. Ol' Mossy Horns: The Del Austin Buck, 1962 105
Dick Idol

24. Spider and Double Down: The Rachel Kechely and
AJ Ahern Bucks, 2016 116

25. Midday: The Kellen Meyer and Jordan Owens Buck, 2010 122

26. Double Drop Tine: The Bill Klawitter Buck, 1963 127

27. Public Land: The Dave Oates Buck, 1985 131

28. Working Man: The Jack Grevson Buck, 1962 134

29. Spanky: The Spanky Greenville Collection 137

30. Goliath: The Jacob Gipson Buck, 2017 144

31. Buck Jam: The Dan Boliver Buck, 1996 148

PART 3. TYPICAL AMERICAN ELK

32. That Guy: The Russel Coffey Bull, 2018 155

33. Family Affair: The Dillon Mortensen Bull, 2017 158

34. Flip of the Coin: The Curtis James Bull, 2015. 163

35. Imperial: The Jason Mosel Bull, 2015 166

36. Wildcat Hills Wapiti: The KC Merrihew Bull, 2014. 170

37. Bull with a Bow: The John Rickard Bull, 2017 174

38. Thank God He Made It: The Doug Correll Bull, 2014 179

39. First Bull: The Warren Chapin Bull, 1986. 185

40. Pine Ridge: The Robert Marsteller Bull, 2004 190

41. Center Pivot: The Chuck Anderson Bull, 2016. 194

PART 4. NON-TYPICAL AMERICAN ELK

42. Perfect Hunt: The Hannah Helmer Bull, 2016. 201

43. Drought and Fire: The Casey Yada Bull, 2012. 207

44. 400 Club: The Justin Misegadis Bull, 2017 212

45. Elk Hunter: The Frank Meyers Bull, 2016. 216

46. Meadow Monarch: The Dana Foster Bull, 2008. 220

PART 5. TYPICAL MULE DEER

47. Houdini: The Michael Dickerson Buck, 2018. 227

48. Brow Tines: The Terry Sandstrom Buck, 1968 231

49. The Stalk: The Kirk Peters Buck, 1989. 236
   Kirk Peters

50. Symmetry: The Brent Klein Buck, 1984 241

51. Deer Hunting Comes to Frontier County: The Henry
   Koch Buck, 1960. 246

52. Forgotten: The Clarence Dout Buck, 1949 249

53. Western Adventure: The James Skorzewski Buck, 1965 252

54. In Memoriam: The James Pavelka Buck, 1957 255

PART 6. NON-TYPICAL MULE DEER

55. Rearview Mirror: The Barry Johnson Buck, 1992 261

56. Wrong Buck: The Eric Johnson Buck, 2017 265

57. Full Velvet: The Mike Lutt Buck, 2014 270

58. HisStory: The Art Thomsen Buck, 1960 275

59. Making Headlines: The Bill Glenn Buck, 1963 279

60. A Hunting Tradition: The Charles Hogeland Buck, 1994 283
   Charles J. Hogeland

61. Tough as Nails: The Dave Davis Buck, 1961 288

62. The Little Girl with a Spoon: The Delman Tuller Buck, 1965 292

63. Working Cattle: The Matthew Lake Buck, 2017 298

64. Nebraska's Oldest Trophy: The R. A. Wirz Buck, 1945 302

65. Better Late Than Never: The Leo Dwyer Buck, 1959 306

66. 30 S 10 W: The Jack Kreycik Buck, 1963 310

67. Dreaming about Nebraska: The Paul Mecouch Buck, 2007 313

68. So Much Horn: The Ken Hollopeter Buck, 1979 318

Notes 323

Index 327

Foreword

Randy Stutheit

Nebraska enjoys a rich heritage of big-game hunting with established seasons for whitetail and mule deer, pronghorn antelope, American elk, and bighorn sheep. That we are able to experience the thrill of hunting for these species in our state is a testament to the success of modern-day wildlife management and regulated hunting.

After a slow but steady recovery of the state's deer herd from unregulated hunting in the nineteenth and early twentieth centuries, the first modern deer season was held in 1945 with a harvest of 275 mule deer and two whitetails from the Nebraska National Forest near Halsey. Since then deer hunting has become a treasured tradition enjoyed by countless hunters who over the years have harvested more than two million whitetail and mule deer in Nebraska.

In addition to both species of deer, Nebraska now also enjoys a hunting season for American elk. At one time elk were mostly extirpated from Nebraska, but by the 1970s a resident herd became established near Chadron in the northwest corner of the state. Eventually, as the population continued to increase, landowner complaints concerning elk damage to crops and fences led to Nebraska establishing its first modern-day elk hunt in 1986. Today the population estimate for the state averages around 2,500 elk.

In 1962 Nebraska introduced the state's Big Game Trophy Records Program utilizing the trophy scoring system established by the Boone and Crockett Club in 1950, the organization that maintains records of all North American big-game trophies. Nebraska trophies meeting the state minimum scores established for firearm, archery, muzzleloader, and crossbow are entered into the records, and certificates are issued to the owners. Currently there are thirty-two categories of trophies in the Nebraska records book based on species, type of rack, and method of take. These records are a documentation of the success of big-game management in Nebraska.

As the current director of the Nebraska Big Game Trophy Records Program, I am excited about the publication of this book. It represents the first comprehensive effort to compile the records, photos, and stories surrounding some of Nebraska's finest deer and elk trophies. Those represented in this book span decades of successful big-game hunting. The stories told by the hunters present a fascinating history of deer and elk hunting through those decades. Joel Helmer is to be commended for his passion and dedication to authoring *Nebraska's Bucks and Bulls*.

Acknowledgments

I express my gratitude to Randy Stutheit for providing office space, access to the Nebraska Big Game Trophy records books, and leads on potential trophies; to Julie Tripp at the Boone and Crockett Club; to the Pope and Young Club for providing the Nebraska trophy list; and to Concordia University, Nebraska, for financial support. Special thanks to Megan Boggs for helping in numerous ways and to Laurie Zum Hofe for her encouragement. Thanks also to Robert Taylor and everyone else at the University of Nebraska Press for seeing the value in this project and making the book writing process enjoyable.

I especially want to thank my wife, Holly, for patiently listening to my incessant book talk and for being an amazing hunter's wife.

Introduction

In September 2016 fourteen-year-old Hannah Helmer peered through the spotting scope, trying to focus on the giant bull elk herding his harem of cows down into a pine tree–rimmed valley in far northwestern Sioux County. Seeing the bull clearly, she whispered, "Dad, he's huge." The following morning, on opening day of the firearm season, Hannah found that same bull moving up and out of the valley, bugling and chasing smaller satellite bulls away from his cows. Later, with the bull bugling right at her, Hannah made the shot, taking down the 426⅞-inch bull, one of the largest non-typical American elk ever shot in North America.

Two years later, on the diagonally opposite end of the state in the rolling hills of southeastern Richardson County, sixty-five-year-old Peggy Easterwood glanced out the kitchen window of her farmhouse and spotted a giant non-typical whitetail walking across her alfalfa field. Grabbing the binoculars she keeps handy for just such an occasion, she watched the massive buck breed a nearby doe. "I knew right away he was a monster . . . and I knew where I would be hunting the next week," remembers Peggy. Indeed a week later, after watching the buck step from the thick oak and red cedar forest bordering the edge of that same alfalfa field, she dropped the buck with a single shot from her Browning .243. After walking up on the massive buck, Peggy knelt down, crying and counting points. Her thirty-point buck scoring 235⅛ inches is currently the ninth-largest non-typical ever killed in the state, and the largest ever by a woman.

In early September 2018 Michigander Michael Dickerson was hunting Houdini, an incredibly tall and wide typical mule deer that made its home in the Badlands of northwest Nebraska. Knowing Houdini was so named for his propensity for disappearing into the wide-open grasslands, gullies, and ravines of northern Sioux County, Mike knew everything had to go perfectly for him to get within bow range. After spotting the buck in the early morning and watching it bed down, he began a three-hour stalk, eventually closing the distance to just over fifty yards. Pulling back his bow, Mike thought to himself, *This is the opportunity you have been waiting for your whole life, take a deep breath and aim small.* His arrow found the buck's vitals, and after going a short distance it fell dead on a sagebrush-and-cactus-covered hillside. Mike's 197⅛-inch typical broke the Nebraska archery state record that had stood for twenty-nine years.

These three excerpts encapsulate not only the diversity and quality of big-game hunting in Nebraska but also the wonderful variety of natural landscapes we have to hunt in. Sometimes wrongly overlooked as a trophy big-game state, Nebraska's unique geography creates a diversity of eco-regions producing some of the largest whitetail, mule deer, and elk found in North America. This is why big-game hunting in Nebraska has a long and rich tradition and is still one of the state's most popular and economically important pastimes. In fact the single largest sporting event in the state each year is deer firearm season, when a Sea of Blaze Orange, numbering well over one hundred thousand, takes to the field, eclipsing the Sea of Red at Memorial Stadium. This book tells the hunting stories and shares the photographs of some of Nebraska's greatest big-game trophies while weaving in a good bit of geography, history, and ecology.

Being a passionate hunter for over forty years and an official Boone and Crockett Club (B&C) and Pope and Young Club (P&Y) measurer, I understand how important stories and storytelling are to those of us who hunt. It is not only how we reminisce and relive our own adventures; it is how we connect with others, especially other hunters. As I often say, trying to tell a hunting story to a nonhunter is difficult, much different than sharing it with another hunter. Hunters get other hunters. That said, storytelling still bonds us with our nonhunting friends, but more so with our children, spouses, and relatives.

Collecting and writing these Nebraska hunting stories also preserves them. Many stories are from decades ago and over time can fade from memory, change, or if never written down disappear altogether when the hunter passes away. Therefore this book is essentially a historical archive, preserving stories and pictures for future generations who can learn from them, share in the excitement, and appreciate more fully the wonderful history of hunting in Nebraska.

Knowing what I know about hunting stories made writing this book challenging. I have tried my best to tell each story as accurately and completely as possible. To limit mistakes I collected most of the stories through face-to-face interviews, although a few people sent them via email, regular mail, or shared them over the telephone. Regardless I am certain I made mistakes or omissions in relation to details or timelines. For this I apologize; it was unintentional.

Finally, as a professional geographer, researching and writing this book gave me a newfound appreciation for Nebraska and Nebraskans. I traveled thousands of miles collecting stories from thirty-nine counties, driving down roads I had never driven and through countless small towns I had never visited. From the Missouri breaks to the sagebrush-and-yucca-sprinkled hills west of McCook, through the Sandhills to the Badlands of Sioux County, across the flat expanse of the Platte River valley to the rugged buttes of the Wildcat Hills, there was one constant: welcoming, friendly people. They invited me to dinner, shared their cold beer, offered access to their hunting lands, and most importantly were willing and eager to share their stories.

I hope you enjoy the stories as much as I enjoyed collecting and writing them.

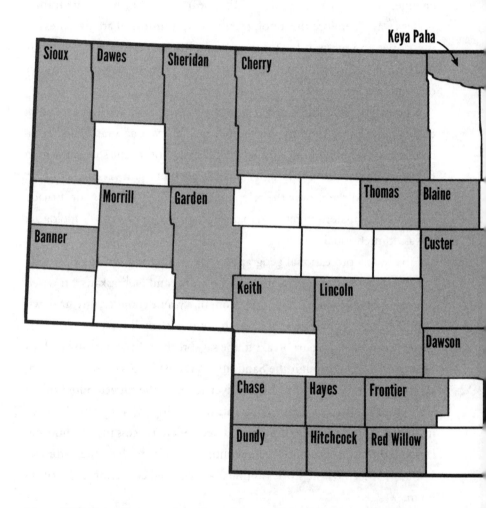

Map 1. The Nebraska counties where these hunting stories unfolded.

NEBRASKA'S BUCKS AND BULLS

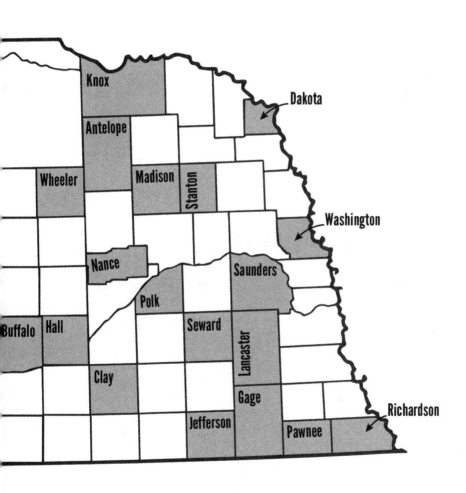

PART 1
Typical Whitetail Deer

1

Barn Find

The John Harvey Buck, 1963

· 196⁴/₈-inch typical

· Antelope County

For John Harvey 1963 was a very good year. One evening while roller-skating at the Plainview Roller Rink, he met a pretty young girl from Illinois who was in town visiting relatives. Later that year he married her. Afterward John and his bride Betty moved onto the family dairy farm near Orchard, Nebraska.

In early November John decided to go deer hunting with his father, something he had never done before. On that fateful hunt, in the fall of 1963, he would shoot the only deer of his life—a massive state-record buck that some believe is the most beautiful typical whitetail ever shot in North America.

Sitting with Betty Harvey in her home in Hastings, I could sense the memories for her are still sharp. "I was just a city girl who married a farmer," she says with a chuckle. Living on the same farm for fifty-three years, she knows dairy farmers seldom take a day off work. "At that time John was just too busy working to go deer hunting. But one day he just came in and said, 'I think I'll go hunting with my dad.'"

On November 7, dressed in his work clothes and carrying a .30-30 rifle borrowed from his brother-in-law, John and his father made their way along a neighbor's creek bottom north of their farm. With sunlight fading, John stood leaning against a tree, scanning the creek bottom for movement.

FIG. 1. John Harvey with the only deer he ever shot—a state record. Photo courtesy of Betty Harvey.

Appearing suddenly over a small knoll, he saw a good-sized buck walking straight toward him. Snapping the rifle to his shoulder, he squeezed the trigger. The buck spun, white tail bounding back down the trail. Thinking he missed, John followed the trail anyway. He found the buck lying dead sixty feet from where he shot it.

Hauling the deer back home, John and his father found some rope and hoisted the gutted deer by its antlers into a tree near the farmhouse. "When he came home that night, he brought that big old deer with him and said, 'This is the only one I got,'" remembers Betty with a shake of her head. "At the time, he didn't know that it was a trophy; he just thought it was a nice buck." Fortunately Betty ran into the house to retrieve her "little Kodak camera," snapping several pictures of John standing next to the hanging buck. After cutting up the meat and sawing off the antlers, it was back to work.

The following year John went deer hunting one last time, helping his father bag a small buck. Meanwhile the giant six-by-six rack from his buck was largely forgotten, left to hang, unmounted, on a wall of the barn. It sat collecting dust for seventeen years!

In 1980 a cousin noticed the rack hanging in the barn and encouraged John to get it officially scored. Heeding his cousin's advice John took the rack into Lincoln, to the Nebraska Game and Parks Commission (NGPC) headquarters. "John bet the men at the Game and Parks some cake that it would beat the state record. And it did," remembers Betty.

The John Harvey buck is a truly spectacular, clean six-by-six. Both main beams eclipse twenty-five inches, with an inside spread of over twenty-one inches. The ten scorable points include brow tines of over seven inches and all four G2 and G3 points over eleven. However, the symmetry is what makes it such a stunning trophy. The buck grosses 202⁶/₈ inches and nets 196⁴/₈ inches, equating to only 6²/₈ inches of total deductions.

After hanging in the barn for seventeen years, John's buck became the Nebraska firearm typical state record, replacing the 194¹/₈-inch Keith Fahrenholz buck from 1966. "After we had it scored we put it on the wall in the house and used it for a hat rack," shares Betty. The buck stills stands as the third-largest typical in the Nebraska records book.

"After it became the state record, guys would ask if they could come by and see it. And the phone just kept ringing with people offering to buy it," remembers Betty. The Harveys did eventually sell the rack to someone from the Y.O. Ranch in Texas. "I asked John what happens if the guy's check bounces after you ship the rack. Come to find out, the man owned the bank down there in Texas, so we didn't have to worry about that!"

2

Hold Low

The Bob Vrbsky Buck, 1978

- 189⁴/₈-inch typical
- Buffalo County

Trophy rooms hold something priceless—memories. The walls of seventy-four-year-old Bob Vrbsky's modest-sized basement in Kearney are covered with a lifetime of outdoor memories: big-game heads, waterfowl and fish mounts, awards, knives, feathers, and countless pictures.

Being in the room stirs Bob's memories, and he begins telling stories. He shares the story of arrowing a P&Y black bear in Canada, the full body mount in the center of the room providing a perfect prop. Then the stories of arrowing a bull elk from a tree stand in Colorado, and how his daughter shot the impressive Nebraska whitetail buck mounted on the far wall.

Reaching the far end of the basement, Bob pauses and points, "There he is." Hanging in the corner is one of Nebraska's longest-standing state records, the massive 189⁴/₈-inch typical Bob arrowed in the fall of 1978. Pointing again, Bob says, "And that's the bow I shot him with." Reaching up and carefully taking the recurve down from its nails, he brushes off the dust and reads aloud the two words scrawled in bold letters on the riser: "HOLD LOW. I sometimes would shoot over deer, so I took a black marker and wrote that on my bow as a reminder," explains Bob with a grin.

Coming of age in the 1950s, Bob grew up like many other Nebraskans of his generation, fishing and hunting small game, pheasants, and waterfowl. "I was raised on it. My dad began leasing property on the Platte River soon after moving to Kearney. I grew up out there. We leased that ground for fifty years, with my own kids growing up out there as well," recalls Bob.

In the early 1960s Bob began hunting deer with a bow, something quite rare for the time. "I don't really remember why I started bowhunting, probably because it gave me a longer season," explains Bob. The equipment we associate with bowhunting today—compound bows, electronic rangefinders, mechanical releases, and illuminated sights—is a far cry from the simple gear Bob carried into the woods. With the first compound bow not patented until 1969, hunters were carrying bows similar to Bob's Pearson recurve and shooting wooden arrows with finger releases. "I practiced a lot with my bow, but it took me six or seven years to finally kill my first buck. It was a little fork horn, but I was thrilled," remembers Bob. "In those days I would shoot just about any buck for the meat."

And it was meat that paid the bills. After high school Bob went to work in a meatpacking plant, spending the next forty-five years in the meat business. While working at the Kearney Locker, he would process as many as two hundred deer in a season. "I was foolish enough one year to offer to cut up someone else's deer at home for a small fee. After working all day cutting meat, I would come home and cut up meat," Bob shares.

Although a self-described meat hunter, he eventually sought the challenge and reward of taking mature bucks. To make that happen Bob and his longtime hunting partner and family friend Steve Trybus began paying more attention to scent control and wind direction. They also began venturing deeper into the Platte River bottoms. "The more we hunted, the farther back into the river we went," recalls Bob. "Those big bucks get out on those islands and become nocturnal, only leaving at night to wade the channels to feed on corn."

During the 1977 rifle season Bob shot his first records book buck, a beautiful 175⅝-inch non-typical. With that success fresh in his mind, he began the 1978 season hoping to finally arrow a mature buck. On the evening of

FIG. 2. Bob Vrbsky with his long-standing 189⅛-inch state-record typical he shot with a longbow. Photo courtesy of Bob Vrbsky.

November 4, with rifle season only a week away, Bob waded across multiple river channels to reach his tree stand on a large island. "That evening I got into my stand, which was just a couple of boards nailed across the crotch of a tree about fifteen feet in the air. I noticed Steve in his stand about one hundred fifty yards to the west," remembers Bob.

A doe soon appeared from the east, making its way toward Bob's stand. "I wanted to start duck hunting, so that doe was looking pretty darn good. At the time you were only allowed one deer, and I decided to shoot her if she came close," shares Bob with a smile. Readying his recurve Bob watched the doe walk into some thick cedars to the north and, fortunately for him, never offer a clean shot.

Shortly thereafter Bob spotted movement from the same direction the

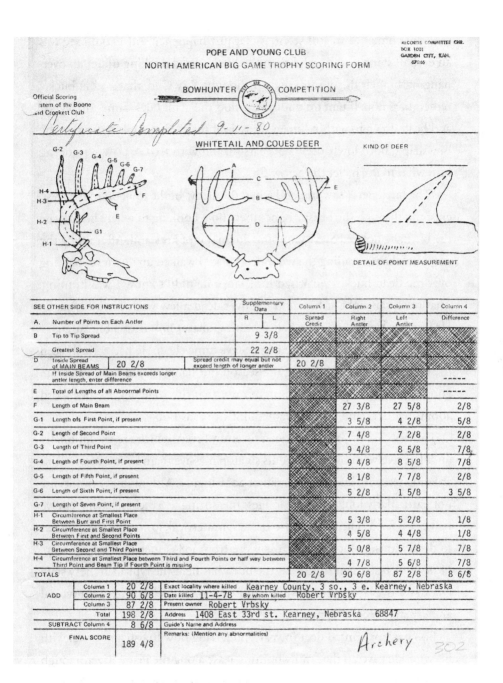

POPE AND YOUNG CLUB

NORTH AMERICAN BIG GAME TROPHY SCORING FORM

RECORDS COMMITTEE CHR.
BOX 1001
GARDEN CITY, KAN.
67846

BOWHUNTER COMPETITION

Official Scoring System of the Boone and Crockett Club

Certificate Completed 9-11-80

WHITETAIL AND COUES DEER

KIND OF DEER

DETAIL OF POINT MEASUREMENT

SEE OTHER SIDE FOR INSTRUCTIONS		Supplementary Data R	L	Column 1 Spread Credit	Column 2 Right Antler	Column 3 Left Antler	Column 4 Difference
A.	Number of Points on Each Antler						
B	Tip to Tip Spread	9 3/8					
	Greatest Spread	22 2/8					
D	Inside Spread of MAIN BEAMS 20 2/8	Spread credit may be equal but not exceed length of longer antler		20 2/8			
	If Inside Spread of Main Beams exceeds longer antler length, enter difference						-----
E	Total of Lengths of all Abnormal Points						-----
F	Length of Main Beam				27 3/8	27 5/8	2/8
G-1	Length of First Point, if present				3 5/8	4 2/8	5/8
G-2	Length of Second Point				7 4/8	7 2/8	2/8
G-3	Length of Third Point				9 4/8	8 5/8	7/8
G-4	Length of Fourth Point, if present				9 4/8	8 5/8	7/8
G-5	Length of Fifth Point, if present				8 1/8	7 7/8	2/8
G-6	Length of Sixth Point, if present				5 2/8	1 5/8	3 5/8
G-7	Length of Seven Point, if present						
H-1	Circumference at Smallest Place Between Burr and First Point				5 3/8	5 2/8	1/8
H-2	Circumference at Smallest Place Between First and Second Points				4 5/8	4 4/8	1/8
H-3	Circumference at Smallest Place Between Second and Third Points				5 0/8	5 7/8	7/8
H-4	Circumference at Smallest Place between Third and Fourth Points or half way between Third Point and Beam Tip if Fourth Point is missing				4 7/8	5 6/8	7/8
TOTALS				20 2/8	90 6/8	87 2/8	8 6/8

ADD	Column 1	20 2/8	Exact locality where killed Kearney County, 3 so., 3 e. Kearney, Nebraska
	Column 2	90 6/8	Date killed 11-4-78 By whom killed Robert Vrbsky
	Column 3	87 2/8	Present owner Robert Vrbsky
	Total	198 2/8	Address 1408 East 33rd St. Kearney, Nebraska 68847
SUBTRACT Column 4		8 6/8	Guide's Name and Address
FINAL SCORE		189 4/8	Remarks: (Mention any abnormalities) Archery 302

FIG. 3. Bob Vrbsky scoresheet. It is especially rare to see the G6 line filled out on a scoresheet since this signifies a seven-by-seven typical. Courtesy of the Pope and Young Club.

doe had come. "I can still see it as if it just happened. All I could see was an eyeball staring at me, and then the buck's head ducking under an overhanging branch thirty yards away. I thought, 'My God, that's a big buck,'" remembers Bob. Intent on trailing the doe, the giant buck came stiff-legged and head down to within fifteen yards. Feeling his finger tab resting on the bowstring, Bob slowly drew his Pearson, and with HOLD LOW reminding him what to do, he let the arrow fly.

"The buck never saw me, and when the arrow hit he took off to the west, crashing through the brush," remembers Bob. Looking to where he last saw the buck, he noticed Steve climbing down out of his stand. After doing the same Bob began trailing the wounded buck. "I walked up on Steve standing over the dead buck. I surprised him, since he didn't know I was hunting. That buck ran right at him and fell over dead a few yards from his stand. He was wondering who the hell shot him," shares Bob with a big laugh.

While admiring the massive buck, Steve came clean. He had actually seen the buck several times during the season but had not told Bob. "We were good about sharing information. But not that time. He never said a word about that deer, and I don't blame him," explains Bob.

The Bob Vrbsky buck is a clean seven-by-seven, which are exceptionally rare. The twelve measurable points sit atop massive main beams of 27⅜ and 27⅝ inches, with an inside spread of 20⅔ inches. Although the points are not particularly long, with the longest measuring 9⅛ inches, having twelve makes up for it. The buck is also quite symmetrical, losing only 8⅝ inches to deductions, reducing the gross score from 198⅔ inches to a final score of 189⅞. A testament to its size, the buck has held the typical archery state record for over forty years, a span eclipsed only by Del Austin's non-typical archery state record from 1962.

Bob has not hunted deer in years, preferring now to fish and travel with his wife. He gave up the family hunting lease along the Platte River, a tough decision he sometimes still regrets. But he will always have something no one can take away—his memory of wading into the Platte River to arrow one of Nebraska's greatest whitetails.

3

Next Generation

The Kyle Newcomb Buck, 2016

· 190⅛-inch typical
· Hitchcock County

It is comforting to know there are still young men who love to hunt. We hear so much about the impending demise of hunting, how we are losing our American hunting traditions. The numbers are disturbing. Hunting peaked in 1982, when nearly seventeen million hunters purchased licenses.[1] Since then it has been a slow, steady decline, with only eleven million hunters taking to the field in 2016. Currently only about 5 percent of Americans ages sixteen years and older hunt. Why the decline? The causes are many and complex, but changing demographics, declining rural populations, changing attitudes about wildlife, cost, access to land, and increasing screen time are but a few.

However, it's not all doom and gloom. There are still many young, passionate hunters out there, keeping the hunting tradition alive in Nebraska and across the country. Young men like Kyle Newcomb.

Born in 1997, Kyle grew up hunting pheasants, geese, and deer with his father, Doug, in southwestern Nebraska's Hitchcock County. In this area you have a choice, hunt mule deer in the more open country or chase whitetails in the thicker creek drainages. Kyle became a mule deer hunter. "I have shot some pretty nice mule deer north of Stratton but never a whitetail. So when I didn't draw a mule deer tag in 2016, I didn't know what I was going to do," shares Kyle.

While talking with his boss's son, Kyle found out they had been getting trail camera pictures of a nice buck living along the Republican River. Making a last-minute decision, Kyle purchased a statewide whitetail buck tag and then went to the Orscheln store and bought a two-person ladder stand. "The night before the season started, we went in and set up that tree stand. We even took a leak on the tree," Kyle remembers with a grin.

The next morning, with the temperature hovering in the low twenties, Kyle sat shivering in the darkness, holding his Remington 700. As the sky slowly lightened and shapes and colors came into focus, he noticed a massive rub on a cedar tree thirty yards in front of his ladder stand. Sitting near a slough on the river, the area around him was a tangle of cedars, brush, and cottonwoods. In front of the stand was a small clearing—the spot felt good.

"Just after sunrise I heard a noise, and I see a doe walk out twenty yards from my stand. And right behind her was the biggest whitetail buck I had ever seen," recalls Kyle. "When I saw how big he was I started shaking."

With the buck intent on trailing the doe, Kyle quickly shouldered his .30-06 and found the buck's vitals in the crosshairs. "By the time I got the rifle up, he was forty yards away, but at that distance all I saw in the scope was deer," laughs Kyle. With the buck now quartering slightly toward him, Kyle settled the crosshairs as best he could and sent a bullet into the buck. Instead of running, the buck slowly walked away and bedded down behind some trees. Through his scope Kyle could see the buck lifting and lowering his massive rack.

Hearing the gunshot from his stand about one hundred yards away, Kyle's hunting partner soon arrived to see what had happened. The two slowly made their way toward the massive buck. "I thought the buck was down for good, but when we got to about twenty feet of him, he jumped up and ran straight away from us. It really surprised us," remembers Kyle. Fortunately, after running about one hundred yards, the buck paused broadside near a pile of dead cedars. Kyle's next shot dropped the buck for good.

"I thought it was a really nice buck when I first saw it, but I didn't think it was that huge. Later that day I took it to my taxidermist who green-scored it at 203 inches. That's when I realized how big he was," shares Kyle.

FIG. 4. Kyle Newcomb posing with his giant 190⅛-inch Republican River six-by-six. Photo courtesy of Kyle Newcomb.

The Kyle Newcomb buck is one of only a handful of Nebraska typicals to gross over 200 inches. The buck is a clean six-by-six with a 22⅛-inch inside spread and main beams measuring 28⅝ and 28⅛ inches. The brow tines are exceptional, with both measuring over seven inches. The rest of the points form a "picket fence" of tines, with five of these measuring over ten inches. Although quite symmetrical, the G5 point on the left side is over four inches shorter than the right, accounting for much of the 13⅝ inches of total deductions. With a net score of 190⅛ inches, it currently ranks as the seventh-largest firearm typical in the Nebraska records book.

4

Platte River Giant

The Vernon Virka Buck, 1983

- 199^2/$_8$-inch typical
- Saunders County

Overshadowed by the likes of Mark Twain and Will Rogers, Edgar Wilson "Bill" Nye was one of the most popular American humorists and authors of the late 1800s.[1] His critique of the Platte River, usually condensed to "a mile wide and an inch deep," is part of our national lexicon, often used in describing shallow thinking.

Nye accurately described the Platte River of his day. A classic braided stream, it was wide and shallow, with multiple channels creating a maze of ever-shifting sandbars. Intense flooding was commonplace, sweeping away any plants seeking a tenuous roothold on the sandbars or along the banks. Sandhill cranes, piping plovers, least terns, and millions of other waterfowl used the open sandbars to rest and roost.

Then came the dams. Seven reservoirs on the North Platte and four on the South Platte altered the hydrology of the entire basin by limiting flooding and reducing the amount of sediment carried downstream. Coupled with diversions for irrigation, there was now less water, less sediment, and less flooding. The Platte River slowly changed, cutting fewer but deeper channels, allowing grasses and other early successional plants to encroach on the sandbars. Mature stands of cottonwood, elm, and willows soon followed, with a brushy understory of red cedar, dogwood, chokecherry, sumac, and wild plum. Perfect whitetail habitat.

Over time the Platte River floodplain became a three-hundred-mile-long trophy deer corridor, accounting for many of Nebraska's greatest bucks. Del Austin arrowed Ol' Mossy Horns, his legendary 279⅞-inch state-record non-typical in 1962—on an island in the Platte River. In 1978 Bob Vrbsky killed his 189⅜-inch state-record typical—on an island in the Platte River. Finally in 1983 Vernon Virka shot his long-standing 199⅜-inch state-record typical—in the floodplain of the Platte River.

Now seventy-five years old, Vernon Virka sits in his living room south of Morse Bluff on a cool spring morning reminiscing about life, farming, and the buck that cemented his name into Nebraska's deer hunting lore. "My father passed away when I was only a year old. I didn't have anyone to teach me how to hunt. I just went by myself, taught myself. I grew up hunting small game and then ducks on the Platte River," remembers Vernon. "I think my first deer hunting season was about 1970. I shot my first deer in the Sandhills with my lever-action .250-3000 Savage. It's the only rifle I've ever shot."

During the 1970s Vernon shot multiple deer, including some decent bucks. But nothing even remotely close to the giant buck he would shoot in the fall of 1983. That hunt began with rumors. Rumors of an incredibly symmetrical and long-beamed buck living in the Platte River bottoms near Morse Bluff. Fortunately for Vernon, people were seeing the buck only a couple miles from his house, sometimes on land where he had multiple deer stands. "The school bus driver told me that he would see the buck about every morning. Other people had seen him too. I never did until hunting season," recalls Vernon.

The first five days of the rifle season were uneventful, despite Vernon taking off from his farmwork to sit mornings and evenings. "It was getting toward the end of the season, and it was raining. I wasn't sure if I wanted to go but decided to give it a shot anyway," remembers Vernon. Grabbing his Savage, he jumped into his pickup and drove to get Ed Virka, his uncle and hunting partner. The two made the short drive to the Platte River for a late afternoon hunt.

FIG. 5. Vernon Virka grasping the unbelievably massive rack of his 199⅞-inch state-record typical. Photo courtesy of Vernon Virka.

After dropping Ed off, Vernon parked the truck and began walking toward his stand, Savage rifle in one hand and a thermos of coffee in the other. In the distance he could see the plywood platform. "I had just nailed a piece of plywood up about ten feet high in a cedar tree. It was the only good tree around," remembers Vernon. Although not much to look at, it was his favorite stand, situated along a travel corridor between a winter wheat field and the thick, brushy cover along the river.

With rain slowly soaking into his jeans, Vernon sat shivering while scanning the thick river bottom for movement. After thirty long minutes he watched as a doe and fawn made their way toward the wheat, followed shortly by another doe. That doe spotted Vernon and began head bobbing and foot stamping while staring directly at him. After a tense stare-down the doe silently slipped away toward the wheat.

Soon after, a slight movement caught Vernon's attention. "The buck came in behind me, only twenty-five yards away. When I turned he was rubbing on a cedar with his antlers, but I really couldn't see his rack," remembers Vernon. Slowly raising the lever-action, he settled the crosshairs on the buck's chest and squeezed the trigger. The buck dropped.

With darkness closing in, Vernon climbed down from his stand and headed toward the dead buck. Suddenly the buck jumped to its feet and ran, quickly disappearing into the thick undergrowth. Reaching the spot where the buck had been lying, Vernon found nothing. No blood, no hair, nothing!

Following the trail the buck had run down, Vernon found no blood. After searching for a considerable distance and still finding no sign, he figured his shot had only grazed the buck. Deciding he should go and get Ed before it was dark, Vernon walked quickly toward his pickup. Circling a large cedar tree, he saw the giant buck lying on the ground, staring right at him! He finished the hunt with one last shot from his Savage.

The first thing Vernon noticed about the buck was the size of its body. Later weighed at over two hundred forty pounds field dressed, the buck's massive body made the rack seem deceptively small. Tying a rope around the buck's antlers, Vernon and Ed dragged the massive buck through the rain to the truck. "I didn't really think too much about the rack, more about the fact that it took two of us to get him in the truck bed. When we finally got him in, his horns stuck up above the side. Then I knew he was big," recalls Vernon with a smile.

Hauling the buck back to the farm, they hung it from the barn rafters and snapped some pictures. Like many hunters at that time, Vernon was concerned far more about the meat than the rack. He never even considered mounting it, and instead cut off the rack with a saw and put it in the shed. "The horns were getting all dusty and the mice were chewing on them," remembers Vernon. Fortunately a neighbor noticed the antlers hanging in the shed and convinced Vernon to get the rack officially measured. Incredibly, the buck was the new Nebraska state record, while falling only inches short of a world record!

The Vernon Virka buck is one of the greatest typical five-by-five bucks ever shot in North America. The main beams are simply amazing, with both

FIG. 6. Vernon Virka admiring the matching 31⅞-inch main beams of his Platte River buck. Photo courtesy of Vernon Virka.

measuring exactly 31⅞ inches, accounting for over sixty-three inches of antler! They currently rank as the ninth-longest whitetail beam lengths in the B&C records book. The rack is also exceptionally wide, with an inside spread of 24⅛ inches. Point length is excellent, with the G2 points measuring 15⅝ and 14⅛ inches, while the G3 points are both over a foot long. Extremely symmetrical as well, the buck grosses 204⅞ inches and nets 199²⁄₈.

The buck easily broke the Nebraska state record of 196⁴⁄₈ inches held by the John Harvey buck from 1963. If not for a shorter G4 point on the right side, it would have been a new world record typical. The right G4 point measures 3²⁄₈ inches compared to 6⅞ inches on the left side. Without this

3⅝-inch deduction, it would have broken the 206⅛-inch world record, then held by the famous James Jordan buck from Wisconsin. The James Jordan buck, although no longer the world record, is still the only typical five-by-five in the B&C records book larger than the Virka buck!

After word got out, antler collectors and reporters were soon contacting Vernon about his state-record buck. *North American Whitetail* magazine co-founder and writer Dick Idol wrote an article about the buck for the July 1986 issue. Vernon later leased the rack to Dick and eventually lost track of it entirely. The B&C now lists Brad Gsell as the owner.

Vernon still often drives the few miles of Highway 79 from his farm through Morse Bluff and into North Bend. While crossing the Platte River floodplain, he often looks eastward, remembering that cool, rainy November day when he killed one of North America's greatest typical whitetails.

OFFICIAL SCORING SYSTEM FOR NORTH AMERICAN BIG GAME TROPHIES Scored 4-3-84

Records of North American Big Game

BOONE AND CROCKETT CLUB

205 South Patrick Street OCT 31 '84
Alexandria, Virginia 22314

1st ~~#27~~ 1992 Saunders 1983 Vernon Virka Morse

Minimum Score: 112
whitetail 170
Coues' 110

TYPICAL
WHITETAIL AND COUES' DEER

Kind of Deer whitetail

#1

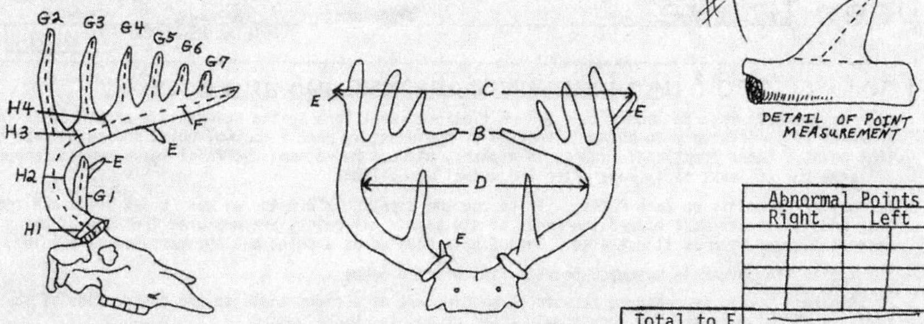

Abnormal Points			
Right	Left		
Total to E			

SEE OTHER SIDE FOR INSTRUCTIONS			Column 1	Column 2	Column 3	Column 4
A. Number of Points on Each Antler	R. 5	L. 5	Spread Credit	Right Antler	Left Antler	Difference
B. Tip to Tip Spread		12 —				
C. Greatest Spread		27 2/8				
D. Inside Spread of Main Beams 24 4/8	Credit may equal but not exceed length of longer antler		24 - 4/8			
E. Spread exceeds longer antler, enter difference. Total of Lengths of all Abnormal Points						—
F. Length of Main Beam				31 - 1/8	31 - 1/8	—
G-1. Length of First Point, if present				5 —	5 - 4/8	— 4/8
G-2. Length of Second Point				15 —	14 - 4/8	— 4/8
G-3. Length of Third Point				12 3/8	12 - 2/8	— 1/8
G-4. Length of Fourth Point, if present				3 3/8	6 - 7/8	3 - 5/8
G-5. Length of Fifth Point, if present				—	—	—
G-6. Length of Sixth Point, if present				—	—	—
G-7. Length of Seventh Point, if present				—	—	—
H-1. Circumference at Smallest Place Between Burr and First Point				5 - 3/8	5 3/8	—
H-2. Circumference at Smallest Place Between First and Second Points				4 - 7/8	5 —	— 1/8
H-3. Circumference at Smallest Place Between Second and Third Points				5 - 4/8	5 6/8	— 2/8
H-4 Circumference at Smallest Place between Third and Fourth Points (see back if G-4 is missing)				4 - 6/8	5 2/8	— 4/8
TOTALS			24 - 4/8	88 —	92 3/8	5 - 5/8

ADD	Column 1	24 - 4/8	Exact locality where killed ~~1.5 East of Morse Bluff~~ Saunders County Nebraska
	Column 2	88 —	Date killed 11-18-83 By whom killed Vernon Virka
	Column 3	92 3/8	Present owner Same
Total		204 7/8	Address Morse Bluff Nc, 68648
SUBTRACT Column 4		5 5/8	Guide's Name and Address None
FINAL SCORE		199 2/8	Remarks: (Mention any abnormalities or unique qualities) OK 142

FIG. 7. Vernon Virka scoresheet. The 3⅝-inch difference between the two G4 measurements kept this buck from being a world record. Courtesy of the Boone and Crockett Club.

5

Deer Drive

The Greg and Mike Hansmire Bucks, 1996 and 2006

- 203$^{2}/_{8}$-inch non-typical and 187$^{2}/_{8}$-inch typical
- Jefferson County

On the second day of the 1996 rifle season, Greg Hansmire stood behind an oak tree, his thumb tucked through the thumbhole stock of his .30-06, scanning the thick timber along Buckley Creek. Greg knew this piece of bottom ground well, including how the deer reacted and where they ran when pressured. A quarter mile up the creek, his thirteen-year-old son Mike and the other hunters in their party were working their way slowly down the drainage, hoping to push a buck his way.

Spotting a flash of brown, Greg watched as a doe popped out of the brush, followed by another, then another, and another. After watching eight does move past his tree, Greg caught a brief glimpse of antlers. "He let all those does go first, and then he peeked out and then went back in. When he couldn't take it any longer, he went," remembers Greg.

Greg knew immediately the buck was a shooter, and wasting no time he tucked the butt plate of his right-handed bolt-action rifle into his left shoulder and found the buck in the crosshairs. "My first shot killed him, but I was taught to keep shooting until they drop," explains Greg. After four quick shots the giant non-typical tumbled dead into the leaves. "Dad never takes that gun off his shoulder when he's shooting. With that thumbhole

FIG. 8. Greg (*left*) and Mike Hansmire with Greg's 203⅞-inch non-typical. Photo courtesy of Greg Hansmire.

stock, he just keeps cycling the action and pulling the trigger," shares Mike. "The guys ribbed me that it sounded like I was shooting a semi-auto," Greg adds with a laugh.

Having never seen this buck before, Greg and Mike were amazed at the buck's antlers and body size. An extremely old buck with a gray Roman nose, it was later aged at between nine and eleven years old. The buck's typical six-by-six frame grosses 186⅞ inches and nets 181⅛, with an inside spread of over twenty inches. With six abnormal points totaling 21⅝ inches, the buck scores 203⅜ inches as a non-typical.

Greg shot his records book buck using one of the oldest and most effective methods of hunting whitetails—the deer drive. Driving game animals like deer, bison, antelope, or wild boar over cliffs, into rivers, or toward human blockers has been in use for thousands of years. Why? Because it works. "We always sit on opening day, but the next day we post blockers and the others push through the timber," shares Greg. "I'll go on record that my dad never walks. Me and the younger guys were always the walkers," Mike shares with a grin toward his dad.

Ten years after Greg shot his buck, Mike found himself once again pushing the same stretch of timber along Buckley Creek. With Greg and another hunter posted as blockers, Mike and two others made their way down the drainage. With his .270 resting in the crook of his arm, Mike walked slowly, scanning ahead for signs of movement. He knew from experience that bedded deer often hold tight, bursting out unexpectedly at the last second.

"We came to this little finger of cover, and all of a sudden I see a couple does take off about one hundred yards away. Then I saw another deer, and horns, and I just lifted my rifle and shot," recalls Mike. The offhand shot sent the bullet through the buck's neck, dropping it instantly. "Shooting them in the neck is like throwing them off the courthouse. Instantly dead," notes Greg.

"I knew he was a good deer when I saw him running but didn't think he was that big. My dad's buck was on the wall outside my bedroom, so growing up I always knew what a big buck looked like," shares Mike. "After everyone arrived they began slobbering over the buck. That is when I knew he was big."

FIG. 9. Mike Hansmire holding his enormous Jefferson County six-by-six. Photo courtesy of Mike Hansmire.

The Mike Hansmire buck is definitely slobber-worthy. The buck's symmetrical six-by-six typical rack grosses an amazing 203⅞ inches. The main beams measure 27⅜ and 26⅞ inches with an inside spread of over twenty-one inches. Mass is impressive, with seven of the eight circumference measurements over five inches. With six abnormal points totaling 11⅛ inches, the buck nets 187²⁄₈ inches, making it currently the eleventh-largest firearm typical in the Nebraska records book.

"Mike and I shot these two bucks on our ground, about two hundred yards apart," says Greg proudly. "My grandfather homesteaded this place we are sitting on. I remember as a kid back in the early 1960s, that if you saw a deer it was a big deal." Talking with them you realize how important hunting their own land is to the Hansmire family. And you can bet that next deer season they will once again post blockers and begin another push down Buckley Creek.

6

Handgun

The Jerry Lauby Buck, 1983

· 180⁴/₈-inch typical
· Dawson County

Jerry Lauby could not believe his eyes as he watched the same symmetrical and incredibly high-racked ten-point buck he saw on opening morning trail a doe directly toward his tree stand. Only twenty-four hours before, this same giant whitetail snuck to within fifty yards before catching Jerry's scent and crashing off into the thick undergrowth along the Platte River.

"Of course after opening morning I thought I would never see him again, especially not from the same stand," recalls Jerry. As the buck and doe crept closer Jerry had a decision to make: reach for the obvious choice, his .25-06 rifle, or for the s&w Model 28 handgun resting on his hip. Slowly cocking the hammer back, he lined up the giant buck in the iron sights of his .357 Magnum revolver.

Jerry credits the U.S. Army for turning him into a handgun nut. Although he now owns multiple handguns, it wasn't until he traveled from his boyhood home near Lexington, Nebraska, to Fort Gordon, Georgia, for military training in 1966 that he became enamored with pistols. Assigned to a company of nearly four hundred service members training to become military policemen, he spent a lot of time sending bullets down range through an

M1911 semiautomatic. "At the end of our thirteen weeks of training we fired for record, and out of the entire company I scored second," Jerry proudly shares.

After completing training, Jerry was stationed in Germany at Landstuhl Regional Medical Center near Ramstein Air Base, witnessing firsthand the thousands of wounded service members arriving daily from war-torn Vietnam. "I was fortunate; they sent me to Germany instead of Vietnam. I still feel somewhat guilty about that," says Jerry.

After serving his country, Jerry returned to Lexington and began operating a truck wash along newly completed Interstate 80. Although he grew up hunting pheasants and quail, and eventually became an avid waterfowler, it wasn't until the fall of 1976 that he began deer hunting. He did not waste much time getting into the records book.

His first trophy buck, a 153⅝-inch typical whitetail, came the following year as the sun was setting on the last day of rifle season. He shot another state citation buck in 1980, a beautiful 156⅝-inch typical. Despite these early successes he still considered himself a rather "green" deer hunter, often taking the first buck he saw. "I found myself wanting more of a challenge and setting my sights a little higher," remembers Jerry.

That is when Jerry started thinking about deer hunting with a handgun. He purchased the aforementioned Model 28 revolver, aka the Highway Patrolman, and began practicing regularly. Chambered in .357 Magnum, it was the most powerful handgun available until the debut of the .44 Magnum. Although Jerry was using a powerful cartridge, the factory ammo available at the time did not meet the legal requirement for deer hunting, which mandated four hundred foot-pounds of energy at fifty yards. "Fortunately I was friends with Bob Thompson, a state trooper from the area, and we struck a deal. Since I was a Federal Firearms License holder, I could get him the reloader he wanted at cost. In return he'd load me some hot .357 loads so I could deer hunt," explains Jerry.

Jerry was soon entering his deer hunting haunts along the Platte River with both his rifle and the Model 28. He knows the area well, with some of the land being in the family for well over one hundred years. Stretching nearly a mile along the banks of the Platte River in Dawson County, it contains thick bottomland cover, protective islands, and bordering croplands.

All conducive to growing monster whitetails. "I've never shot a deer outside the river bottoms," Jerry confesses.

Although his hunting land currently has fourteen different deer stands, with most being manufactured ladder stands, on November 11, 1983, Jerry quietly made his way into the river bottom toward one of his handmade stands. "Back in those days you nailed up a couple two-by-fours and laid a piece of plywood between them," explains Jerry. After climbing up he sat with anticipation in the cool air, legs dangling over the plywood platform. Then the buck appeared.

Attentive to the doe he was trailing, the buck came to within thirty-five yards, but sensing something wasn't right, he paused in a plum thicket. Seeing a small opening through the brush, Jerry settled the .357's iron sights on the buck's vitals and dropped the hammer. At the shot the buck's front legs buckled, and he went down. Just as quickly the buck jumped back to its feet, circling toward Jerry. Shooting instinctively, Jerry got off three more rounds as the monster buck ran to within ten yards. After shakily climbing down from his platform, Jerry found the buck dead one hundred yards from the plum thicket. He had connected with all four shots!

"I didn't realize how big he was. If I had known, I wouldn't have been dragging him by the antlers! I'd have been afraid of breaking them off," recalls Jerry. After showing off the buck around town, someone snapped a photograph of Jerry sitting with his young daughter Heather on the tailgate of his pickup, with both grasping the buck's giant antlers.

Friends encouraged Jerry to get the buck officially measured for entry in the B&C records book. "I was still pretty green in 1983; I hadn't been hunting long. I don't think I even knew what a Boone and Crockett buck looked like," Jerry recalls with a smile. He did now.

The Jerry Lauby buck scores 180⅛ inches, sporting an extremely symmetrical ten-point rack, with only 2⅛ inches of total deductions. The nearly matching main beams measure 26⅝ on the right and 26⅜ on the left. The G2 and G3 points are also noteworthy, with each measuring over eleven inches and the longest eclipsing thirteen.

Unfortunately neither the B&C nor the Nebraska records book differentiates

FIG. 10. Jerry Lauby and his daughter, Heather, with the 180⅛-inch buck he killed with a .357 Magnum revolver. Photo courtesy of Jerry Lauby.

between trophies shot with a rifle or handgun, so there is no way to determine whether the buck is the largest ever shot with a handgun in Nebraska. Considering the rarity of hunting deer with handguns, and the size of the buck, it is probably safe to say Jerry killed one of the largest typical whitetails ever shot with a handgun in North America.

Jerry still hunts deer, having only missed one season since 1976. "That year I was busy with work and raising a family and I just forgot to buy a tag. It about killed me," Jerry remembers. Although multiple surgeries and age have slowed him down, he still sits through cold mornings in one of his many stands, now sometimes carrying a crossbow. "With my health issues, I shouldn't even be here. But I still have the hunting fire in me."

In the fall of 2017, thirty-four years after his fateful hunt in 1983, Jerry again watched as a B&C-caliber buck made its way toward his stand. "He caught me reaching for my .44 Magnum handgun and was gone."

7

Back-to-Back Booners

The Adam Zutavern Bucks, 2009 and 2010

· 178⅝-inch and 172⅜-inch typicals
· Blaine County

Confluence—where two rivers join. Many of America's great cities began at these geographically advantageous locations—Philadelphia, Pittsburgh, and St. Louis. Many Nebraska towns did as well—North Platte, Niobrara, and tiny Dunning, nestled in the triangle of land at the confluence of the Middle Loup and Dismal Rivers in Blaine County. Near this confluence the story of two giant typical bucks runs together as well.

Dunning sits in the heart of the Sandhills, where people are few and wildlife, cattle, and sky are plentiful. Blaine County reached its population apex in the 1920s, with just over seventeen hundred people before slowly dwindling down to under five hundred, making it the second least populated county in the state today. The families that remain often have deep roots. The Zutavern family certainly does, having raised cattle in the area since the early 1900s. Their ranch, like many in the Sandhills, spreads across thousands of acres, with some of it bordering the Dismal River. Prime cattle and deer country.

Working on the family ranch, Adam Zutavern keeps close tabs on the cattle as well as the whitetails and mule deer. "We have some nice mule deer, but they tend to stay more in the hills, while the whitetails tend to stay down along the river," explains Adam. "Where I hunt, the whitetails wade across the Dismal River for safety since there are no roads over there."

In the fall of 2008 Adam was sitting in one of his tree stands near the Dismal River, watching a massive six-by-six walk toward his stand. It was a buck he knew well, and although it passed directly under his tree, he never drew his bow. "I estimated him at 175 inches, but I knew he wasn't old enough to shoot," explains Adam. "I had his sheds from the two previous years, so I figured he was only three and a half years old."

Adam's patience paid off, with the buck growing an exceptionally wide seven-by-six rack the following year. Adam made the decision to hunt him. "I was seeing him a mile east of where he usually was, so I put up a stand to hunt him," remembers Adam. Sitting in this stand on an unseasonably warm fall day, Adam watched as the buck made his way into some hay bales and weeds on the edge of an old alfalfa field. Thinking he might be able to stalk to within bow range, Adam climbed down, removed his boots, and crept slowly toward the buck. "I never saw him, and it's a good thing, since my heart was pounding so hard he could have heard it."

On Halloween Adam decided to hunt the buck from a ground blind near a river crossing. After watching the Huskers pound Baylor, he was in his blind by four o'clock that afternoon. "My blind was right where deer cross the river to come feed in the alfalfa and meadows in the evening," explains Adam. Unexpectedly the giant buck came from the opposite direction, moving toward his bedding area. Approaching the river crossing, the buck paused broadside at thirty yards. Adam released his arrow. After waiting a short time Adam crawled out of his blind and walked to the spot of the hit. Picking up his bloodstained arrow he could see a decent blood trail along the river.

After calling some friends to come help, the group began searching for the buck. Making their way through the thick brush, Adam spotted the buck lying down, but still alive. Quickly drawing his bow he sent another arrow toward the buck, only to see it deflect off a branch. The giant buck jumped to its feet and was gone. With darkness approaching Adam decided to wait until morning to continue the search. "I didn't sleep much that night," remembers Adam.

The next morning, with even more people along to help, they found the buck's bed from the night before. Thinking the buck may have waded the river, several people waded across the Dismal to search the opposite bank. "I was standing near the edge of the river, and the guys on the other side yelled, 'He's laying right in front of you!'" remembers Adam. The buck was lying dead, tight up against the bank. "It was good they crossed to the other side, because I was standing right on the bank and couldn't see him."

After the mandatory sixty-day drying period, the buck scored 178⅝ inches, becoming the third-largest typical in the Nebraska archery records book. With an inside spread of over twenty-three inches and main beams over twenty-six, it is incredibly wide. The rack is also unique with respect to point length. The G2 points, measuring 4⅜ and 5⅝ inches are considerably shorter than the G4s, making the rack look even wider. The buck grosses 184⅝ inches, and with only 6⅛ inches of total deductions, nets 178⅝.

"People kept telling me I would never shoot another buck like that," shares Adam. "I would just quietly reply, 'Well, maybe.'" His maybe came from the fact that he knew of another B&C-caliber buck living along the Dismal River.

During late summer and early fall of 2010 Adam began patterning this buck, a giant eight-by-seven. Trail camera pictures clearly showed the buck's signature double split brow tines and the six symmetrical points on each side of the rack. He looked even bigger than his 2009 trophy! However, killing him would prove to be much more difficult.

"I had him patterned and thought it would be cool to have two archery records, so I wanted to kill him with my bow," says Adam. "He would always come out on the center pivot near this same windbreak." Confident in his scouting, Adam snuck in with his bow, sitting on the ground near the windbreak. Sure enough the buck came walking by. "I kind of panicked and didn't range him. I used the wrong pin and just missed him."

With no other opportunities during archery season, Adam hoped the buck would survive rifle season. The week did not start well. "I found him breeding a doe on opening weekend of rifle season, twenty yards from the road," laughs Adam. "I chased him out of there, yelling at him to go do that someplace else and that I wasn't going to shoot him with my rifle."

FIG. 11. Adam Zutavern's exceptionally wide 178⅝-inch archery buck (*middle*) alongside an impressive collection of Sandhills bucks. Photo courtesy of the author.

Fortunately the buck survived, with Adam making the decision to hunt him during the December muzzleloader season. "When the weather gets cold the deer often stay out on the pivots all day long," explains Adam. And that is exactly where Adam spotted him. Approaching the center pivot, Adam closed the distance to two hundred thirty yards and leveled his muzzleloader before touching off the cap. Although Adam was certain he hit him, the buck did not go down, disappearing instead into the brush along the edge of the field. Walking over to the spot, Adam found no sign of a hit. Wanting to be certain, Adam came out again the next morning, searching for blood and scanning the sky for circling crows. "Later that day I saw him, and he looked fine."

Over the next few days Adam patterned the buck again, noting that he was using another pivot farther to the east. Later, while checking that pivot, he spotted the buck bedded down in some thick cover. After sneaking to within range, Adam sat patiently for an hour, waiting for the buck to stand. "I could

FIG. 12. Adam Zutavern with his double split brow tine B&C muzzleloader buck. Photo courtesy of Adam Zutavern.

just see his horns in the brush," recalls Adam. When the buck finally stood Adam missed him a third time. "I was so pissed off. It wasn't like I hadn't shot big deer before, so I wasn't bucky. I was really annoyed, to the point that I was thinking about not hunting him anymore," remembers Adam. "One evening, drinking with some friends, the ribbing began. I was getting a lot of shit about not being able to kill that buck," remembers Adam. "So finally I said, 'Fine, I'll go shoot him tomorrow.'"

As promised Adam found the buck the next day, this time in an old farmstead. Keeping the wind in his favor, Adam snuck in above him to within two hundred yards. Settling the crosshairs behind the buck's shoulder, Adam sent his fourth and final projectile toward the buck. "He dropped in his tracks," Adam smiles. "That buck took a lot of hunting out of me."

It was worth it. Adam's muzzleloader buck scores 172⅜ inches, making it currently the sixth-largest typical whitetail killed with a muzzleloader in the Nebraska records book. A typical seven-by-seven with an unmatched G6 on the left side, it grosses 183⅝ points. Split brow tines add character but account for the majority of the 11⅜ inches of deductions on an otherwise symmetrical rack.

Many spend a lifetime hunting deer without even seeing a B&C-caliber buck, much less shooting one. Killing two in back-to-back years is extremely rare. Adam now focuses mainly on giving others an opportunity to shoot big bucks, especially his three young nephews. "If I find a big one, I might hunt him. But it's more enjoyable taking my nephews," shares Adam.

8

Father and Son

The Frosty Adams Buck, 2000

- 191⅞-inch typical
- Gage County

Hunting with your young children is fleeting. However, the hunting memories you share live on, they become part of your life, your relationships, part of who you are. Rex and Frosty Adams share a special memory. Sitting together in their elevated box blind on a cold, windy opening morning in 2000, they stared in amazement as the most magnificent buck they had ever seen stepped slowly from the wood line into the open field.

Born into a hunting family in 1985, Frosty practically grew up with a bow in his hand. In 1989 his father opened Adams Bottles and Bows in Wymore, which had an archery shop and shooting range on one side and a liquor store on the other. By age twelve Frosty was hunting deer with both a bow and rifle. "We hunted a lot. I bet out of the ninety-day deer season, we were hunting eighty-plus days," remembers Frosty.

Before the 2000 archery opener, Rex and Frosty began their preseason scouting routine. "We would go out to the bean fields and throw a tarp over the back of the truck bed and sit and watch for bucks through our spotting scopes," shares Frosty. They were hoping to see one particular buck. Frosty's uncle Jay had found an immense set of sheds the previous spring, and if the buck was still alive, he would be a truly massive typical.

During one of their evening scouting trips, they finally spotted the giant typical. He was unmistakable, with extremely long G2 tines and distinctive inward curving brow tines so long they crossed.

With Frosty busy playing football, Rex began bowhunting the buck every chance he could. Fortunately the buck's Gage County home range included a property Rex managed intensively for wildlife. The site of an old rock quarry, the property is a maze of oak-and-cedar-choked canyons feeding down into lower-lying agricultural fields. Both Rex and his brother Jay worked hard on improving their ground for deer and other wildlife, planting food plots, clearing brush, and planting trees. Both received Conservationist of the Year awards from the NGPC.

Rex would have two encounters with the huge buck. On the first, the buck paused at thirty yards, but a tree blocked a clear shot at the vitals. The second was even closer. Only a few days before the start of the rifle season and with the rut in full swing, the buck came within ten yards of Rex's tree stand. By the time a clear shot presented itself, the buck was breeding a doe, and with the gun season approaching, Rex decided to pass on the shot. "My dad had that buck twice within bow range. I can't believe he didn't kill him," recalls Frosty. If Rex had shot the buck it would have been a new archery state record, topping the 194⅛-inch typical Bob Vrbsky arrowed in 1978.

After that close call only days before, Rex and Frosty felt good about their chances of shooting the monster typical on November 11, opening day of rifle season. "Opening morning of rifle, we were in the blind early, and it was cold," remembers Frosty. Father and son sat together in their handmade elevated box blind, with a clear view of the surrounding ridgetop. "I asked Dad when the buck was going to come out. He whispers that he'll be out at ten eighteen. And sure enough that buck stepped out at ten fifteen and stood broadside at one hundred fifty yards."

Raising his Browning .30-06 Frosty found the giant buck in the crosshairs and squeezed the trigger. "I hit him, but Dad yelled to shoot him again. With a buck that size we didn't want to lose him, so I ended up shooting him four times before he dropped," remembers Frosty.

As father and son climbed down and began walking toward the buck,

FIG. 13. Rex (*right*) and fifteen-year-old Frosty Adams with his long-tined 191⅞-inch Gage County buck. Photo courtesy of Frosty Adams.

it seemed the rack grew larger with each step. Reaching down and lifting the massive rack off the ground, they were amazed at the size. "My dad and I were both really excited to finally get that buck down," remembers Frosty. Running back to get their phone, Frosty called his mom, Jodi, who drove over and took some pictures of the proud hunters and their buck, its head resting on a chunk of Nebraska limestone. Adding to the excitement they also noticed something unique about the buck's rack. Sprouting from the skull, between the brow tines, was a small one-inch third antler, barely visible above the hair.

After the sixty-day drying period, they took the rack to B&C official measurer Sam Cowan of Beatrice to get it officially scored. Sam noticed the third antler. The B&C rule book bans from entry all deer, elk, caribou, and moose racks having a third antler. The rule states: "This policy applies to a third antler that is completely separated from either of the other antlers with flesh and hide and has its own pedicel and is shed separately from the other two antlers each fall. In some cases the third antler may actually arise from one of the two normal pedicels, but it is shed separately from the other two normal antlers. This policy does not apply to normal points that branch off one of the antlers near the burr. Several of these trophies have been entered in the non-typical categories."[1]

Not sure what to do, Sam placed a call to B&C headquarters in Missoula, Montana, for clarification.[2] They told him the buck did not qualify for entry into the records book. Fortunately a few days later they called back, telling Sam to score it and send in the required documents and photographs so they could make a final decision.

After officially measuring the rack at 191⅞ inches, Sam sent the scoresheet and photographs to B&C, whose officials eventually agreed to recognize the buck. The Frosty Adams buck is a five-by-nine, with the left antler having four abnormal points, including the small third antler growing from the top of the skull plate. The most impressive feature on the buck is the 16⅛-inch G2 point on the right side. It is the longest point of any Nebraska typical in the B&C records book. The buck currently ranks as the sixth-largest typical shot in Nebraska, and one of only seven typicals to score more than 190 inches.

9

Trifecta

The James Hamik Bucks, 2007 and 2008

· 160$^{6/8}$-inch and 160$^{7/8}$-inch non-typicals, 172$^{6/8}$-inch typical
· Clay County

One of the most enjoyable aspects of big-game hunting is the anticipation. Anticipation especially fuels bowhunters, since having a buck within bow range is such an intense, unforgettable adrenaline rush. You sit for hours, hoping and dreaming that a big buck is just over the hill or down the tree line, and when it finally happens it seems unreal. Just ask James Hamik—in two seasons he had three records book bucks within fifteen yards of his tree stand, and arrowed them all.

Thinking back on his 2007 and 2008 archery seasons, James admits, "I was pretty spoiled how it all worked out." Spoiled may not be the right word. Perhaps lucky, undoubtedly a good shot, and definitely blessed. However you describe it, killing three giant bucks with a bow over a two-season stretch is one of the most amazing Nebraska hunting feats of all time.

James grew up in Hastings with a father passionate about bowhunting. Dave Hamik began deer hunting in 1980 and like most others at the time, used a rifle. After a friend suggested he try bowhunting, he liked it so much he quickly gave up rifle hunting. Dave's two sons, Joseph and James, grew up watching their father shoot and hunt with a bow. "My first deer season I actually used a muzzleloader, but I didn't get anything. I always saw Dad practicing and hunting with a bow, so I decided I wanted to try it," shares James.

The summer before eighth grade, Dave bought James his first bow. "I hadn't hit my growth spurt yet, so he wanted to get me something that I wouldn't outgrow," remembers James with a grin. The bow's draw length maxed out at twenty-eight and a half inches, with James ultimately needing a bow with a draw length of over thirty-one. "When I first started it was fine, but eventually I had to shoot that bow with my elbows bent." That summer he spent countless hours practicing with his bow, gaining confidence and looking forward to the upcoming season.

Wanting James to stay safe, Dave set up two tree stands, in two different trees, but side by side. On only his third hunt his practice paid off, with James arrowing his first buck, a small four-by-four. Several weeks later he would do it again, arrowing another four-by-four. James was off to an exceptionally fast and successful start as a bowhunter. It would get even better.

At the time, the Hamiks were hunting a two-hundred-acre property in Clay County that was originally part of the Navy Ammunition Depot.[1] From 1942 until 1966 this massive facility covering over forty-nine thousand acres produced millions of rounds of ordnance and employed thousands. After its closure some of the land transferred back to private ownership, although many of the oddly shaped storage bunkers remain. James and Dave primarily hunted a four-hundred-yard-long shelterbelt that is about thirty yards wide and thick with hardwoods and cedars. They set up four stands along its length.

Now a freshman in high school, James started his 2007 archery season with an evening hunt in late October. Hunting alone, he again arrowed a decent four-by-four. Despite spending a lot of time on stand over the next month, he had no other encounters until Thanksgiving morning. "Before we left for our stands, I asked Dad if I could use his grunt call. He said no, but he gave me his doe bleat can call," recalls James. After reaching his stand in the shelterbelt, James climbed up and settled in, fighting to stay warm until daylight.

About thirty minutes after sunup he spotted five does and a giant buck about seventy-five yards away, getting ready to cross the fence to the adjacent property. "The buck was walking away from me, so I turned the bleat call over. He looked in my direction and made a beeline right toward me," remembers James. Now standing up, James watched as the buck quickly closed the distance. "He came around a tree at fifteen yards, and I shot him." James had his first P&Y records book non-typical buck, a beautiful mainframe five-by-five scoring 160⅝ inches. "That was the first time I really felt buck fever."

The following year's archery season started slowly, with James breaking his collarbone during football camp. "I couldn't pull my bow back very well until October, so I only hunted five times that entire season," shares James. He would make the best of those five days!

With no school on Halloween, James and Dave decided to get in a hunt. That morning Dave spotted a good buck walking down the shelterbelt toward his son, but James never saw him. After the morning hunt they thought the buck had probably bedded down and might move that evening. They returned by mid-afternoon, with James choosing a stand near the midpoint of the shelterbelt and Dave in another several hundred yards away.

"It was about four thirty and I see this buck coming down the middle of the shelterbelt. The stand I was in was a ten-foot ladder stand, up against a fat hardwood, with the main trunk splitting just below the seat. I was hugging up against one of those branches, trying to stay out of sight," remembers James. As James watched another giant non-typical close the distance to fifteen yards, buck fever hit him hard. "I was trying to keep my composure, but my heart was beating so fast. It's almost like I was holding my breath. The buck reached a tree where I knew he would have to go right or left. Either way he would be broadside. When he went behind it, I drew, and when he appeared, I let it rip," remembers James.

Knowing the hit was good, James called his dad. Sitting in disbelief about his son shooting yet another big buck, Dave waited an hour before heading down the shelterbelt. On his way he found the buck lying dead. It was bigger than the first one! James's second P&Y records book non-typical buck scored 160⅞ inches, an eighth of an inch more than his first. Having bowhunted deer for over twenty years, Dave could not believe his son had

FIG. 14. James Hamik with the three records-book bucks he arrowed in back-to-back seasons. Photo courtesy of James Hamik.

already shot two bucks bigger than anything he had ever taken. It would only get worse (better?).

With busy schedules and not wanting to hunt during the nine-day rifle season, James and Dave only bowhunted one other time prior to November 28, a few days after the close of rifle season. That cold morning found James sitting once again in the shelterbelt. "I had not seen anything all morning and was getting restless. My dad told me that if he didn't see anything by about eight thirty he was going to try and push some deer my way," recalls James.

Soon after eight thirty Dave did crawl down from his stand and drove toward the west end of the property to begin his walk toward James. Nearing the end of the property, Dave spotted a nice buck bedded down with a doe. Not wanting to spook the buck, he drove past. Parking the truck a good distance away he began walking in hopes of pushing the buck to James. Instead the big buck jumped and ran in the wrong direction. Dave continued on, thinking he may still push a good buck toward his son.

Unbeknownst to Dave, his plan actually worked. "All of a sudden I see does and fawns running down the shelterbelt right toward me. There were probably ten of them, and right behind them I see this big old rack, just bobbing up and down, making a beeline for my tree," remembers James. With the giant high-racked buck running hard, James bleated at him with his mouth, trying desperately to stop him. The buck kept running. He bleated again. Nothing. Then again but even louder. "By the fourth time it was obnoxiously loud. I don't know how the hell he stopped, but he did." With the giant buck standing broadside at fifteen yards, James center-punched him through the vitals. "It happened so fast I didn't have time to get nervous."

Dave, still a couple hundred yards away, felt his phone vibrate. Once again it was James breathlessly telling him that he had shot another monster. Looking down the tree line Dave saw his son emerge from the trees, celebrating with his bow held high in the air. When they walked up on the buck lying dead seventy yards from the shot, Dave threw up his hands and just walked away. "My dad was in disbelief again," smiles James.

Scoring 172⁰⁄₈ inches, the James Hamik typical from 2008 is one of the most impressive in the Nebraska archery records book. Both main beams are incredibly long, measuring 28³⁄₈ and 28²⁄₈ inches, with an inside spread of 23²⁄₈ inches. Symmetry is exceptional with only 3²⁄₈ inches of total deductions, with 1⁴⁄₈ inches of that from an unmatched G4 point on the left side. With long points, including brow tines of over seven inches and G2s over twelve, it is a beautiful typical whitetail. It currently ranks as the eighth-largest archery typical in the Nebraska records book.

Now twenty-seven, and living and working in Lincoln, James still takes time each year to hunt with his dad. "I can't hunt as much anymore. It kind of puts it in perspective, how lucky I was. I give all the credit to my dad, that's for sure. He knew what he was doing. I thank him the most."

10

Giant of the Bohemian Alps

The Kevin Petrzilka Buck, 2010

- 198$^{2}/_{8}$-inch typical
- Saunders County

Attend a parade in eastern Nebraska and you are guaranteed to see at least one Czech queen. More likely three or four. Beginning in the late 1800s thousands of Czechs immigrated into Nebraska from central Europe, especially from the region called Bohemia. With surnames sprinkled liberally with z's and v's, they built strong farming communities like Prague, Brainard, Bruno, and especially Wilbur, the official "Czech Capital of the USA." So many settled in the rolling glacial hills of Seward, Butler, and Saunders Counties, the area became known as the Bohemian Alps.

Czech culture still survives through Czech festivals, ornate Catholic churches, Friday-night fish fries, and the passing down of *kolache* recipes. There is also a strong affinity for meats. Although most are now gone, a few family-owned meat markets will still custom-process what patrons bring in, including whitetail deer.

The Kevin Petrzilka farmhouse sits off a long, winding driveway in Saunders County, near the center of the Bohemian Alps. Kevin was born in 1959, and his parents owned and operated the bar in the nearby village of Loma. "I grew up walking the railroad tracks and shooting grasshoppers with my

BB gun," remembers Kevin. "I also hunted squirrels with my grandpa and a few bunnies with my dad. Deer were not particularly common in those days, but I did take a few with my dad's old .30-.30."

After marrying, he and his wife, Donna, purchased the home they have lived in for thirty years, and raised two sons, Dillon and Mason. Hunting trophy bucks was an important part of their family life. "My boys knew early on not to shoot scrubs, what we call small bucks," said Kevin. A windmill in the farmyard attests to past hunting successes, with the legs wrapped in bleached-out racks, racks most people would have mounted on the wall. "We're not big mounters," laughs Kevin. That would change in the fall of 2010.

Already six days into the 2010 November rifle season, Kevin drove Mason to one of his favorite stands a quarter mile south of the house. Two years prior Mason had shot his biggest buck out of that stand, a giant 166⅝-inch typical. Meanwhile Dillon drove the six miles to hunt his grandfather's farm. Approaching the farm he spotted a bull in the road and called his mom and dad to come help him get it back in and fix the fence.

As Dillon was watching after the bull, Mason was walking into his deer stand. Looking across the field he spotted four does followed by an unbelievably giant buck. Quickly shouldering his .22-250, he shot at the buck standing broadside two hundred fifty yards away. With no reaction from the buck, Mason tried cycling another round into the chamber, but the cartridge tore, jamming his bolt-action Weatherby. The giant buck and four does disappeared into a knot of cedar-infested draws.

As Mason's hunt was unfolding, Kevin and Donna were heading toward Dillon. "We were going to help with that bull, when Dillon comes flying past us in his truck, heading back home," explains Kevin. After missing the buck, Mason had called Dillon to tell him to come home and help him. Mason's next call went to his dad, yelling at him to "Come home now!" Soon the entire family was back home, drawing up a plan to go after the massive buck.

"We usually don't go into the area that buck went, even during the season. It's a sanctuary for big bucks," Kevin explains. Due to the size of this buck, they decided to ignore that rule and be aggressive. Dillon drove around and entered the area from the south, while Mason walked in from the west, near

FIG. 15. Kevin Petrzilka with his massive 198 2/8-inch Saunders County typical. Photo by the author.

where he first saw the buck. Kevin and Donna meanwhile drove around and started walking in from the north and east.

Carrying his old Remington 788 in .22-250, Kevin worked his way down into the creek, soon spotting four does. "Then I see this buck running away from me and I see horns, but I can't tell how big he is," remembers Kevin. Then, as if on cue, the giant seven-by-seven stopped, spun, and headed right back at him! "He must have seen or smelled Dillon, because he came right at me." Instinctually shouldering his Remington, Kevin snapped off a shot through the thick cover. The buck disappeared.

Seeing Dillon coming up out of the draw, Kevin yelled to see if he had seen the buck. "He's right here, and he's big, big, big!" Dillon replied. As the family gathered around the unbelievably giant buck, Kevin admits they had no idea what would unfold over the next few days. "We knew he was a great buck but had no idea he would be a state record," shares Kevin. After loading the buck into the bed of his truck, they did what farmers do: went back, returned the bull to the pasture, and fixed the fence.

Pictures of the buck spread quickly via cell phones, with family and friends calling, texting, and coming by to see the buck. "It was like the State Fair; it was just nonstop," remembers Kevin. Mike Luben, the local conservation officer, arrived and green-scored the buck. "That's when we first realized what we had." The story and pictures soon made their way into state and even national publications and websites. Kevin's phone wouldn't stop ringing.

Following the mandatory sixty-day drying period, the buck was officially measured at 202 6/8 inches. This was earth-shattering news in the Nebraska hunting world. Not only was it the new state-record typical, breaking Vernon Virka's state record from 1983; it was the first Nebraska typical buck to eclipse the magical 200-inch mark, something fewer than twenty bucks in North America have ever done. Numerous articles in hunting magazines and newspapers soon appeared, proclaiming the buck as the new state record.

Three years later the story takes a rather unfortunate turn. After the measurements were officially entered into the B&C records book, Kevin and his buck were invited to attend the organization's 28th Big Game Awards banquet in Reno, Nevada, in July 2013. At this triennial banquet the five largest trophies in each of thirty-six big-game categories gets an automatic invitation, with all the trophies put on public display. Kevin and Donna decided to make the trip to Reno.

As part of the event, an awards program judges panel of veteran official measurers convenes to remeasure and verify all potential world record trophies. In addition the top five trophies entered into each category are also remeasured, certifying them for additional B&C medals and certificates. Unfortunately, after remeasuring Kevin's buck, the panel reduced the score by 3 4/8 inches, dropping it to 198 2/8 inches. After three years as the state record, it moved into second place, one inch behind the Vernon Virka buck. "Probably my worst decision was to take it to Reno," says Kevin. You could tell by the look in his eyes that it still hurt. As it would any deer hunter.

Although now officially the second-largest Nebraska typical whitetail, the Kevin Petrzilka buck is still unquestionably one of the most impressive

Kevin S. Petrzilka ~Not Awarded~ 2021
Brainard, NE   ID: 41
typical whitetail deer   2
Date of Kill:
Kill Location: n/a
Method: n/a

Records of North American Big Game

BOONE AND CROCKETT CLUB
OFFICIAL SCORING SYSTEM FOR NORTH AMERICAN BIG GAME TROPHIES

TYPICAL WHITETAIL AND COUES' DEER

KIND OF DEER (check or
- ☑ whitetail
- ☐ Coues'

MINIMUM SCORES	AWARDS	ALL-TIME
whitetail	160	170
Coues'	100	110

ENTERED

Detail of Point Measurement

Mod Firearm

Abnormal Points	
Right Antler	**Left Antler**
2 0/8	4 0/8
1 7/8	
SUBTOTALS 3 7/8	4 0/8
TOTAL TO E	7 7/8

SEE OTHER SIDE FOR INSTRUCTIONS		COLUMN 1	COLUMN 2	COLUMN 3	COLUMN 4
A. No. Points on Right Antler	9	No. Points on Left Antler	8	**Spread Credit**	**Right Antler**	**Left Antler**	**Difference**

	COLUMN 1 Spread Credit	COLUMN 2 Right Antler	COLUMN 3 Left Antler	COLUMN 4 Difference
A. No. Points on Right Antler 9 / No. Points on Left Antler 8				
B. Tip to Tip Spread 15 6/8 / C. Greatest Spread 24 6/8				
D. Inside Spread of Main Beams 21 1/8 / SPREAD CREDIT MAY EQUAL BUT NOT EXCEED LONGER MAIN BEAM	21 1/8			
E. Total of Lengths of Abnormal Points				7 7/8
F. Length of Main Beam		26 7/8	24 6/8	2 1/8
G-1. Length of First Point		5 3/8	5 4/8	3/8
G-2. Length of Second Point		12 2/8	12 1/8	1/8
G-3. Length of Third Point		8 9/8	10 0/8 8 7/8	2 1/8
G-4. Length of Fourth Point, If Present		10 6/8	12 5/8 11	1 7/8
G-5. Length of Fifth Point, If Present		6 3/8	7 7/8	1 4/8
G-6. Length of Sixth Point, If Present		4 3/8	4 5/8	2/8
G-7. Length of Seventh Point, If Present				
H-1. Circumference at Smallest Place Between Burr and First Point		4 7/8	5 0/8	1/8
H-2. Circumference at Smallest Place Between First and Second Points		5 0/8	4 7/8	1/8
H-3. Circumference at Smallest Place Between Second and Third Points		6 4/8	5 4/8	6/8
H-4. Circumference at Smallest Place Between Third and Fourth Points		7 4/8	7 4/8	0/8
TOTALS	21 1/8	97 1/8	100 7/8	7 7/8

RECEIVED JAN 27 2011 PAID

B.&C. BIG GAME AWARDS 28 2010~2012

ADD	Column 1	21 1/8	Exact Locality Where Killed: Hills Southeast of Brainard, Saunders County NE
	Column 2	97 1/8	Date Killed: 11-19-10 — Hunter: Kevin J. Petrzilka
	Column 3	100 7/8	Trophy Owner: Same — Telephone #:
	Subtotal	219 7/8	Trophy Owner's Address: 980 32rd Brainard NE 68626
SUBTRACT Column 4		17 7/8	Trophy Owner's E-mail: — Guide's Name: None
FINAL SCORE	202 0/8		Remarks: (Mention Any Abnormalities or Unique Qualities) aged at 4 1/2 yr.
(198 2/8)			skull plate intact 3 nontyp points 2-R1-L OM I.D. Number K 0 6 1

COPYRIGHT © 2008 BY BOONE AND CROCKETT CLUB®

FIG. 16. Kevin Petrzilka scoresheet. Note the change in the final score from 202⅙ to 198⅜. Courtesy of the Boone and Crockett Club.

whitetails ever shot in North America. A typical seven-by-seven with two abnormal points on the right antler and one on the left, it currently ranks thirty-fourth in the B&C records book. The buck's inside spread is 21⅛ inches, while the main beams are 26⅞ and 24⅝ inches long. Both brow tines measure over five inches, while both G2 points measure over a foot. The mass of the main beams is probably the most impressive feature on this buck, with the circumference measurements increasing from 4⅞ and 5⅝ inches near the bases to over seven inches at the H4 measurements.

11

Perfect Eight

The John Woloszyn Buck, 1994

· 160⅛-inch typical
· Cherry County

Nebraska whitetail deer hunters shoot lots and lots of eight-pointers. Although fine trophies, the vast majority of these lack enough antler to reach the 160-inch minimum for entry into the B&C records book. Hampered by only three point measurements to a side, an eight-pointer must be exceptional in every other way—long points and beams, wide inside spread, good mass, and exceptional symmetry—to become a Booner.

The striking difference in the number of typical eight-pointers versus ten-pointers in the B&C records book proves the point. A mere one hundred sixty-eight eight-pointers are currently listed in the B&C records book, compared to nearly twenty-seven hundred ten-pointers. And how many of those B&C eight-pointers are from Nebraska? One.

Dr. John T. Woloszyn, an orthopedic surgeon from Jonesboro, Arkansas, lays claim to that one Nebraska B&C eight-pointer. A self-described "first generation American from pure Polish heritage," John came into deer hunting late in life. His parents grew up in Poland, with both spending time in German concentration camps during World War II. "They were sent despite not being Jewish. They were considered political prisoners," explains John.

After emigrating from Poland the family settled in New York, where John and his two brothers grew up without ever going hunting.

Eventually completing his medical training at Chicago Medical School, he began his residency at Metropolitan Northwest Detroit Hospital. "I was twenty-nine years old when my friend James Bicknell, an emergency room resident in training, taught me how to shoot a bow," remembers John. In the fall of 1985, toting a round-wheel compound bow shooting 500-grain arrows, John bagged his first whitetail near Saginaw Bay. "No one in my family were or are hunters. But I was hooked."

"That first deer began a long-term love, and sometimes hate, relationship with hunting," continues John. Immersing himself in his newfound passion, John became an expert on ballistics, hand-loading and testing his own ammunition. Using this knowledge and his medical training, he began researching the treatment of gunshot wounds, resulting in the publication of an article titled "Management of Civilian Gunshot Fractures of the Extremities."[1] "At the time, it was the largest study in the previous twenty-five years, helping to establish a course of treatment originally not thought viable," explains John.

Eventually moving to Jonesboro, Arkansas, John began exploring and hunting other states. In 1991 he made his first trip to Cherry County to hunt the Twisted Pine Ranch near Merriman, Nebraska. "The ranch is owned by Ken Moreland, a big, kindhearted man who knows deer hunting and how to judge deer on the hoof," shares John. "I was still quite a novice on judging deer, so I began hunting with one of Ken's buddies, Mike Westervelt. We call him Pellet, since he raises rabbits, but he taught me how to judge whitetails, and the patience to pass on what I thought were nice deer."

Enjoying both the area and the people, John made hunting the Twisted Pine an annual event. In November 1994, after again making the long drive from Arkansas, John sat on a high bluff overlooking the Niobrara River valley. Sitting alongside him scanning the thick plum thickets was Pellet. "I notice this buck coming from my left, and watch him as he got to within two hundred fifty yards. He looked like a giant to me. I ask Pellet if he was a good one, and he whispers, 'Too small,'" remembers John.

Watching as the buck closed the distance to two hundred yards, John was second-guessing Pellet's field judging. "I kept nagging him, wondering what the heck has to show up to be a good deer," recalls John. "At that point the buck starts to walk off into a plum thicket and catches Pellet's eye. He grabs me and says, 'Shoot that buck!'" By that time it was too late, with the giant buck melting into the brush. Looking at each other they realized Pellet had been watching a 120-class eight-pointer, not the giant buck John was watching.

"I went to bed that night feeling that I let a buck of a lifetime go. I figured, what are the chances of ever getting another opportunity on a buck like that?" John remembers thinking. To make matters worse there was a full moon that night, convincing John that all the bucks would bed down well before first light.

The next morning John and Pellet sat in the exact same spot as the morning before. Scanning the valley in the graying dawn, John knew that if the buck showed again he would have to make a long shot. "I was shooting a .300 Winchester Mag, custom built by Kenny Jarrett, and some of my hand-loads, which I measure and seat one at a time. I still have that rifle today, and it can shoot half-inch groups at one hundred yards. I was a fantastic shot, if I do say so myself," explains John.

He would get a chance to prove it. Stepping out of the brush on the opposite side of the river was the giant eight-pointer from the previous morning. Shouldering his .300 Mag, John watched as the buck turned and ran back into the brush. Thinking he may be chasing a hot doe, John watched as the buck made his way slowly through the thicket. "I see his chest through an opening, and I wasn't about to let him go," shares John. Settling the cross-hairs on the buck's chest, John sent one of his hand-loaded 180-grain Nosler bullets across the river toward the buck. "We saw no movement, no deer running away, no motion at all."

With the river too wide, deep, and cold to cross, John and Pellet made their way back to the truck. "We had to drive around to the other side, the longest twenty minutes of my life," remembers John. Parking the truck, they hiked down toward the plum thicket, and lying right where he should

FIG. 17. John Woloszyn with the only true Nebraska eight-pointer in the B&C records book. Photo courtesy of John Woloszyn.

be was the most massive eight-pointer either hunter had ever seen. "It was surreal, almost like a dream. He was a giant. We field dressed him and took him back to camp where we weighed him at two hundred thirty pounds. A veterinarian who was in camp aged him at four and a half years old."

The John Woloszyn buck is a perfect case study in demonstrating what it takes for an eight-pointer to make the B&C records book. Symmetry is vital, since deductions especially hurt a buck with only six scorable points. The Woloszyn buck is very symmetrical, with only 4²⁄₈ inches of total deductions on a rack grossing 164³⁄₈ inches. Although not particularly wide, with an inside spread of 18⅛ inches, point length is exceptional, with both brow tines over seven inches, both G2 points over twelve inches, and both G3 points over ten. Finally, both main beams are over twenty-four inches long with good mass extending to the fourth circumference measurement. With a final score of 160⅛ inches, it is a perfect eight.

John hunted the Twisted Pine Ranch several more times, taking a nice twelve-pointer scoring 156⅝ inches. "The Sandhills are a great place to hunt. It was always a good time in camp, meeting hunters from other parts of the country and hearing their stories. Just all around good fun. God has truly blessed me," says John.

12

Missouri River Breaks

The Keith Fahrenholz Buck, 1966

· 194⅛-inch typical
· Dakota County

"I should have done it," Keith Fahrenholz says with a shake of his head. Everyone has regrets.

Born in 1942, Keith grew up twenty miles west of Sioux City, Iowa, in Allen, Nebraska, a town that could never quite lay claim to five hundred residents. A good athlete in high school, he excelled at playing middle linebacker but also pole-vaulted and high-jumped. Keith's regret—not accepting Bob Devaney's offer to play football for the Huskers.

However, his true passion was hunting. "I hunted all the time. Squirrels and rabbits mostly, with my .22 rifle, but also some pheasants," remembers Keith. Although not certain, he thinks he first went deer hunting in either 1958 or 1959.

By the fall of 1966 Keith was working in a meatpacking house in Sioux City. With three whitetail deer already under his belt, as well as a western Nebraska pronghorn, his main hunting area was north of Jackson, in Dakota County. The property was located along what Keith calls the "Missouri breaks," the transition line between the Missouri River floodplain and the rolling farmland to the west. With oak-and-cedar-covered hills and draws, these breaks are excellent whitetail habitat, providing cover yet easy access to nearby crops.

FIG. 18. Keith Fahrenholz's 194⅛-inch six-by-six from Dakota County held the state record for a decade. Photo by the author.

In November 1966 Keith drove to his hunting area for an afternoon hunt. Parking his 1963 Ford sedan, he grabbed his lever-action Model 99 Savage from the backseat and quietly eased shut the car's heavy doors. "I walked in about a mile and was sitting up on a hill, smoking a cigarette, which you did at that time, and drinking a cup of coffee," remembers Keith. About two hundred yards below him was a house-sized clump of brush, with thick stands of trees on either side. Sitting on the hill in the late afternoon sun, Keith swung his binoculars back and forth, searching for movement or the glint of antlers.

"All of a sudden this giant buck stood up in the middle of that patch of brush below me. It shocked me, because I had been sitting there for half an hour and hadn't seen anything!" remembers Keith. Rattled by the sudden appearance of such a large buck, Keith's first shot from his .308 was a clean miss. The buck bolted, bounding uphill toward the safety of the trees. "I hit him through the neck on the second shot, running up the hill. It dropped him."

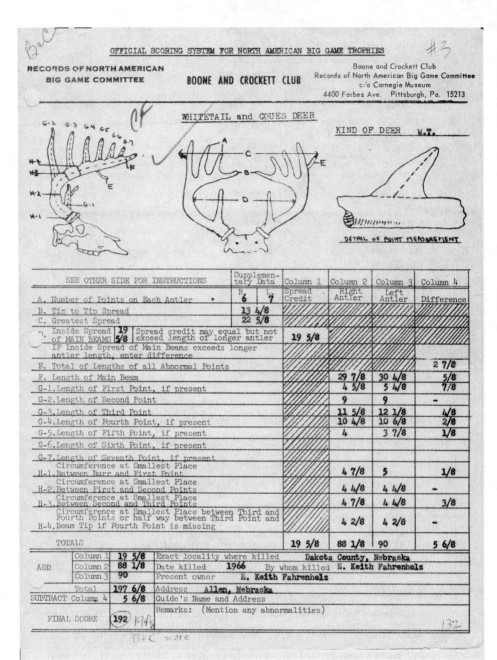

RECORDS OF NORTH AMERICAN BIG GAME COMMITTEE

BOONE AND CROCKETT CLUB

Boone and Crockett Club
Records of North American Big Game Committee
c/o Carnegie Museum
4400 Forbes Ave. Pittsburgh, Pa. 15213

WHITETAIL and COUES DEER

KIND OF DEER **W.T.**

DETAIL OF POINT MEASUREMENT

SEE OTHER SIDE FOR INSTRUCTIONS	Supplementary Data R	Supplementary Data L	Column 1 Spread Credit	Column 2 Right Antler	Column 3 Left Antler	Column 4 Difference
A. Number of Points on Each Antler	6	7				
B. Tip to Tip Spread	13 4/8					
C. Greatest Spread	22 5/8					
D. Inside Spread **19 5/8** of MAIN BEAMS — Spread credit may equal but not exceed length of longer antler			19 5/8			
IF Inside Spread of Main Beams exceeds longer antler length, enter difference						
E. Total of Lengths of all Abnormal Points						2 7/8
F. Length of Main Beam				29 7/8	30 4/8	5/8
G-1. Length of First Point, if present				4 5/8	5 4/8	7/8
G-2. Length of Second Point				9	9	-
G-3. Length of Third Point				11 5/8	12 1/8	4/8
G-4. Length of Fourth Point, if present				10 4/8	10 6/8	2/8
G-5. Length of Fifth Point, if present				4	3 7/8	1/8
G-6. Length of Sixth Point, if present						
G-7. Length of Seventh Point, if present						
H-1. Circumference at Smallest Place Between Burr and First Point				4 7/8	5	1/8
H-2. Circumference at Smallest Place Between First and Second Points				4 4/8	4 4/8	-
H-3. Circumference at Smallest Place Between Second and Third Points				4 7/8	4 4/8	3/8
H-4. Circumference at Smallest Place between Third and Fourth Points or half way between Third Point and Beam Tip if Fourth Point is missing				4 2/8	4 2/8	-
TOTALS			19 5/8	88 1/8	90	5 6/8

ADD	Column 1	19 5/8	Exact locality where killed	Dakota County, Nebraska
	Column 2	88 1/8	Date killed 1966 By whom killed	E. Keith Fahrenholz
	Column 3	90	Present owner E. Keith Fahrenholz	
	Total	197 6/8	Address Allen, Nebraska	
SUBTRACT Column 4		5 6/8	Guide's Name and Address	
FINAL SCORE	(192) 194 1/8		Remarks: (Mention any abnormalities)	

B&C score

FIG. 19. Keith Fahrenholz scoresheet. Note the increase in the final score from 192⅝ to 194⅛. Courtesy of the Boone and Crockett Club.

Walking down the hill, Keith approached the fallen buck. "The first thing I thought about when I walked up on him was, 'How the hell am I going to get him in my car?'" recalls Keith with a chuckle. "And I didn't dare gut him and have him bleeding all over my trunk." Driving his car up as close as possible to the buck, Keith dragged the un-gutted buck the rest of the way to his car. "He was a big-bodied buck, and I had to figure out how to get him in the trunk. Using a board, I just kind of slid him up and in." With the trunk lid bouncing, Keith drove to his brother-in-law's farm, where the two gutted the buck while marveling at the size of the antlers.

Although Keith knew the buck was big, he never bothered getting it officially scored until four years later. In 1970 the game warden in Norfolk scored the six-by-seven at 192⁰⁄₈ inches, making it the new Nebraska firearm typical state record! But the story doesn't end here.

After entering the buck into the B&C records book, the B&C sent Keith an invitation to attend the 1970 Big Game Awards. Since 1970 these awards ceremonies have honored the largest big-game animals taken in North America during each three-year period. All invited trophies are put on public display. "I had to make a big box to ship it to the Carnegie Museum in Pennsylvania. For some reason they would not take it on the train, so I had to ship it by airplane. I just about didn't send it, since it cost me four hundred dollars, which was a lot of money at that time," shares Keith.

Here is where the story gets strange. After the Big Game Awards, the B&C published the book *North American Big Game, 1971 Edition*, which lists Keith's trophy at 192⁰⁄₈ inches. The 1981 edition subsequently listed it at 192⁰⁄₈ inches as well. Keith is not sure who or exactly when, but someone at the B&C eventually noticed the score was added incorrectly on the official scoresheet. "They sent me a letter saying it was scored correctly, but someone had added the score wrong," remembers Keith. Twenty years after he shot it, Keith's buck "grew" by 2⅛ inches, now netting 194⅛ inches!

The Keith Fahrenholz buck is an amazing six-by-six typical, with extremely long main beams measuring 29⅞ and 30⅛ inches, and an inside spread of nearly twenty inches. Although it has good point length and mass, the symmetry between the two sides makes it special. The 5⅝ inches of total deductions include one abnormal point of 2⅞ inches, meaning the buck has less than three inches of difference between the two typical antlers. Over fifty years later the buck still ranks as the fourth-largest firearm typical in the Nebraska records book.

One thing is certain, Keith does not regret going hunting on that cool November afternoon in 1966.

13

Plane Crash

The Keith Houdersheldt Buck, 1985

- 184⁵/₈-inch typical
- Polk County

Keith "Skip" Houdersheldt's life is typical of his generation. Born in 1931 during the Great Depression, he grew up near Shelby, Nebraska, working hard, farming, fishing, and hunting. Serving four years in the U.S. Air Force during the Korean War, he fell in love with flying and a girl named Marilyn Euse, who became his wife for the next fifty-one years.

After the war Skip began farming and raised three children, Roger, Roy, and Christine, on his land in Polk County. By the 1970s he was a pilot and partner in Shelby Flying Service, a crop-dusting business. Obviously a hardworking man, he also found time to play semipro baseball, make yearly fishing trips to Minnesota, and teach his children and grandchildren to love the outdoors. Skip passed away in 2014 at the age of eighty-two.

Sitting with his sons Roger and Roy in their Creston Fertilizer office south of Shelby, it is clear that Skip was successful in turning his boys into outdoorsmen. Their office is full of big-game heads, hunting pictures, memorabilia, and on one wall, their father's stunning five-by five typical whitetail.

"When we were growing up we hunted pheasants, waterfowl, deer, and we ate everything we shot. Dad made sure we learned how to hunt. As soon as we were old enough, we were hunting," remembers Roger. Roy agrees,

FIG. 20. Pilot Keith "Skip" Houdersheldt safely on the ground with his exceptionally symmetrical Polk County ten-pointer. Photo courtesy of Roger Houdersheldt.

"Dad loved to hunt, especially deer. When I was in college in Minnesota, Dad would sometimes fly up and bring me home for the weekend so I could hunt, and then fly me back!"

By the fall of 1985 Skip had shot numerous deer, including some decent bucks, mostly off his ground near the Big Blue River. "Back then there was a lot of milo being grown in this area. You don't see much of it anymore," remembers Roger. Harvesting his milo prior to the season, Skip spotted a nice eight-pointer with a distinctive white rack.

Opening morning of the 1985 rifle season dawned cold and windy. Driving his 1979 Ford pickup, Skip spotted a small buck as he drove into his two-hundred-forty acres of cut milo. Parking the truck and grabbing his Remington 700, he began walking through the field, making his way toward the center pivot. Scanning the horizon he suddenly saw the unmistakable outline of two bucks standing in the stubble. Peering through the scope he saw solid antlers and squeezed the trigger. The buck didn't move. Racking another round into the chamber, Skip sent another round toward the buck. The buck did not flinch, taking a couple steps forward and stopping. Quickly cycling a third round, Skip steadied the crosshairs and dropped the buck into the stubble. He later estimated the shot at four hundred yards.

After the buck dropped out of sight, the other buck ran right at Skip, causing him to lose the location of the first buck. Walking toward the spot he thought the buck fell, he began searching in the tall deer-colored milo stalks. After a fruitless search Skip drove home and got Roy to help him look. "I was bouncing around in the back of that pickup as we drove through the milo field. I didn't have a clue as to what he shot," remembers Roy.

After searching for well over an hour, they finally found the buck lying dead in one of the milo rows. When Roy saw the buck he shouted, "Oh my God, Dad, do you know what you've shot here?!" remembers Roy. "We had never seen a buck like that before." Not only did the buck have an amazingly symmetrical and massive ten-point rack, but its body was huge, weighing in at over two hundred thirty pounds field dressed.

After waiting sixty days for the rack to dry, it was time to get it officially measured. Wanting to save time Skip decided to fly the rack to Bassett, Nebraska, to get it scored. With Roger strapped in next to him and the rack in the back, Skip eased his Beechcraft Bonanza down the runway, lifting off and turning the plane northwest toward Bassett. "We caught a tailwind coming into the airport, and Dad couldn't stop the plane in time. We ended up crashing, flipping the plane over at the end of the runway," Roger remembers with a laugh. After getting the buck officially scored, Skip borrowed another plane and flew back home. "That was an expensive trip," adds Roy.

The Keith Houdersheldt buck is a clean five-by-five with an inside spread of over twenty-one inches, main beams of 26⅝ and 25⅛ inches, and good point length and mass. The buck is extremely symmetrical, grossing 187⅞ inches and netting 184⅝. In 1985 it was the ninth-largest typical firearm buck in the Nebraska records book, while today it ranks fourteenth.

14

High Five

The Kevin Wood Buck, 1999

· 183⅝-inch typical

· Lincoln County

Typical, *adj.*, showing the characteristics expected of or popularly associated with a particular person, situation, or thing.

When deer hunters visualize a typical whitetail rack it is most often a five-by-five with tall symmetrical points spaced evenly along massive main beams curling inward toward the tips, all balanced perfectly between long matching brow tines. This is exactly the buck Kevin Wood saw standing fifteen yards from his tree stand the first morning he ever hunted the Cornhusker State.

Kevin lives in arguably the most whitetail-obsessed state in the union—Michigan. Where school districts still have "deer day" on the school calendar, upholding the long tradition of canceling class on the first day of gun season to allow their students time to hunt with family. Although down from a historic high of nearly eight hundred thousand in the mid-1990s, six hundred thousand deer hunters still venture out into the Michigan woods, harvesting over three hundred fifty thousand deer. In comparison Nebraska hunters generally shoot fewer than fifty thousand.

"I started hunting deer when I was fourteen, after starting out on small game with my brothers," shares Kevin. "We would also go north to deer camp every year with the family." After graduating high school Kevin joined the

FIG. 21. Michigan native Kevin Wood with the 183⅜-inch buck he shot opening morning of his first Nebraska deer hunt. Photo courtesy of the Boone and Crockett Club.

navy, serving his country for six years before returning home. "I wasn't able to hunt for a few years, but when I came home I started hunting again at the old deer camp. A few years later my brothers bought a cabin in the Upper Peninsula, where I still hunt today."

After returning home Kevin also started a successful heating and cooling business. It was through work that he met Russell Newton, who needed heat and air installed in his new Michigan home, but who also worked as an outfitter near Gillette, Wyoming. "The next year I went out West with Russell for the first time and shot a mule deer and an antelope. I had so much fun, I went again the next year," recalls Kevin. Eventually doing some guiding of his own in Wyoming, Kevin discovered that Russell had a friend in Nebraska who would take them whitetail deer hunting.

So on opening morning of the 1999 rifle season, Kevin Wood, from tiny Grant, Michigan, found himself sitting in a tree stand in Lincoln County,

Nebraska, near the Platte River. "We had just set up that stand a few days before; it was a new spot," recalls Kevin. The morning began well, with several does and some smaller bucks working past his stand. With the rut in full swing Kevin soon spotted two small bucks fighting a short distance away. "All of a sudden they stopped fighting and ran right under my stand, before looking back."

Following their gaze Kevin spotted a giant typical five-by-five standing fifteen yards from his stand. "He ran off the two small four-pointers, and my 7mm Remington Mag came up instantly," remembers Kevin. The well-hit buck didn't go far, dropping dead after running twenty yards. After climbing down from his stand, Kevin was shocked at what he found. "I really couldn't believe it; it was such a great buck. It is a hunt I will never forget."

The Kevin Wood buck is what one calls "high racked." The extremely long points on the proportionally narrow 18 2/8-inch inside spread make it look even higher than it is. The G2 points are 15 1/8 and 14 6/8 inches, while the G3 points are both over eleven. The 26 6/8- and 24 7/8-inch main beams curve inward, resulting in a tip-to-tip spread of only 5 1/8 inches, giving the rack a beautiful, classic shape. With only 4 1/8 inches of total deductions, the buck grosses 187 1/8 inches while netting 183 0/8.

Since his Nebraska hunt Kevin continues hunting Wyoming today, while also pursuing whitetails in Illinois and bears in Canada. But during Michigan's deer season, you will find him in the Upper Peninsula, sharing a hunting cabin with family. Tradition.

PART 2
Non-Typical Whitetail Deer

15

Kitchen Window

The Peggy Easterwood Buck, 2018

- 235⁴/₈-inch non-typical
- Richardson County

Not many women scout for deer from their kitchen window. But not many women love deer hunting as much as Peggy Easterwood does.

On an early November evening in 2018 Peggy bustled around the kitchen of her one-hundred-thirty-year-old farmhouse on the edge of tiny Dawson, Nebraska. While cleaning and putting away dishes, she stole quick glances out the kitchen window, hoping to see a buck she might want to hunt.

Glancing out the window once again, Peggy's heart skipped. Walking into the eight-acre alfalfa field behind her house was the biggest buck she had ever seen. Reaching for the binoculars she always keeps handy, she focused in on the buck's massive non-typical rack as he made his way toward a doe. "I could tell right away he was a monster. I watched him as he bred that doe, and even got a picture," recalls Peggy. She knew exactly where she would be sitting the following week on opening morning of rifle season.

Peggy became a deer hunter later in life than most. In her thirties, she went on her first deer hunt with her boyfriend at the time. She would later shoot her first deer, a whitetail doe, in the mid-1980s. "When I finally started deer hunting, I got the fever bad, and haven't missed a season since," shares Peggy. When she met her future husband Jim, they connected through hunting,

69

often sharing a deer blind together. Eventually shooting some nice bucks, Peggy still dreamed of shooting a true monster.

"My monster buck is actually a family joke," shares Peggy. About fifteen years ago her son-in-law Eric was seeing a big buck crossing the road on his way to work. Hoping to get a crack at the buck, Peggy set up along a tree line near where the buck was crossing. "I'm looking into the sun and this buck comes down the hedgerow, and thinking it was the monster buck, I shot him. He was just a tiny buck, but I called my son Joshua to help me load him." On seeing the buck Joshua teased, "A little ground shrinkage, huh, Mom." As a joke Joshua had his mom's "monster" buck European-mounted and gave it to her as a Christmas present.

On opening morning of the 2018 rifle season Peggy was thinking about the monster buck she had seen from her kitchen. For her and Jim, getting to their blind that morning was easy—just open the back door of the house and walk a few hundred yards. Once in their ground blind overlooking the alfalfa field, they waited quietly for sunrise.

Opening morning passed with no buck sightings, as did their evening hunt. The next three days followed the same routine: up at five thirty, hunt until late morning, eat lunch, head back out at one o'clock, and sit until dark. Four straight days without even a glimpse of the big buck. "Eric kept telling me to hunt other properties, but I kept saying, 'I'm not leaving, I'm hunting right here,'" Peggy shares with a smile.

Determined to continue hunting the big non-typical, Peggy and Jim went out again on Wednesday morning, counting twenty-two does on their alfalfa field. With the rut in full swing it was just a matter of time before a buck came to scent-check the does. Sure enough that evening a nice buck entered the field, but with the sun in her eyes and the monster buck still on her mind, Peggy decided to pass. Soon a second shooter buck appeared, with Jim encouraging her to shoot it. Shouldering her Browning .243 and centering the crosshairs on the buck's vitals, she hesitated. "No, I'm not shooting him. I'm waiting for that big buck," Peggy whispered.

It was a great decision. With only a half hour of daylight remaining, the big non-typical suddenly appeared on the edge of the field, standing

FIG. 22. Peggy Easterwood with the 235⅛-inch non-typical she first spotted from her kitchen window. Photo courtesy of Peggy Easterwood.

broadside at one hundred twenty yards. "I've had my scope on some big bucks and missed them because of buck fever. I think putting my scope on those first two bucks got rid of my buck fever. I knew I better not hesitate, so I just fired," remembers Peggy.

The buck lurched forward, going only twenty-five yards before piling up. Seeing the buck go down, Peggy burst into tears. "I walked up on him in the dark and started counting points. His rack was so heavy I could hardly hold his head up, but I counted thirty points. I was just crying; I couldn't even talk," shares Peggy, again wiping tears from her eyes.

Peggy began making phone calls to share the news and get help loading the giant-bodied buck. "I called Joshua, who only lives three miles away. I guess he thought I shot another little one since he didn't come help," recalls Peggy. Soon a small crowd of friends and family was gathered in the shed behind the house, taking pictures and enjoying the fun and excitement a world-class whitetail generates.

As word spread, a more complete and intriguing story of this magnificent buck emerged. Like most other big bucks, this one too had been pursued by multiple people who were hunting him but keeping it quiet. Peggy's neighbor to the east had four years of trail camera pictures of the buck and was hunting him hard that fall. Another person on the west side of town had found his shed antler from the year before. Someone from Lincoln, who hunts a mile east of Peggy, sent her a camera picture of the buck from the year before. "This buck had quite a home range, at least a couple miles. And he was traveling right through Dawson," shares Peggy.

The Peggy Easterwood buck is currently the seventh-largest non-typical firearm whitetail in the Nebraska records book and the largest by a woman. Scoring 235⅛ points, it is an amazing example of a non-typical buck. A mainframe five-by-five with a 20⅛-inch inside spread and main beams of 24⅛ and 25⅝ inches, its typical rack is not exceptionally large, grossing 164⅛ inches and netting only 153⅛. However, the number and size of its abnormal points are incredible, totaling 82⅛ inches! The right antler includes nine abnormal points totaling 39⅛ inches, while the left side has eleven totaling 42⅛. Official scoresheets include only ten blanks for abnormal points on each side of a rack, forcing the measurer of Peggy's buck to squeeze two into one blank!

Peggy was sixty-five, with seven grandchildren when she finally shot her monster buck. She plans on hunting as long as she can and has set a goal of taking a deer with a bow. And you can be sure that when she is in her kitchen this coming fall, she will be scouting for deer.

16

Twenty-Five Points

Hunter Unknown, 1990

- 252⅜-inch non-typical
- Pawnee County

Sometime, most likely during the 1990 hunting season, an unknown teenager hunting in Pawnee County shot one of Nebraska's greatest bucks. The massive non-typical has a beautiful twenty-five-point chocolate-colored rack with a mule deer–like inside spread of 29⅜ inches. Scoring an incredible 252⅜ inches, the buck is currently the second-largest Nebraska non-typical listed in the B&C records book. Whoever the young man or woman was, they must have been ecstatic.

The little information we have about this buck comes from the official scoresheet and a photograph and brief notes included in the buck's official file at B&C headquarters in Missoula, Montana. The scoresheet includes a stamp mark in the upper left corner showing it was received by the B&C on August 20, 2007. The official measurer, now deceased, wrote "Nebraska purchase from teen" in the blank after "Exact Locality Where Killed." The blank after "Hunter" is empty. According to the notes in the official file, the hunter needed money and therefore sold the rack to the DLJM Collection, which is listed as the trophy owner.

When exactly the buck was shot is even more confusing. Next to "Date Killed" it says, "1990 or unknown." However, someone using a different-colored

FIG. 23. Unfortunately we do not know who shot this 252⅜-inch giant from Pawnee County. Photo courtesy of the Boone and Crockett Club.

pen drew a line from that note and wrote "2000," before scribbling it out. In the blank under "Remarks" it says, "This trophy was hunter taken in 1990 in Neb- & purchased By the *DLJM* Collection." The buck was never entered into the Nebraska records book.

Regardless of when it was shot and by whom, the buck is a magnificent example of a non-typical whitetail, and worthy of inclusion in this book. Scoring 252⅜ inches, it is smaller than only two other non-typical Nebraska bucks, the Del Austin archery buck from 1962 scoring 279⅞ inches and the Wesley O'Brien firearm buck from 2009 scoring 284⅝ inches. The buck's typical five-by-five rack is enormous, with an inside spread of 29⅜ inches, main beams of 29⅜ and 28⅝ inches, and long points, including a G2 point on the right, of 14²⁄₈ inches. The buck's typical rack grosses 208²⁄₈ inches and nets 197⅛. The fifteen abnormal points, five on the right antler and ten on the left, total 55²⁄₈ inches. Mass is noteworthy as well, with all eight circumference measurements over five inches, and the third measurements both over six inches.

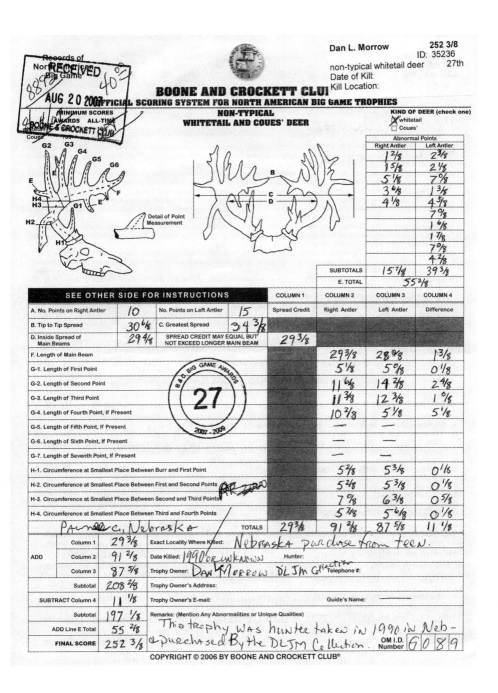

FIG. 24. Unknown scoresheet. Note the "purchase from teen" on the "Exact Locality Where Killed" blank. Courtesy of the Boone and Crockett Club.

17

Pocket Cover

The Jon Allen Buck, 2007

· 212⅝-inch non-typical
· Lancaster County

Big whitetail bucks don't require much cover. A small, out-of-the-way pocket of brush or trees and some nearby food and water is all they really need. If you can find a spot like this, especially on private ground in the middle of a 640-acre section away from any roads, hunt it. Big bucks are notorious for using these out-of-the-way sanctuaries, places they can live, loaf, and grow massive racks without being harassed.

In the fall of 2007 Jon Allen was hunting just such an area in eastern Lancaster County. "There is really not much there, just a creek running through a little draw between two fields, with a two-acre patch of timber on the neighbor's ground across the fence," shares Jon. "You really can't see it from anywhere; it's just a small pocket of cover."

Born in 1971, Jon began deer hunting in the mid-1980s near his boyhood home in Nemaha, Nebraska. Although his family did rifle hunt, their passion was bowhunting. According to Jon, his grandfather Leonard was the first hunter to check in an archery-killed deer in Nebraska. "I grew up hunting with my dad, who was a bowhunter. I went with him even before I could hunt, and would sit with him in the tree stand," remembers Jon. "I've always had a passion for it. Some people ride motorcycles; I go and sit in a tree stand."

After moving to Eagle, just east of Lincoln, Jon began hunting the aforementioned small patch of cover only a mile from his house. While shed-antler hunting the property in the spring of 2006, he and some friends found three sheds in the small wooded draw, including an impressive set of non-typical sheds from a buck he saw the year before.

A year later, on a hot June day in 2007, Jon dragged a ladder stand into that same draw and after leaning it against a tree, went home. On a much cooler early September day before archery season, he snuck back in to finish the job. "There was corn planted on each side, and really tall grass growing in the draw. I heard something coming out of the corn, and looking up I saw a big buck standing about fifty yards away. I just dropped everything and left. I didn't want to spook him," recalls Jon.

Not wanting to chance disturbing the buck, Jon began glassing the area from the road, hoping to determine just how big the buck was. "I could never get a good look at him since he was a long way away and always came out at dusk. I saw him several times, but all I knew was that he was wide and tall," shares Jon. Sometimes it's better not to know.

With the temperatures finally dropping in late September, Jon decided it was time to hunt the big non-typical. After walking in and securing the ladder stand to the tree, he climbed up and sat, enjoying the cool evening. With a busy work schedule and his wife due to have a baby in late November, Jon knew his days on stand were limited. Despite hunting as much as possible over the next few weeks, he never saw the buck.

On October 24, with the temperature in the mid-fifties and the pre-rut phase just beginning, Jon left work to meet up with his hunting partner, Jerry Steinmeyer. After arriving at the property, Jerry dropped Jon off on the road before making his way around the section to another tree stand. After quietly walking in and crawling up into the ladder stand, Jon glanced down at his watch—five o'clock.

He sat quietly for an hour, waiting for prime time—those few golden minutes before dark when bucks begin moving. Hearing rustling in the nearby standing corn, Jon slowly tipped his Primos can call back and forth, sending soft doe bleats into the cool evening air. Fifteen minutes passed—nothing.

FIG. 25. Jon Allen with the fourth-largest non-typical archery buck in the Nebraska records book. Photo courtesy of Jon Allen.

He tried again. This time he spotted a buck coming from the south, along the edge of the corn. "I knew right away it was the big buck, but he was still eighty yards away. I really couldn't see his rack very well," remembers Jon.

Jon watched as the buck moved away toward the timber. Reaching this time for his grunt tube, he blew one soft grunt. The buck ignored it and kept walking. Jon blew it again but louder, and the buck stopped, turned, and stared directly at him. "I still couldn't see the rack, but I could see his ears flipping," adds Jon.

The wide-racked buck spun around and began walking directly toward Jon's stand. Reaching slowly for his bow, Jon tried to calm his nerves and focus on the buck's vitals. After closing the distance to forty yards, the buck stopped behind some overhanging limbs. But once again the buck began walking away toward the timber. "I hung my bow back up and grunted at him. The buck then stopped and started making a scrape and raking an overhanging branch with his rack. When he began peeing in the scrape, I pointed my grunt call behind me and grunted again. He stopped peeing," laughs Jon.

Again the buck changed directions, coming stiff-legged and ears back toward Jon. "I still hadn't seen his rack from the front, which I'm glad I hadn't," remembers Jon. With the buck now angling slightly away at thirty yards, Jon slowly drew and released an arrow from his Bear compound. He saw the arrow sink to the fletching on the buck's front shoulder. "The arrow went through his front shoulder and embedded in the opposite shoulder, pinning his legs together." Struggling to walk, the massive buck broke the arrow in half before pausing at a barbed-wire fence. Turning parallel to the fence the buck went another sixty yards before toppling over and disappearing into the tall grass.

"After finally seeing how big he was when he was walking away, I almost dumped out of my stand. I had to sit down," shares Jon. Not wanting to take any chances on jumping the buck, Jon sat until well after dark and then crept silently to the road where he met Jerry. After going home and changing into some warmer clothing, they went back to look for the buck.

"I found the broken arrow, and there was blood everywhere," remembers Jon. Following the blood trail, Jon spotted a crab-claw point jutting up from the grass. "I reached down and pulled the rack up out of the grass. That is when I finally realized how big he was. I was just in awe."

The Jon Allen buck is definitely awe-inspiring. The buck's thick, nearly matching main beams are exceptionally long, measuring 27⅛ and 27⅛ inches, with an inside spread of 21⅝ inches. With five scorable points on each side, the typical rack grosses an amazing 196⅛ inches and nets 187⅘. Add in seven abnormal points, including double split brow tines totaling 25⅛ inches, and you reach a final score of 212⅝ inches. The buck is currently the fourth-largest archery non-typical in the Nebraska records book.

Unfortunately Jon lost access to the property where he shot his trophy buck. But he continues hunting other properties, constantly on the lookout for an out-of-the-way pocket of cover. "I don't need two hundred acres, just give me a little out-of-the-way draw or pocket of timber," says Jon.

18

Talk of the Town

The Robert Snyder Buck, 1961

- 242⁵/₈-inch non-typical
- Nance County

Nebraska is full of small towns. With the exception of Omaha and Lincoln, every other town is, by most standards, small. Rank Nebraska's five hundred thirty or so incorporated places and nearly five hundred have five thousand or fewer people. And the vast majority of these, nearly four hundred, aren't even considered towns; they are villages with populations of eight hundred or less.

Small towns make Nebraska what it is—a great place to live, work, farm, and raise a family. These are close-knit communities, where people know and help one another. Residents sit together in pews, on bar stools, and uncomfortably on cold metal bleachers at football games. Inevitably they also share news, gossip, and perhaps most importantly, stories.

In the late fall of 1961 the residents of Genoa were sharing the story of a giant whitetail buck shot by longtime resident Rick Snyder. Some were even saying the buck was a new state record.

Genoa is typical small town. About twenty miles west of Columbus, it sits just north of the Loup River in eastern Nance County. In 1960 it had one thousand nine residents; in 2010 it had six fewer. Today it has four churches, two bars, and a football field where the Twin River Titans battle it out on Friday nights.

Robert "Rick" Snyder was born here in 1923. Like other Nebraskans of his generation, Rick spent his youth only dreaming about deer hunting, since there were few deer and there was no deer season. His son Scott explains, "He told me that when he was a kid in the 1940s and 1950s, if someone saw a deer, it was the talk of the town."

By the mid-1950s Nebraska's deer population was on the rise, with the NGPC slowly adding hunting seasons in select counties. It was an amazing few years to be a deer hunter, since with no hunting season for decades there were a lot of mature, records book whitetails roaming the state. The Nebraska records book is full of big bucks from the early 1960s.

Although Rick and his hunting partners had already taken some decent bucks since the first Nance County season in 1959, they had no idea what was in store for them in the fall of 1961. On that eventful day Rick and locals Jim Weldon, Dale Pearson, and Roy Walker drove eight miles west of Genoa for a deer hunt. Having hunted the property before, they knew it was great whitetail country, with deep, cedar-filled draws bordering corn, milo, and soybean fields.

Arriving at the property Rick uncased his Model 88 Winchester in .243 and along with his buddies began walking out the property. Having no luck, the group decided to head to town for lunch. On their way back to the pickup they spotted a massive non-typical buck standing a little over a hundred yards away. Quickly shouldering his Winchester, Rick swung on the now running buck and dropped it cleanly with a single well-placed shot.

For lack of better words, the Robert Snyder buck is just cool looking. The eighteen non-typical points total 49⅞ inches and include it all—three drop tines, stickers off bases and points, a forked brow tine, and a sawlike row of points coming off the front of the right side G2. All these points sprout from a very symmetrical five-by-five typical frame grossing 185⅝ inches and netting 181⅛.

With a final score of 242⅝ inches, it was the Nebraska non-typical fire-arm state record for an amazing forty-eight years, until the Wesley O'Brien buck eclipsed it in 2009. On a side note, there is actually a larger non-typical

FIG. 26. The Robert Snyder buck stood as the non-typical firearm state record for forty-eight years. Photo courtesy of the Boone and Crockett Club.

from Nance County, a 246⅝-inch buck shot in 1960 that is listed in the B&C records book but not in the Nebraska records book. The hunter is unknown.

"When Dad shot his buck, he knew it was big but never imagined it was that big. There was no ground shrinkage," shares Scott. In 1972 Rick and his wife, Emily, purchased Rock's Bar in downtown Genoa, a local watering hole where you can still get a beer. For years Rick's buck hung in the bar, prompting the telling of many a deer hunting story, and presumably a few lies. After Rick passed away in 1983, Scott eventually sold the rack to an antler collector but still has a replica of the antlers in his home.

"After shooting that buck, he was the talk of the town for years," remembers Scott.

19

Records Are Made to Be Broken

The Wesley O'Brien Buck, 2009

- 284⅝-inch non-typical
- Richardson County

As they say, records are made to be broken. But surely not this one. Not Ol' Mossy Horns, a buck so famous it's known throughout Nebraska and the country by its nickname. So famous, you can purchase paintings, prints, coffee mugs, dinner plates, replicas of the antlers, and sculptures depicting its incredible 279⅞-inch non-typical rack. For almost forty years it was the archery world record. Shot with a bow in 1962 by lifelong Nebraskan Del Austin, the gnarly thirty-nine-pointer was "Nebraska's buck," the highest-scoring whitetail ever shot in the state.

Then the unthinkable happened. Not only was the record broken; it was broken by a Texan!

On November 14, 2009, somewhere on private ground in Richardson County, Wesley O'Brien from Lexington, Texas, lifted his .270 Weatherby Magnum, centering the crosshairs on the largest buck ever shot in Nebraska.[1] With a slow squeeze of the trigger, he rewrote the records book.

Hunting the evening of opening day with Brandon Rhodus, also of Lexington, Texas, and Dave Haveman of Louisville, Nebraska, the trio spotted the massive buck through the timber two hundred fifty yards away. With only a few minutes left of legal shooting light, Wes closed the distance to

FIG. 27. Wesley O'Brien with his 284⅛-inch non-typical, the highest-scoring buck ever killed in Nebraska. Photo courtesy of *Nebraskaland* magazine/ Nebraska Game and Parks Commission.

about one hundred yards and made a solid broadside shot on the buck. After running about thirty yards, the giant non-typical hit the cold Nebraska dirt.

Taking the buck to the Ak-Sar-Ben Aquarium, near Gretna, it was green-scored at an amazing 281⅛ inches by aquarium director and official measurer Tony Korth.[2] Text messages, word of mouth, hunting forums, and online articles quickly spread the story and pictures of a possible new Nebraska state record. For twenty-four-year-old Wes the sudden attention and notoriety was undoubtedly shocking. Wes and his buck were instant hunting celebrities.

And when you see the Wesley O'Brien buck, it is easy to understand why. It is freakishly non-typical, with a crazy tangle of antlers sitting atop its head. Eventually scored at 284⅛ inches, it's the type of rack that makes an official measurer ask: Where do I even start?

Official measurers begin by identifying the typical points. All non-typical bucks, regardless of how gnarly they look, have a typical rack hidden somewhere in all those points. Often using different-colored tape, measurers stick a

Wesley A. O'Brien BASS PRO 284
Lexington, TX ID:3987£
non-typical whitetail deer 28th
Date of Kill: 11/14/2009
Kill Location: Richardson Co., NE

BOONE AND CROCKETT CLUB
OFFICIAL SCORING SYSTEM FOR NORTH AMERICAN BIG GAME TROPHIES

NON-TYPICAL
WHITETAIL AND COUES' DEER

MINIMUM SCORES	AWARDS	ALL-TIME
whitetail	185	195
Coues'	105	120

KIND OF DEER (check on
☒ whitetail
☐ Coues'

Mod Firearm

ENTERED

Detail of Point Measurement

PAID
JAN 2 5 2010

BOONE & CROCKETT CLUB See attachment →

	Abnormal Points	
	Right Antler	Left Antler
	2 0/8	2 1/8
	3 5/8	1 0/8
	3 3/8	4 4/8
	1 0/8	7 1/8
	2 3/8	6 0/8
	2 1/8	1 6/8
	20 5/8	2 1/8
	5 7/8	1 4/8
	1 5/8	7 5/8
	7 1/8	7 0/8
SUBTOTALS	49 6/8	40 6/8
E. TOTAL	90 4/8 + 43 7/8 = 134

SEE OTHER SIDE FOR INSTRUCTIONS		COLUMN 1	COLUMN 2	COLUMN 3	COLUMN 4
		Spread Credit	Right Antler	Left Antler	Difference
A. No. Points on Right Antler 22 14	No. Points on Left Antler 24 14				
B. Tip to Tip Spread 6 6/8	C. Greatest Spread 23 7/8				
D. Inside Spread of Main Beams 16 1/8	SPREAD CREDIT MAY EQUAL BUT NOT EXCEED LONGER MAIN BEAM	16 1/8			
F. Length of Main Beam			22 2/8	24 2/8	2 0/8
G-1. Length of First Point			10 6/8	9 7/8	7/8
G-2. Length of Second Point			8 5/8	10 1/8	1 4/8
G-3. Length of Third Point			6 5/8	9 6/8	3 1/8
G-4. Length of Fourth Point, If Present				5 1/8	5 1/8
G-5. Length of Fifth Point, If Present					
G-6. Length of Sixth Point, If Present					
G-7. Length of Seventh Point, If Present					
H-1. Circumference at Smallest Place Between Burr and First Point			7 4/8	7 1/8	3/8
H-2. Circumference at Smallest Place Between First and Second Points			4 2/8	4 3/8	1/8
H-3. Circumference at Smallest Place Between Second and Third Points			4 7/8	5 2/8	3/8
H-4. Circumference at Smallest Place Between Third and Fourth Points			3 1/8	4 5/8	1 4/8
TOTALS		16 1/8	68 0/8	80 4/8	15 0/8

ADD	Column 1	16 1/8	Exact Locality Where Killed: Richardson Co. Nebraska
	Column 2	68 0/8	Date Killed: 11-14-09 Hunter: Wesley A O'Brien
	Column 3	80 4/8	Trophy Owner: Wesley O'Brien BASS PRO SHOPS Telephone #:
	Subtotal	164 5/8	Trophy Owner's Address: 1031 CR 348 Lexington TX. 76947
SUBTRACT Column 4		15 0/8	Trophy Owner's E-mail: Guide's Name: N/A
	Subtotal	149 5/8	Remarks: (Mention Any Abnormalities or Unique Qualities)
ADD Line E Total		134 3/8	See attachment for additional points
FINAL SCORE		284 0/8	

B&C BIG GAME AWARDS 28 2010-2012

OM I.D. Number P 0 7 2

COPYRIGHT © 2008 BY BOONE AND CROCKETT CLUB®

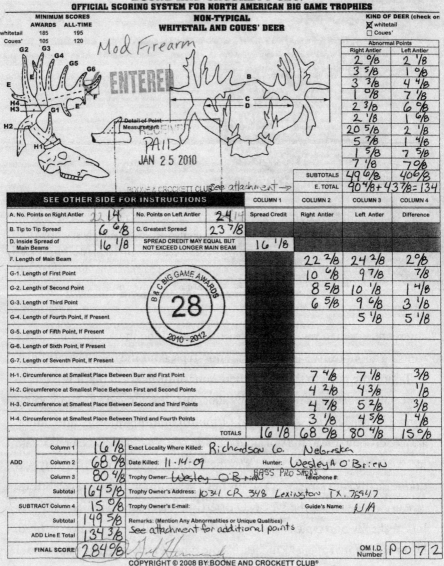

FIG. 28. Wesley O'Brien scoresheet. Note the amazing 134⅜ inches of abnormal points on Line E. Courtesy of the Boone and Crockett Club.

piece on the tip of each point to differentiate typical points from non-typical. After measuring each point the tape is removed and the length recorded.

For a buck netting 284⁰⁄₈ inches, the O'Brien buck's typical four-by-five frame is quite small and unsymmetrical. Out of the seven typical points, only two are over ten inches, including the brow tine on the right antler that measures an impressive 10⁶⁄₈ inches. The left brow tine is also long, measuring 9⁷⁄₈ inches. The rack is also narrow, with an inside spread of only 16⅛ inches, while its main beams are not particularly long, measuring 22²⁄₈ and 24²⁄₈ inches. The typical frame grosses 164⁵⁄₈ inches, and with 15⁰⁄₈ inches of deductions, nets only 149⁵⁄₈. In comparison Ol' Mossy Horns has a symmetrical five-by-five typical rack grossing 191³⁄₈ inches and netting 184⁵⁄₈.

However, the O'Brien buck makes up for a smallish typical frame with twenty-seven abnormal points, including one branching off the right base measuring 20⁵⁄₈ inches. The eighteen abnormal points on the right side total an incredible 90⁴⁄₈ inches, while the nine on the left total 43⁷⁄₈, resulting in 134³⁄₈ inches of abnormal points! Ol' Mossy Horns actually has more abnormal points, with twenty-nine, but they total only 95²⁄₈ inches.

The Wesley O'Brien buck actually knocked two long-standing records out of their number one spots in the Nebraska records book: Ol' Mossy Horns, as the largest non-typical regardless of category, and the state record non-typical firearm buck scoring 242⁵⁄₈ inches, shot in 1961 by Robert Snyder. Eventually purchased by Bass Pro Shops, the O'Brien buck is currently the fourteenth-largest non-typical listed in the B&C records book.

The O'Brien buck begs the question: Will a lucky Nebraska hunter ever break this amazing record? Remember, records are made to be broken.

20

Like Father, Like Son

The Gary and Adam Stohs Bucks, 1994 and 2015

> Train up a child in the way he should go: and
> when he is old, he will not depart from it.
> —Proverbs 22:6

· 180⁴/₈-inch and 218⁴/₈-inch non-typicals
· Gage County

Gary Stohs raised two boys into men. Two of his goals: raise Christian men, and raise bowhunters. Sons watch their fathers, soaking up not only what they do but also what they say. It is how they learn to be men. If you want a churchgoing man, then take your boy to church. If you want an outdoorsman, then take your boy hunting, fishing, trapping, and camping.

Gary began bowhunting in 1988, the year his oldest son Adam was born. Over the next few years his bowhunting skills grew along with his son. In 1993 he had his best hunting year to date, arrowing a bobcat and two bucks, with one grossing, but not quite netting, enough to make the records book.

"I fully expected the 1994 season to be somewhat of a downer in comparison," remembers Gary. That didn't stop him from going at it hard-core and full bore. "I hunted long and hard, scouting, still-hunting, using scents, grunting, rattling. You name it, I tried it." By late October he was genuinely frustrated, since he hadn't even seen a shooter buck. "On the twenty-seventh I decided to try one of my best stands, the one I had shot the big buck from the year before." The stand was located in an eight-hundred-acre pasture of native grass, intersected by oak canyons and thick cedar draws. Perfect big buck habitat.

Taking six-year-old Adam along with him, they settled into the tree stand for an evening hunt. "It turned out to be an exciting evening for both of us," remembers Gary. Adam had a blast, spotting several squirrels and two raccoons, all the while helping his dad scan the woods for deer. Soon a group of five does came trailing by, only fifty yards away. Scanning their back trail Gary spotted a giant non-typical buck following the does. Sensing something amiss, the buck stopped, waiting and watching. After legal shooting light the buck slowly ambled past Gary and Adam at thirty-five yards. Soaking it all in Adam looked up and smiled at his dad.

Gary's work schedule over the next week was busy, allowing for only one evening hunt during which he saw four does. Finally, with a free evening on November 5 and the rut heating up, he drove toward the same property, hoping for another encounter with the giant non-typical. Pulling up to the gate his heart sank. The owner had moved a couple hundred head of cattle onto the property. He backed out and drove home.

Try as he might Gary couldn't get the giant buck out of his mind, especially with the rut now in full swing. "I couldn't stand it any longer . . . cattle or no cattle," shares Gary. The following evening, after only an hour on stand, he spotted three does followed by a fork horn and the big non-typical. The big buck, after chasing the fork horn away, nosed around the does, eventually pushing them to the south. After working over a low-hanging branch with his antlers, the buck followed the does down a trail that would bring him within bow range. "He was trotting toward the does, and I grunted at him. He stopped at forty yards but was alert and looking in my direction," remembers Gary. He let the buck walk.

Two days later, with a new ladder stand in the back of his truck, Gary drove hard toward the property. Arriving late and throwing caution to the wind, he worked as quickly and quietly as possible erecting the new stand. "As I climbed down to get my bow and gear, I glanced out into the pasture and the same two bucks were standing fifty yards away!" recalls Gary. Scrambling back up the ladder, Gary sat glassing the big five-by-six, thinking he may score in the 160s.

"The next afternoon, before leaving work, I told everyone that tonight was the night!" remembers Gary. Donning his "lucky camo" he devised a meticulous game plan. After spraying down with scent killer, he opened a can of deer scent, laying a trail all the way to his stand. He also paused to cut some cedar branches, rubbing those on his clothes as well. Arriving at his stand he did one last thing: he placed the scent canister in a locust tree, eighteen yards away.

A few minutes later, hearing rustling leaves, Gary glanced over his shoulder and spotted a doe. Hoping to call in any trailing bucks, Gary grunted softly. The doe trotted past, and once again the same fork horn buck was following, with the big non-typical not far behind. "I whistled, and the big buck stopped right on the scent trail I had laid down. He put his head down and followed it straight toward me," remembers Gary. Stopping at the scent canister and facing directly at Gary, the buck let out three snort-wheezes.

Already at full draw, Gary waited for the buck to turn broadside. Hearing a grunt, Gary glanced down to see the fork horn buck standing only fifteen yards away. Fearing the big buck might bolt, he centered the pin on the base of the buck's neck and pulled the trigger on his release, sending an arrow into the buck's heart. After running only seventy yards, the giant toppled over.

Shaking with excitement Gary walked up on the fallen buck, realizing it was much bigger than he imagined. "I gave thanks to the Lord for such a beautiful animal," shares Gary. Soon family and friends gathered to take pictures. Adam, dressed proudly in his own camo coat, posed next to his dad.

The Gary Stohs buck's typical six-by-five rack includes main beams of 25⁴⁄₈ and 26⅛ inches, good mass, and nearly matching brow tines of over six inches. With the missing G5 on the left antler accounting for 2⅝ inches of the 7²⁄₈ inches of total deductions, the typical frame grosses 176⅝ inches and nets 169³⁄₈. Add in four abnormal points totaling 11⅛ inches and you reach a final score of 180⁴⁄₈ inches. It was the largest archery whitetail buck killed in Nebraska in 1994 and at the time the eighth largest in the Nebraska records book.

Fast-forward twenty-one years to Halloween 2015, and Adam, now thirty-one, is perched in his own Gage County deer stand. Hearing what sounds

FIG. 29. Gary (*left*) and young Adam Stohs pose with Gary's 180⅛-inch non-typical, the largest archery buck killed in 1994. Photo courtesy of Gary Stohs.

like a deer jumping, he stands up, readies his bow, and waits. Five minutes pass—nothing. Sitting down and hanging his bow back up, Adam looks up, and standing broadside at twenty yards is the giant non-typical he's been hunting all season! "The air was dead calm, and I knew if I moved he would spot me instantly," remembers Adam. "I watched him feed and slowly walk away, and I couldn't do anything about it." With the buck now moving directly away, Adam slowly stood, lifting his bow and drawing in one smooth motion. "He turned down another trail and stopped forty yards away. I settled my pin and released an arrow." Jumping the string the buck spun and ran. Adam immediately called his dad, and the two looked for sign of a hit. Nothing. Amazingly they captured a trail camera photograph of the buck later that night in the same area.

The story of Adam's 2015 buck actually began in late July when a coworker showed him a trail camera picture of the giant non-typical, taken about three-quarters of a mile from a piece of family ground. "I never saw the buck until the end of October when they started picking corn. That's when I started getting pictures of him on my trail cameras," recalls Adam. "The area I was hunting is just a little five- or six-acre patch of timber in the middle of a section. It's surrounded by open ground and isn't much to hunt, but one thing Dad taught us is to hunt where everyone else doesn't."

Following his clean miss on Halloween, Adam and Gary went in on November 4 and hung another stand, allowing Adam to hunt the forecasted wind direction for the coming weekend. On November 7 Adam snuck in and, despite staying on stand all day, saw little.

"The next morning, I got set up and it was like flipping a light switch, the rut was on," remembers Adam. Seeing does and a fork horn at first light, and then later some running deer behind him, Adam felt good about this hunt. At about eight o'clock a doe walked past at twenty yards. Glancing down the trail behind the doe, Adam saw the massive non-typical walking toward him. After the buck came to within twenty yards, a 120-inch five-by-five came in, causing the giant buck to turn and chase him off. "If he had taken a couple more steps I could have shot him."

An hour later Adam spotted the giant buck again, chasing does in a cut soybean field. "He was out there in the middle of the morning, chasing does, acting stupid," Adam shares with a laugh. The buck eventually moved off the field to the south and into a cedar thicket.

The action continued throughout the day with multiple deer sightings. At about four o'clock, with a doe and fawn feeding nearby, the five-by-five from earlier showed up again, grunting and scraping. "The five-by-five had this deep, gnarly grunt. But then I hear this high-pitched, girly grunt and see a buck standing about forty yards away with his head down in a deadfall. He jacks his head up, throwing a six-foot [tree] limb over his ass!" shares Adam. It was the giant non-typical. "He was all postured up . . . like he was the man. He started walking sideways at the smaller buck."

With the big buck working a scrape, Adam stood and slowly turned to his right to get into position for a shot. "I kicked my backpack as I turned, and a fawn that was at the base of my tree spooked," recalls Adam. "But I was

FIG. 30. Adam (*left*) and Gary Stohs with Adam's massive 218⅜-inch non-typical, the third largest in the Nebraska archery records book. Photo courtesy of Adam Stohs.

already at full draw, and the buck came walking down the trail toward me, giving me a perfect broadside shot at twenty yards. I shot, hitting a small limb I didn't see, but the arrow still double lunged him." Adam watched as the giant buck ran for only twenty yards before stopping and tipping over in plain sight. "I was about shaking out of that tree stand."

After calling his wife, he called his dad. "Dad was hunting, so all he says is, 'That's great, I got to go, I'm deer hunting,'" laughs Adam.

Once safely on the ground, Adam approached the fallen buck, trying to comprehend what had just happened. "I knelt down and felt so thankful and blessed to shoot a deer like that. I don't know what I did to deserve it, but I'm glad God put him in front of me," shares Adam. Later that night, dressed in his own camo coat, Gary posed proudly with his son.

Any hunter would feel blessed to shoot a deer like the Adam Stohs buck.

A mainframe five-by-five, the typical rack is not exceptionally large for a buck this size, grossing 172⅞ inches while netting 167⅝. What makes it a world-class archery buck is the number of non-typical points and the mass. The thirteen abnormal points, five on the right and eight on the left, total 50⅝ inches, giving the buck a unique, gnarly appearance. The nearly matching twenty-six-inch main beams are massive, with the eight circumference measurements totaling over forty-six inches! *Bowhunter* magazine put Adam and his buck on the cover of its November/December 2016 edition, a testament to its size. The Adam Stohs buck currently stands as the third-largest archery non-typical in the Nebraska records book and the largest from Gage County.

Adam gives much of the credit to his dad, for turning him into a passionate outdoorsman. "Dad planted the hunting seed in my brother Kyle and me," shares Adam. "I had a bow in my hand when I was four and remember practicing with my dad. I grew up with a bow in my hand." Like father, like son.

21

Crossbow

The Bob Malander Buck, 2017

· 195³⁄₈-inch non-typical
· Nance County

Crossbows are ancient weapons. No one knows for certain, but sometime in the fifth or sixth century BC, someone in China, or maybe Europe, began tinkering with a traditional bow, trying to figure out a way to keep the bowstring back without having to hold it. Perhaps the spark of ingenuity was someone missing a buck after having to hold their bow back too long. Whatever the reason, someone eventually designed and assembled the necessary parts—a stock, limbs, riser, cocking stirrup, barrel, and trigger. Although the materials have changed, the basic design has not.

Ultimately replaced by firearms, the crossbow became somewhat of an oddity seldom seen in the deer hunting woods. In fact for many years most states in the United States severely limited their use for hunting, with some banning them outright. In the 1980s, with deer populations increasing and hunters aging, states began loosening restrictions. Now every state except Oregon allows some deer hunting with a crossbow.

Nebraska first allowed crossbows for deer hunting in 1985 but only for those with a disability preventing them from pulling a bow. Crossbows eventually became legal for anyone during rifle season, and in 2011, during archery season. Bob Malander, a longtime bowhunter, made the switch from compound bow to crossbow for the same reason many do—a sore and aging shoulder.

Bob grew up hunting the rugged Red Rock area north of tiny Belgrade, Nebraska. Toting his BB gun, his first hunts were pursuing cottontails and squirrels in the cedar-and-oak-covered canyons near his home in Nance County. "In 1968 my dad got a deer permit, the only time he ever hunted deer. I got to go along on opening weekend and I really enjoyed it. The next year I bought a permit and tagged a nice four-by-four. I haven't missed a rifle season since," shares Bob. In the early 1970s Bob bought his first bow, a Bear recurve.

Over the next fifty years Bob became an experienced deer hunter, while also passing his passion on to his six children and eventually his nineteen grandchildren. "I took my children along as soon as they were big enough to follow, sit, and be quiet," explains Bob. "Hunting is such a special way of bonding with family, friends, and God. Nowhere else do I feel closer to God than when I'm out in nature."

With five decades of deer hunting under his belt, Bob knew immediately what he had on his game camera in early August of 2017. The huge non-typical was by far the biggest buck he had ever seen. He also knew the early season is one of the best times to kill a giant buck, since their feeding patterns are predictable. "I started scouting and planning how to hunt him right away," recalls Bob. Hoping to pattern the buck, Bob began glassing the field where he had captured the game camera images. In early September coworker Justin Meyer spotted the buck in the field and snapped a picture through his binoculars. Giant.

After studying Justin's picture Bob set up a new tree stand in hopes of ambushing the buck. After sitting fruitlessly in this stand for two evenings, he decided to scout the edge of the field for another stand site. He found a perfect tree for a stand, but it was four hundred yards from where he wanted to be. Moving on, he continued looking until finally giving up and heading back toward the pickup. "When I passed that tree again, it seemed to be telling me to move the stand there," remembers Bob. He listened to the tree.

On his first sit in the new stand, two small bucks came directly underneath. "I knew I had the right spot."

The next day, September 10, was warm and sunny, with Bob traveling to Columbus to watch his grandson play football. Arriving back home Bob decided to get in a quick evening hunt. After crawling up into his stand, he sat swatting mosquitoes and scanning the soybean field for deer. At seven forty-five, the massive non-typical stepped clear of the woods and entered the beans, only one hundred yards away. Unfortunately the buck began slowly feeding away from Bob. "I was thinking I wasn't going to get a shot, so I took out my phone and began videoing the buck so I would have something to show the kids," recalls Bob. Then for some unknown reason the buck turned and ran straight toward his stand! Quickly dropping his cell phone and grabbing his Horton crossbow, Bob tried to calm his nerves as the massive non-typical came running toward him.

FIG. 31. Bob Malander with his 195⅜-inch state record, his first deer with a crossbow. Photo courtesy of Bob Malander.

After closing the distance to forty yards, the buck stopped broadside. Fighting the shakes Bob centered the crosshairs and watched the bolt disappear through the buck's vitals. "I heard the hit and knew it was right on," remembers Bob. But the buck didn't move. Slowly lifting his binoculars Bob could clearly see the entry wound. As if nothing had happened the buck slowly walked away, disappearing down the same trail he had entered the field on. As the sky darkened Bob sat quietly in his tree stand replaying the shot over and over in his mind.

"After returning home and talking with my sons, we decided to wait until daylight and not risk losing him. It was a very long night, and I started second-guessing my shot placement," recalls Bob. After a fitful night's sleep Bob and his son Justin headed out at first light. Following the trail the buck exited on, they found him lying dead only thirty yards from the edge of the field.

"That buck got bigger as I walked up on it, a true monster," remembers Bob. After his son Dan arrived the three hunters celebrated by taking pictures and just relishing the experience. "We gave thanks to God and enjoyed the moment. I was feeling very blessed to have fulfilled a lifelong dream of taking a records book buck."

The Bob Malander buck is definitely a buck of a lifetime. The buck's five-by-five typical frame is 20⅛ inches wide and is quite symmetrical, grossing 168⅝ inches while netting 157⅝. The buck has five abnormal points on the right and three on the left, totaling 37⅝ inches, including a unique drop tine curling down off the front of the right beam. With good mass extending to the ends of both beams, the buck nets 195⅜ inches.

After becoming legal during archery season, crossbow hunting in Nebraska increased in popularity, necessitating the creation of a separate crossbow category in the Nebraska records book. Bob's buck is currently the non-typical state record. Not bad for his first deer with a crossbow!

22

2 County

The Jeff Moody Buck, 2003

· 223⅜-inch non-typical
· Lancaster County

Like most born-and-bred Nebraskans, Jeff Moody knows his license plate numbers. Growing up in McCook, 48 was on his plate. He knew nearby counties—79 for Red Willow, 60 for Frontier, 79 for Hayes. Mostly the bigger numbers, from less populous western Nebraska counties. The smaller numbers he knew by city, 15 for North Platte, 9 for Kearney, 2 for Lincoln, and 1 for Omaha.

Since 1922 the state of Nebraska has issued license plates using a prefix number to identify counties.[1] These prefix numbers were assigned by the number of registered vehicles in the county in 1922, so Douglas County, having the most vehicles, claimed 1, Lancaster 2, and so on, all the way down to Hooker County at 93. For rural Nebraskans, license plates provide a quick and easy way to identify nonlocals.

Following a job-related move in 2001, Jeff found himself doing something he never anticipated—swapping his 48 plates for 2. Now living in Hickman, just south of Lincoln, he was in unfamiliar country. "I didn't think there was a single deer in Lancaster County," laughs Jeff.

With the 2002 bow season approaching and no place to hunt, he began scouting the back roads of southern Lancaster County. "I went for a drive one evening and spotted a massive non-typical buck just standing on the edge of a field, only four miles from my house. I couldn't believe it," remembers Jeff. After looking up the landowner, he realized they both worked for the BNSF Railway Company. "I went to his door to ask permission, but since I was new at work he didn't recognize me. At first he told me no, but after talking for a while he changed his mind."

After gaining permission Jeff realized he had discovered a deer-hunting honey hole. Consisting of two quarter sections divided by a gravel road, the property is mainly cropland, except for two patches of timber, brush, and grass bordering waterways near the center of each parcel. Each of these brushy patches is about ten acres, with one abutting public land. Sweetening the pot further, the entire three hundred twenty acres sits in a landscape dotted with homes and small acreages, providing deer cover and food but limited hunting pressure.

By 2002 Jeff was already an accomplished bowhunter, having taken trophy-caliber whitetails and mule deer. After shooting his first mule deer with a rifle in the mid-1980s at the age of twelve, he discovered archery. "None of my buddies bowhunted, but my dad had an old Bear Whitetail bow, and I began shooting carp with it, just messing around," explains Jeff. "After purchasing my own bow, I really got into shooting paper and 3D targets. I started hunting turkey and deer, and after shooting a really nice five-by-five on the Republican River in 1995, bowhunting became an infatuation."

Jeff began planning and preparing to hunt the monster non-typical. Experience taught him to hunt the wind, and after studying the shape, size, and orientation of the two patches of timber, he knew northerly winds were ideal. Hanging a tree stand in each patch, he waited for opening day. Despite hunting every chance he could, the first month passed without a single sighting of the giant buck. With the rut and rifle season approaching, Jeff decided to roll the dice and try an especially aggressive move. Posting one of his hunting partners on the road separating the two stand sites, he walked through one of the patches of timber to see if the buck was still around. "Sure enough I jumped him, and he ran out across the open field. He was huge," remembers Jeff.

Thinking the buck might come back into his sanctuary later that evening, Jeff snuck in and climbed into his tree stand. With a light northwest wind, the conditions were perfect. A small buck soon appeared, making his way to a scrape thirty yards downwind of Jeff's stand. Catching his scent the buck bolted. Soon after, with the sun setting, Jeff spotted the massive buck sneaking back into his refuge. "He came in quick and made his way toward the same scrape. After the buck made it to the scrape, I just knew if he took another step he would wind me," remembers Jeff. Drawing his bow Jeff noticed one small opening between the branches and let an arrow fly. "I hit him too high and too far forward." The buck ran only a short distance with the arrow dropping from his side to the ground. "I was sick to my stomach. How could I have messed that up?"

Wanting to be certain the previous evening's hit was nonfatal, Jeff went back in the next morning, not bothering to carry his bow. His hunting partner was hunting the other stand across the road. Reaching the scrape, Jeff followed the meager blood trail for a short distance before finding his arrow. Seeing no sign of the buck, he decided to cross the road and look in the other patch of cover. On entering the woods he spotted the buck fifty yards away, bedded down with a doe! The buck jumped to its feet and was gone. Jeff never saw him again that season.

Throughout the winter Jeff wondered and worried whether the buck was still alive. Not hearing anything about a giant buck being killed in the area kept his hopes alive. That spring Jeff found solid proof that the buck was indeed still alive—an unmistakably massive shed antler.

After a long summer spent shooting his bow and wondering whether he would get another chance at the buck, the 2003 archery season finally arrived. "I started hunting hard, but except for seeing some large tracks just before the season, I didn't see him the whole first month," Jeff remembers. However, his favorite time to hunt was just starting. Like many bowhunters, Jeff considers the late October pre-rut an especially productive period, with bucks on their feet during daylight hours searching for the first does to come into heat.

October 28 dawned cool, with winds gusting to forty miles per hour.

FIG. 32. Jeff Moody holding his 223⅞-inch Lancaster County archery buck, the second-largest non-typical in the records book. Photo courtesy of Jeff Moody.

Thinking it best to stay home, Jeff skipped the morning hunt. By early afternoon, with the giant buck on his mind, he decided to give it a shot. In his stand by two thirty that afternoon, he sat swaying in his tree stand, only to watch as the farmer began disking corn a short distance away. Jeff thought to himself, *This just isn't going to work.*

Deciding to wait it out, he sat for two hours before finally spotting a group of does and a small buck browsing through the trees. Jeff watched as they slowly fed out of sight. Then, as bucks often do, the massive non-typical just appeared, walking directly toward Jeff's stand. "He acted like he didn't have a care in the world, just walking with his head down, right at me," recalls Jeff with a wide smile. "He was coming fast and I didn't know which side of the tree he was going to pass on. I positioned myself to shoot the left side, and of course he went directly under my tree on the right."

"At this point I knew he was big and I was trying not to look at his antlers, but everything was happening so quickly. Turning, hoping the stand wouldn't squeak, I got my bow around to the other side of the tree and came to full draw. I remember putting my yellow top pin on him, and him being so close I could move the pin around on different parts of his back. I kept thinking I should wait for him to turn, but he was moving directly away, so I shot him right through the back at fifteen yards," continues Jeff.

At the shot, the buck jumped forward and took off on a dead run. "I watched him the entire time; he made it about one hundred yards and then flipped over backward," remembers Jeff. Staring in disbelief, Jeff realized the buck, which had consumed his thoughts and dreams for two years, was lying dead in the cut corn.

After sitting in his stand until pitch dark, Jeff returned home and got a flashlight before making his way toward the buck. "Walking up on him was the biggest adrenaline rush I've ever had! He was way bigger than I thought," recalls Jeff. After sitting next to the buck and enjoying the moment, he called his hunting partner and told him the news. His next call went out to his mother and father. "My mom answered, and in my excitement I shouted, 'I just shot the biggest &$#@ deer you have ever seen,'" laughs Jeff. "I never talk to my mom that way, so she knew it was big."

Shooting a buck the size of the Jeff Moody buck would make anyone cuss. Scoring an even 223⅝ inches, it ranks second in the Nebraska non-typical archery category behind Ol' Mossy Horns, the legendary 279⅞-inch buck shot by Del Austin in 1962. The buck's typical six-by-six rack grosses 189⅞ inches while netting 181⅝, and includes extraordinary main beams of 29⅝ and 28²⁄₈ inches and an inside spread of 21⅛ inches. Add in the ten abnormal points totaling 41³⁄₈ inches and you arrive at a world-class archery buck scoring of 223⅝ inches. The largest ever arrowed in 2 County.

Now living back in McCook, Jeff continues pursuing his passion of hunting big bucks. However, his time in Lancaster County made him a better hunter. "Moving to Lancaster County changed me as a bowhunter. I went from hunting the Republican River bottoms and wide-open country for mule deer, to hunting hedgerows and small pockets of cover. I learned that you don't have to hunt something incredible; you can just hunt something small coming off something that is incredible," explains Jeff. Solid advice.

23

Ol' Mossy Horns

The Del Austin Buck, 1962

Dick Idol

· 279⅞-inch non-typical
· Hall County

Surprisingly few of the top whitetails in the record book were taken by serious hunters who knew of their presence and hounded them for any substantial amount of time. However, the story of the archery world record non-typical is perhaps history's most classic saga of a big buck hunt, even though the bowhunter who pursued the deer most fervently never got him.

This story begins back in the 1950s, along the Platte River south of Shelton, Nebraska, an area of open prairie and farmland that rolls for seemingly endless miles. Cover lies at the bottom of ravines and gullies, with most of the larger blocks of trees and brush being along the river and its major tributaries. Because of fertile soil in the bottoms, substantial crop fields also lie along this major waterway. The river is wide but fairly shallow, with much of the basin featuring islands of various shapes and sizes. Some are small, house-sized landmasses, while others are more than a mile in length. Most are choked with heavy underbrush, especially willows, and some have large cottonwoods. The edge of the river itself is covered with the same types of trees and brush.

Back in 1958, rumors began to leak out about a giant buck with a "weird" rack that lived along the river and had been seen on the farm of Dan Thomas.

This buck's most relentless pursuer turned out to be Al Dawson, who had heard the rumors. At that time Al was thirty-one years old and lived in Hastings, about thirty miles southeast of Shelton. He'd recently started bow-hunting, and he was so taken with it that he'd totally given up deer hunting with a gun.

Dan's farm was one Al especially enjoyed hunting, and one day during the 1958 season, he walked across a freshly cut cornfield to look for deer sign. He'd stopped at a fence to look over an adjoining alfalfa field and the timbered river bottom beyond when he caught a glimpse of movement. Five or six deer had broken out of the timber and were heading straight for him.

In the lead was a tremendous buck. Not only was the deer huge, with a high, massive rack, but the antlers were also the most unusual Al had ever seen. "There were heavy, scraggly points, long and short, growing from the main beams in all directions," he said. "Strangest of all, he had these long prongs curving out and down on either side of his head, between eye and ear. They extended below his jaws, giving him an odd, lop-eared appearance."

It appeared the deer wanted to cross the fence on the trail where Al stood. The hunter had been caught in the open, so he risked taking a couple steps backward, sank to one knee, and nocked an arrow. By now the non-typical and other deer had approached to within fifty or sixty yards, but suddenly the buck swerved off to the side and cleared the fence seventy yards from Al. The monster then stopped broadside and looked directly at him. Al knew he wasn't going to come closer, and in the heat of the moment he decided to take a shot. Not surprisingly the arrow fell short, and the buck whirled around and led the entire herd back to the same wooded bottom from which they'd come.

Al retrieved his arrow and followed the huge tracks across the field for some distance. He knew there would be no hope for another shot though, so he finally left the tracks and headed back to his car. That morning the name "Mossy Horns" came to him, as it seemed to fit that irregular set of antlers. (Today this name is still attached to the deer.) And that same morning, the bowhunter vowed he'd keep after that buck until the great trophy was his.

Al hunted the remainder of the bow season, which ended after Christmas, and had a half-dozen chances at lesser deer. But on each occasion the thought of Mossy Horns kept him from shooting, as he had only a single deer tag. If he waited there was always a chance. As it turned out he did see the huge buck twice more that season but never got a shot.

During the 1958 season, Al had hunted the buck alone. But the following year he'd be joined by a couple of fellow archery hunters. Gene Halloran, a retired farmer, and Charley Marlowe, a Hastings advertising executive and the only member of their Oregon Trail Bowhunters Club who'd killed a deer with a bow up to that time, also would become obsessed with the hunt for Mossy Horns.

By now Dan Thomas had his own reasons for wanting the buck dead. A couple years earlier, he'd planted fifty young spruce trees as a windbreak about thirty yards from his house and the big buck had taken it upon himself to destroy them. In one season he'd killed all fifty with his antlers!

In the fall of 1959 Al, Charley, and Gene built tree blinds in a half-dozen locations. In those days portable tree stands were just being developed, so their ambush sites consisted of small platforms ten to twenty feet off the ground. Despite their best efforts, most of the archery season passed without anyone even glimpsing the huge buck. By now the old second-guessing game had begun. Charley shot a doe, ending his season. Al finally resigned himself to the possibility that the buck had moved to another area or was dead.

Still, he kept hunting. Then late one November evening he saw Mossy Horns about one hundred fifty yards away, following a slough. His movement was extremely slow and cautious, and it was clear that he'd pass well out of range. Several times he stopped at the edge of thickets to test the wind and listen for danger. This was the first time Al had seen him all year, and his rack appeared nearly identical to the one he'd worn the previous season.

Finally Al decided he had nothing to lose by trying to stalk close enough for a shot. A strong wind was blowing from the deer to the archer, and there was enough brush that Al just might be able to stay out of sight.

For a half mile he moved along on the most careful stalk he'd ever made. Three times the buck stopped to thrash trees with his huge rack, and each time the hunter crept closer. On two of those occasions he was in bow range, but there was simply too much brush in the way. Finally the buck paused at the edge of a thicket to work over another willow clump just twenty-five yards from Al. Two steps around a willow clump and the excited bowhunter would have an open shot. But just then a dry twig broke underfoot and the buck was gone.

Al didn't see him again until the final evening of the season. As the tired hunter walked out of the river bottom at dusk, realizing the buck had eluded him for another season, he noticed a dark form standing in the open. Al finally made out the white throat patch and huge antlers as the buck stood calmly, watching him from just out of range. Then the monster turned and disappeared into the gloom, drawing the season to a fitting close.

Al muttered, "Okay, Mossy. Next year will be different."

During the summer of 1960 Dan saw the buck about once a month, each time near his old hangout in the river bottom. The same three hunters would once again do their best to get the deer, but now a fourth had joined the quest. A warehouse manager from Hastings, Del Austin was an enthusiastic convert to bowhunting and would hunt with the group for the next three seasons.

By the time the bow opener rolled around on September 10, all four archers knew Mossy Horns was still alive and well, and everyone felt confident they had his travel pattern down cold. Stands had been built long before the season. Al had the greatest faith in one stand he'd erected near the corner of a cornfield, where it joined the river bottom. Here he had found numerous fresh tracks that he felt could belong only to the non-typical, and he resolved to hunt this spot until the great buck showed.

For seven weeks Al sat in the stand every chance he had. Over time he grew progressively more impatient. Then one cool afternoon toward the end of October, two bucks stepped into the cornfield about two hundred yards down the fence line from the stand. They were certainly not in the class of Mossy Horns, but they were good bucks, and it had been a long dry spell. Once the deer had disappeared into the standing corn, Al climbed down and began to stalk them.

The hunter had gone only about seventy yards when, for some reason, he looked back toward his stand. Mossy Horns was standing under it! The gigantic buck stared toward Al, not sure what he was. Then the big deer caught human scent and was gone.

The following week Charley was in his stand when four deer walked past. He too succumbed to temptation and arrowed a young buck, which promptly ran into the cornfield and dropped. Charley had filled his deer tag for the year. But before he could even climb down, Mossy Horns stepped out of the brush and stood broadside at thirty yards!

Finally he blew and ran back toward the river.

Near the end of that same season, Al had yet another chance at the great buck. This time his wife, Velma, was sitting in another tree about fifty yards from where Al sat. It was getting dark, and Al was almost ready to depart. Then the snap of a twig froze him as he looked into the brush. Mossy Horns was walking slowly toward him!

Al let the buck walk beneath his stand and a short distance beyond. The bowhunter was at full draw when the buck passed, and Al shot for the front shoulder. The arrow hit with a solid thud, and the deer instantly flinched and bolted. Beneath the stand where Velma sat, a woven-wire fence was nailed to the tree. As the buck crashed away, he hit the fence so hard that the tree shook, nearly knocking Velma from her perch. But the buck kept going.

In the poor light Al and Velma looked for blood but found none. Finally they decided to wait a half hour then return with a flashlight. Al still remembers that wait as being the longest thirty minutes of his life. When they returned, they found where the buck had crashed into the fence; they even recovered the feathered end of his arrow, but it had no blood on it. Even after further searching the next day, they encountered no trace of blood or the buck.

Al was haunted the rest of the season by concern that he might have killed the deer. Had he crawled into a thicket and died, or could he have been carried away by the river, never to be seen again? During the last week of the season, Al finally filled his tag with a big eight-pointer, which was his first deer with a bow and his third whitetail ever. The season ended with no more sightings of Mossy Horns.

During the summer of 1961 Dan didn't see the non-typical. This was unusual, as the farmer had observed the deer in each of the past three summers. Perhaps Al's arrow really had killed the buck, or maybe he'd simply died of old age. Judging from the size of his rack back in 1958, he now was presumed to be at least eight years old.

Later, one bitterly cold afternoon near the end of the 1961 season, after the other hunters had given up, Al again was sitting in the stand from which he'd shot at Mossy Horns the previous year. Just before dark he spotted a button buck making his way through the willows about one hundred yards off. Following him was a large buck, and behind that buck was the one whitetail Al had expected never to see again—Mossy Horns!

Suddenly the season took on an entirely new dimension. The giant moved as cautiously as ever while he worked his great rack through the willow bushes. His rack looked the same as before, and if anything, even bigger. Despite the cold, Al began to sweat.

Before dark, the two other bucks headed out into the field, but Mossy Horns remained in the willows. Then a half-dozen does came out under Al's stand and began feeding. Soon two younger bucks joined them, and all eight milled around near the stand until dark. Mossy Horns finally entered the field just before dark, but he would come nowhere near Al's tree. It was as if he remembered the shot from a year earlier—and he probably did.

In the spring of 1962 Dan had the good fortune to find a matching pair of shed antlers from Mossy Horns, not far from where the guys had been hunting the buck. Now it was clear that the buck was as big as Al had always claimed. (Charley was the only other hunter in Al's group who'd even seen the buck in four years!) Al had believed Mossy Horns was a new archery world record, but he'd had no proof. The evidence now was in hand.

The giant sheds had an 11-inch drop point off one base and one of 13 inches off the other base. Approximating the inside spread, the rack would have scored in excess of 281 non-typical points, easily making this buck just what Al had claimed—a Pope and Young world record.

As it turned out, the sheds probably were from the previous year—the 1960 hunting season—which was the year Al thought he had hit the buck. Near the end of one of the long, clublike drop tines off the bases was what appeared to be a three-edged broadhead mark that had penetrated the antler about a half inch! Instead of the arrow hitting the shoulder, as had been intended, it apparently had hit that antler tip! This would account for the buck's excessive crashing and hitting the fence, as he was temporarily stunned from the shock.

In 1962 Al's fifth season of hunting Mossy Horns, he decided to try a new tactic. For weeks in the summer, the archer cut trails through the heavy brush in places where he'd seen the buck most often. At the most likely crossings he built tree stands. Then, starting a full month before bow season, Al kept away from the area to allow Mossy Horns time to get used to the changes. Once again no one saw the old buck prior to the season.

At the time, Interstate 80 was being built on the north side of the bottoms where Mossy Horns lived. As a result the Platte had been temporarily dammed upstream. One day early in the season, as Al walked the dry riverbed, he found the fresh, unmistakable tracks of the non-typical. From the looks of it, the buck had been traveling to an alfalfa field. Al backtracked to a small island choked with willows, where he jumped the deer at close range. His rack looked just as big as ever.

During the next few days, Al was careful to keep away from the island and the primary trails the buck was using. One evening while he sat in a tree where a runway crossed a big slough, several does walked under his stand, followed by an eight-point buck that stopped to rub his antlers on a bush. Mossy Horns showed up just after the smaller buck but eventually moved off without coming close enough for a shot. That same week Al had one more distant look at him.

The following week the monster wasn't seen, so Al searched the dry riverbed again to find out what he was doing. Here the bowhunter found a trail the buck hadn't been using previously. Early bow season was drawing to an end, so Al decided to set up a new stand as a last-ditch effort. A nine-day rifle season would begin soon, and too many other local hunters knew of the legendary deer. He'd be lucky to survive the onslaught.

On Al's first evening in the new blind, an hour before dark, he saw the great buck slip out of the willows on an island and head his way. Mossy

Horns crossed the dry channel and walked to within fifteen yards of Al's stand. It appeared it was all over but the shot.

But as always before, something went wrong: The buck stopped in heavy brush. Finally the buck circled the tree at twenty yards, but he never left the brush for a clear shot. He locked up not twenty feet from Al's stand, where a fence came down to the river, but there was no chance to draw. After another ten agonizing minutes Mossy Horns jumped the fence and walked into the alfalfa field. He stopped broadside at forty-five yards . . . and Al sent an arrow just over his back.

The last afternoon in October rolled around, and the early bow season was about to end. Al and Gene got to the bottoms early and chose their stands. Del and Charley left Hastings after work and hurried out to the farm to get in a last-minute hunt.

Originally Del had planned to sit in one of Al's stands but now feared he wouldn't be able to find it quickly. So he brought along a portable platform and placed it on a large island of thick brush and liberally sprinkled buck lure on the ground all around his tree.

Del stood on the platform until just before dark; then, as he was starting to get down, a loud crash from upwind caught his attention. It was hard to see antlers in the dim light and heavy cover, but the hunter could tell the buck was big. For some reason he ran toward Del and stopped twenty yards from his tree, turning almost broadside. The archer drew his 45-pound Oneida recurve and drove a Bear Razorhead behind the shoulder of the deer, which promptly bolted.

Al and the other hunters waited for Del until an hour after dark, but still there was no sign of him. Finally, with flashlights, they headed toward the river and met him halfway. He relayed his story, noting that he wasn't sure if the deer he'd shot was Mossy Horns or another buck.

From the blood, it appeared Del had made a hard hit. After some searching, they found the broken arrow, which had been snapped off ten inches above the head. For three hours the hunters trailed the buck through slough grass and willow thickets until the blood and their flashlights were nearly gone. They decided it would be best to wait until daylight to continue the search.

FIG. 33. Del Austin and Ol' Mossy Horns, which has stood as the Nebraska archery state record for nearly sixty years. Photo courtesy of the Boone and Crockett Club.

The next morning, within one hundred yards of where they had stopped the previous evening, they found the buck lying dead in a clump of willows. He was indeed Mossy Horns! It was a bittersweet moment for Al Dawson. The five-year quest had ended with someone else taking "his" buck. On the other hand, one of his buddies had been fortunate, and that was reason enough to celebrate.

Mossy Horns was showing signs of age. He had no fat on his body, and his loins were sunken. Even so, he dressed two hundred forty pounds, and Al felt sure he would have been sixty pounds heavier during earlier years. The rack wasn't quite as massive as it had been earlier, but it still scored 279⅞ points when measured by P&Y's Glenn St. Charles. At the time, this buck was the second-largest non-typical in the world (behind only the 286-point Jeff Benson buck from Texas), and Mossy Horns was far and away the new world record by bow. This buck is indeed a fitting archery world record, and even after all these years, he's faced no serious challenges to that title.

Records of North American
Big Game Committee

BOONE AND CROCKETT CLUB

Address Correspondence to:
Mrs. Grancel Fitz, Secretary
5 Tudor City Place, NYC 17, NY.

NON-TYPICAL WHITETAIL DEER

3-23-65

DETAIL OF POINT MEASUREMENT

SEE OTHER SIDE FOR INSTRUCTIONS	Supplementary Data		Column 1	Column 2	Column 3	Column 4
	R.	L.	Spread Credit	Right Antler	Left Antler	Difference
A. Number of Points on Each Antler	21	18				
B. Tip to Tip Spread	13 7/8					
C. Greatest Spread	29 5/8					
D. of MAIN BEAMS 21 3/8 Inside Spread Spread credit may equal but not exceed length of longer antler			21 3/8			
IF Inside Spread of Main Beams exceeds longer antler length, enter difference						
E. Total of Lengths of all Abnormal Points	95 2/8					
F. Length of Main Beam				27 7/8	28 1/8	2/8
G-1. Length of First Point, if present				7 2/8	6 5/8	5/8
G-2. Length of Second Point				11	11 3/8	3/8
G-3. Length of Third Point				6 6/8	9 6/8	3
G-4. Length of Fourth Point, if present				7 2/8	8 2/8	1
G-5. Length of Fifth Point, if present						
G-6. Length of Sixth Point, if present						
G-7. Length of Seventh Point, if present						
H-1. Circumference at Smallest Place Between Burr and First Point				6 5/8	6 6/8	1/8
H-2. Circumference at Smallest Place Between First and Second Points				5 3/8	5 2/8	1/8
H-3. Circumference at Smallest Place Between Second and Third Points				5	5 2/8	2/8
H-4. Circumference at Smallest Place Between Third and Fourth Points				6 2/8	5 2/8	1
TOTALS	95 2/8		21 3/8	83 3/8	86 5/8	6 6/8

ADD	Column 1	21 3/8	Exact locality where killed Hall Co., Shelton, Nebraska
	Column 2	83 3/8	Date killed 11-1-62 By whom killed Del Austin
	Column 3	86 5/8	Present owner Del Austin
	Total	191 3/8	Address 919 E. 9th St. Hastings, Nebraska
SUBTRACT Column 4		6 6/8	Guide's Name and Address Al Dawson, 2500 W. 7th, Hastings, Neb.
	Result	184 5/8	Remarks: (Mention any abnormalities)
Add Line E Total		95 2/8	
	FINAL SCORE	279 7/8	

FIG. 34. Del Austin scoresheet. Courtesy of the Boone and Crockett Club.

[Currently, the Del Austin buck is the fourth-largest non-typical in the P&Y records book while remaining the Nebraska state record for archery.]

Perhaps the most interesting aspect of this story is what it tells us about the lifestyle of a monster buck. Rarely is there any account through which we can get to know a deer of this caliber and see how he avoids dangers time after time. Despite being subjected to serious hunting pressure, this giant came within minutes, perhaps seconds, that fateful afternoon of perhaps surviving to die of old age. Can you imagine how seldom Mossy Horns would have been seen by casual hunters who didn't know he even existed?

24

Spider and Double Down

The Rachel Kechely and AJ Ahern Bucks, 2016

- 229³/₈-inch and 202²/₈-inch non-typicals
- Richardson County

For Rachel Kechely's entire life, her dad, Kurt, has managed the land. Land that has been in the family for four generations. Land where he learned to love the outdoors and where he taught his two daughters, Katherine and Rachel, how to shoot, hunt, fish, and ride four-wheelers. Land where corn, soybeans, and alfalfa grow in rich Nebraska soil. Land where creeks cut ravines down into the rolling hills of Richardson County. Land where two giant B&C non-typical whitetails were living in the fall of 2016.

Managing land for trophy bucks takes time and trust. Trusting the decisions you make today are going to pay off someday. Kurt started the process twenty years ago by closely aging the bucks on his land and passing on the younger ones so they could reach their full potential. Using game cameras extensively, he began creating lists of bucks—the shooters versus the non-shooters. "I would sit with the girls in the tree stand when they were younger and talk about the different bucks, and whether they were big enough to shoot," explains Kurt.

When Rachel began deer hunting her junior year of high school, Kurt realized his lessons had stuck. Sitting together on opening morning they watched as a mature nine-point buck approached their stand. "I lifted my gun but didn't shoot. If he would have had ten points I would have shot him," recalls Rachel with a knowing glance toward her father.

It was around this same time that AJ Ahern decided to return to the land. Having grown up on the family farm near Shubert, he had moved away to central Nebraska to work for Nebraska Public Power. In 2012 he made the decision to return home to southeast Nebraska to work the family farm with his father. "While I was working office hours in the corporate world I longed to experience nature on a daily basis, like I did growing up," explains AJ. Soon after returning home he connected with Kurt, since their properties adjoin. "It was after a few conversations with Kurt that our wildlife management really took off."

With over three thousand combined acres, the two began working together to manage the property for trophy whitetails. In less productive areas they planted native grasses, while in some agricultural fields crops were left standing to provide cover and feeding areas during the harsh, late-winter period. "I take stewardship of the land very seriously. There is a reason for everything we do," explains Kurt. They also continued monitoring deer with game cameras, seeking to maintain a healthy buck-to-doe ratio while increasing the number of mature bucks. "We really try to let the best bucks mature to five to seven years before we hunt them. It does take believing in the process to let a younger 180-inch buck pass, knowing he needs more time," explains AJ.

The fruits of their labor began appearing on their cameras in July 2016. Both were massive non-typical bucks and both had impressive drop tines. Rachel named one Double Down, due to his long matching drop tines, while the other, with his own impressive drop tine off his left side, she called Spider. When bow season opened Kurt was on a mission to arrow one of the giant bucks. An avid bowhunter with some nice bucks on his wall, he hunted hard, spending at least thirty days on stand. He never saw either buck.

With two B&C-caliber bucks still in the area, anticipation was running high for the opening of rifle season. "I just knew somebody was going to have an opportunity at a tremendous deer, a buck of a lifetime," remembers Kurt. However, Kurt had also set some clear rules. "I told Rachel's boyfriend and my buddy that if you ever want to come back here again, you don't shoot those bucks," explains Kurt.

November 12, opening day of the 2016 rifle season, was unusually warm. Kurt sat overlooking a pond, while twenty-one-year-old Rachel and her boyfriend, Brody, sat in a double stand overlooking a creek bottom. Meanwhile Katherine and Kurt's friend sat in separate stands nearby.

At about eight o'clock Rachel noticed movement along the creek. "I looked and saw a tree moving. I hit my boyfriend and whispered, 'He's right over there.' He said, 'No, he's right over there.' I said again, 'No, he's right over there.' After arguing back and forth we realized that we were looking at two different bucks," Rachel remembers with a smile. Amazingly Spider and Double Down were both standing within rifle range across the creek!

Rachel recognized the larger of the two bucks as Spider. Watching as the massive non-typical sauntered along the creek bottom, Brody hit his grunt call when the buck entered an opening in the brush. Swiveling his head and tangle of antlers toward the sound, the buck stopped broadside, one hundred twenty-five yards away. Shouldering her .25-06, Rachel found the buck's vitals in the scope and pulled the trigger on the first deer of her life. "I thought that I would be really nervous and shaking whenever I shot my first deer. But I was steady, I was ready, and I did it," says Rachel. "Afterward I started shaking. My boyfriend thought I was going to drop the gun out of the tree!"

After the shot both bucks ran, quickly dropping out of sight. "I was hoping Double Down would run toward Katherine, so she could get a shot," remembers Rachel. After the rest of the hunting party arrived, they began tracking the buck. With a solid blood trail it didn't take long for the group to find the monster buck lying dead in a twenty-five-foot-deep ravine. Looking down Kurt thought, *Oh my gosh, he is a lot bigger than I thought.*

Rachel Kechely named the buck Spider due to its weblike tangle of antlers. Within that web is an impressive typical frame, with brow tines of 9⅜ and 8⅜ inches, G2 and G3 points all over a foot long, and main beams of 28⅞ and 26⅝ inches. It grosses 195⅞ inches and nets 184⅞. Spider has five abnormal points on each side totaling 44⅜ inches, including double forked

FIG. 35. Rachel Kechely with 229⅜-inch Spider, the first deer she ever shot. Photo courtesy of Rachel Kechely.

brow tines and a 9⅜-inch drop tine off the left side. With a final score of 229⅜ inches, it is the third-largest non-typical from Richardson County and is currently displayed on a full-body mount at the Scheels store in Lincoln.

Although Spider was now off the hit list, Double Down was not. AJ knew Rachel had shot Spider and was very happy for her. Opening weekend for him was a bit of a scramble, trying to complete fieldwork before the onset of winter. "2016 was a dryer than normal year and harvest was done early, so I knew I was going to get some hunting in. But the second day of the season was also good for spraying weeds," remembers AJ.

Therefore the second morning of rifle season found AJ spraying weeds, but by two o'clock in the afternoon the wind had increased to twenty-five miles an hour from the south, making it difficult to spray. After parking the sprayer AJ ran home and swapped work clothes for hunting clothes.

Arriving at his hunting location, he walked in and found a brush pile on

FIG. 36. AJ Ahern showing off Double Down, the buck Rachel Kechely saw with Spider on opening morning. Photo courtesy of AJ Ahern.

the north side of some timber, about a quarter mile from where Rachel shot Spider. Cradling the Remington .30-06 he received as a Christmas present in high school, he sat down and slowly unwound. "I remember just sitting there, enjoying the warm afternoon and the end of a long harvest," shares AJ.

With only ten minutes of shooting light remaining, he saw Double Down chase a doe out of the timber four hundred yards to his south. "I was super anxious, since the sun was setting and I knew I didn't have much time." Fortunately the massive buck was trailing the doe and the doe was moving across the cut corn toward AJ. The buck closed the distance to two hundred sixty-five yards. "I didn't want to take an irresponsible shot at such a beautiful animal, so I was hesitant to shoot."

While AJ was trying to decide what to do, the buck stopped broadside, offering a clear shot at his vitals. Lifting his Remington, AJ sent a 180-grain bullet screaming across the field. He heard the telltale thump of the bullet hitting the buck. The buck lurched forward and went down. "My heart was beating out of my chest. I couldn't believe I had finally put a nice one down," remembers AJ.

His elation was premature. As AJ watched the downed buck through his scope, it suddenly got to its feet and walked slowly into the timber. "People ask me why I didn't shoot again. I guess I was ready to, but I just couldn't believe what I was seeing, and he was gone so quickly in the fading light," recalls AJ. A feeling of dread set in as the sky darkened. "I wanted so badly to go look for that buck, but I knew I should wait."

After returning home AJ tried his best to get some sleep. "As soon as daylight broke I was out the door like a rocket," shares AJ. Returning to the field, he walked out to where he thought the buck was standing when he shot, and immediately found a blood trail. "I only walked about fifty yards, and lying near the edge of the timber was my buck. I thanked God for letting me have this opportunity."

The AJ Ahern buck is aptly named, with a 12 3/8-inch drop tine on the right side and a nearly matching 11 6/8-inch one off the left. These two drop tines make up the majority of the buck's 30 4/8 inches of abnormal points, giving the rack a uniquely "clean" appearance for a non-typical. The buck's typical five-by-five rack grosses 183 3/8 inches, with impressive main beams of 28 3/8 and 30 1/8 inches and an inside spread of 21 2/8 inches. With a final score of 202 2/8 inches, it stands as the fifth-largest non-typical from Richardson County, a county known for giant non-typicals.

The odds of having two B&C bucks of this caliber on the same property are extremely slim. Having someone shoot them on consecutive days and only a quarter mile apart is astounding. But it didn't happen by chance. Kurt and AJ both put a lot of time, effort, thought, and money into helping it happen. "Now the neighbors up and down the creek are wanting to manage their properties," shares Kurt. "With the work we've done, I think there is the potential every year to shoot a Booner."

25

Midday

The Kellen Meyer and Jordan Owens Buck, 2010

· 232²/₈-inch non-typical
· Seward County

Big bucks are where you find them. Not particularly profound, but true. Sometimes after finding out where someone shot a giant whitetail buck, it is hard to believe that it came from where it did. The massive non-typical Kellen Meyer and Jordan Owens killed in 2010 is a prime example.

Kellen and Jordan know each other and the area in and around Seward, Nebraska, well. Both were born in 1984, and both attended St. John Lutheran grade school together before graduating a year apart from Seward High School. They each shot their first deer near Seward—Kellen a few miles east, Jordan a half mile north. They both still live close to town, with Jordan farming and Kellen selling seed. Each fall they get together with friends and family to hunt whitetails in Seward County. "We've known each other since we were little; our parents were friends. Through the years we have hunted a lot together," shares Kellen. "Our deer hunting tradition is to get together with a bunch of our high school buddies and when we get done we hang out and have a few beers together."

By Wednesday of the 2010 rifle season, neither Kellen nor Jorden had seen a shooter buck. After finishing their morning hunt at separate locations, they met in Seward for a lunch of Godfather's pizza. "It was just a perfect day, not too cold or too warm, one of those days where you just want to be outside," remembers Jordan. After finishing lunch they decided to try something they rarely did, hunt during the middle of the day. "People always say that bucks move during the middle of the day and that no one is hunting them. We decided to give it a try," adds Kellen.

They decided to try a spot on the eastern edge of Seward where Kellen had never hunted but where Jordan had seen a nice five-by-five while harvesting corn. "I was cutting corn, and jumped a really wide buck. His horns were hitting both sides of the row of corn as he ran from the combine," recalls Jordan. Arriving at the property, they drove past the only significant cover in the area, a small two-acre patch of timber and brush. Otherwise the property did not look like prime deer cover. Mostly a cut cornfield near a housing development, it had a U-shaped grassy draw running through it containing a pile of dead trees. What it did have going for it was its location less than a mile from the Big Blue River. "After the first weekend of the season it's a good spot. Hunters down on the river push them out and they go in there," explains Jordan.

Shortly after midday Kellen sat down on the east side of the U-shaped draw, while Jordan found a spot on the west side. Only a couple hundred yards apart, the two could see each other. After sitting for only a half hour they both spotted two does running toward them from the small patch of timber they had driven past on the way in, and right behind them was a giant buck. Thinking it was the wide-racked buck he had seen while harvesting, Jordan lifted his .270 and shot at the running buck. Kellen did the same with his Browning .30-06. The buck did not flinch and kept running. Cycling another round into their chambers, Kellen and Jordan shot simultaneously at the buck. The massive non-typical crumpled dead into the cut corn.

Approaching the buck from opposite directions, they had similar reactions. "We were both just speechless. Neither of us had ever seen a buck like that, and he just kept getting bigger," remembers Kellen. "When I first saw him and noticed the drop tines, I knew it wasn't the buck I had seen during harvest. He was much bigger," adds Jordan. While examining the buck they found two bullet holes, one in the front shoulder and one near the hindquarters. Not certain who actually killed the buck, they decided to share the trophy.

FIG. 37. Lifelong friends Kellen Meyer (*left*) and Jordan Owens shot simultaneously at this buck and are not sure who killed it. Photo courtesy of *Seward County Independent*.

After taking the buck to Jordan's parents' house, word and pictures of the buck spread quickly around Seward. "It was crazy. People started showing up, some we didn't even know. People kept calling and texting," remembers Kellen. The rest of the day was one long deer party, as people came to see and take pictures of the freakishly massive buck.

The Kellen Meyer and Jordan Owens buck is indeed one of the most massive bucks ever shot in North America. The four circumference measurements total an amazing 56⅝ inches, with the last measurement on the left antler an amazing 9⅛ inches, the largest circumference measurement of any Nebraska whitetail in the B&C records book. Nevertheless these eight measurements still do not capture just how massive each individual point is and how the

FIG. 38. The Meyer/Owens buck between Ol' Mossy Horns (*left*) and the Rachel Kechely buck on display in the Lincoln Scheels store. Photo courtesy of the author.

mass extends to the tip of each main beam. The buck's typical five-by-five frame includes main beams of 28²⁄₈ and 26²⁄₈ inches and an inside spread of 18⁴⁄₈ inches and is quite symmetrical, grossing 206⁷⁄₈ inches and netting 199⁶⁄₈. The buck's twelve abnormal points total 32⁴⁄₈ inches, resulting in a final score of 232²⁄₈ inches. The buck currently ranks as the thirteenth-largest non-typical from Nebraska and the largest ever from Seward County.

Kellen and Jordan definitely had their fifteen minutes of fame. Reporters from around the state and country interviewed them, including some from *Field & Stream*, who had them do a photo shoot in the Lincoln Haymarket. "The whole experience was fun. Neither of us had ever been in the spotlight like that. And for a buck like that to be living right by Seward, it was just amazing," shares Kellen. The rack is currently on display on a full body mount at the Lincoln Scheels store, where it stands above a full body mount of Ol' Mossy Horns, making that 279⅞-inch non-typical look somewhat spindly!

The buck also garnered the attention of Gale Sup, a well-known antler collector from Nebraska. As part of the sale of the antlers, he had replicas made for Kellen and Jordan, solving the sticky problem of whose house the rack should hang in.

26

Double Drop Tine

The Bill Klawitter Buck, 1963

· 224⅛-inch non-typical
· Madison County

Bill Klawitter was born in Norfolk, Nebraska, during the height of the Dust Bowl. To combat the impacts of the ongoing drought, President Franklin Roosevelt initiated the Prairie States Forestry Project in 1935, the same year Bill was born. The goal of this ambitious program was to build an enormous network of windbreaks from North Dakota down to Texas.

The first government-funded windbreak in Nebraska was planted about forty miles northwest of Norfolk, near Orchard. Nebraska Historical Marker 296 marked the location from 1985 until May 2017, when the shelterbelt was bulldozed, burned, and the sign removed.[1] That sign read: "From 1935 through 1942, the U.S. Forest Service, working with the Works Progress Administration and Civilian Conservation Corps planted windbreaks throughout the Great Plains. Nearly 220 million seedlings were planted creating 18,600 miles of windbreaks occupying 240,000 acres on 30,000 farms. Nebraskans led this effort planting almost 4,170 miles of windbreaks occupying 51,621 acres on 6,944 farms. The windbreak before you was planted in April, 1935 on the John Schleusener farm and was the first windbreak established under this project in Nebraska."

On an unusually warm day in November 1963, Bill Klawitter stood leaning against a tree in an FDR windbreak, taking an occasional drag from his cigarette. Like other deer hunters, he knew these thick windbreaks of elm, cottonwood, and cedar were excellent whitetail habitat. Cradling his open-sighted, lever-action Winchester .30-30, he knew from past hunts that this particular windbreak, a few miles southwest of Norfolk, often held good bucks.

Catching movement on the opposite side of the thick, fifty-yard-wide shelterbelt, he quickly shouldered his Winchester and snapped off a shot on a running buck. Although it wouldn't be officially measured until forty-six years later, Bill had just put a bullet through one of Nebraska's largest and most unique non-typical bucks.

Fast-forward fifty-five years and one hundred miles south to Kevin Wingard's basement in Milford, Nebraska. Hanging prominently in the corner of the room is Bill's massive double drop tine buck. On a table in the center of the room sits his well-worn Winchester .30-30. "His buck has been part of our family since Bill shot it, and I will eventually pass it down to my son," explains Kevin. While looking through his collection of hunting memorabilia, Kevin shares the twisting tale of Bill's records book buck.

After shooting the buck Bill and his wife, Peg, eventually moved to Rising City to operate a lumberyard. It was in Rising City, when Kevin was twelve

FIG. 39. Bill Klawitter with the gnarly double drop tine buck he felled with one shot from his iron-sighted .30-.30 while smoking a cigarette. Photo courtesy of Kevin Wingard.

FIG. 40. The three-pronged drop tine on the left side of the Klawitter buck looks like a tongue of fire. Photo courtesy of the author.

years old, that he first met Bill's daughter Becky. Kevin began hunting turkeys with Bill a couple years later and eventually married his daughter.

"In those days guys like Bill were more concerned about the meat than the antlers," explains Kevin. Becky agrees, adding, "My dad also couldn't afford to pay for a taxidermist to mount the deer, so he put the head in this big old crock and covered it with salt." The head stayed in the crock for years. Eventually teaching himself taxidermy, Bill pulled the deer head out in the early 1980s and mounted it himself. For years the buck hung over the fireplace in his home, developing a dark, smoky patina.

Knowing his buck was exceptional, Bill then had it unofficially scored by a local measurer at 212⅜ inches non-typical. For many years it was listed in the Nebraska records book at this score.

After Bill contracted cancer, Kevin decided to get the buck officially scored as a gift to Bill. In 2009 Kevin took the rack to Cabela's, which was holding a public scoring event. "When I walked in with the mount and got in line, people said, 'Why don't you go ahead to the front,'" Kevin remembers with a laugh. "I was probably there seven hours. People kept coming up and taking pictures. It was a cool day."

When Kevin reached the front of the line, the B&C official measurer balked at rescoring the buck. Fortunately Randy Stutheit, the Nebraska Big Game Trophy Records coordinator, was also there and made the decision that the buck needed to be rescored. After forty-six years Bill's buck was officially measured, with the score increasing from 212⁰/₈ to 224⅛ inches! "It was great that Bill lived to see his buck officially scored. He was always really proud of it," shares Kevin. Sadly, after fighting a long battle with cancer, Bill passed away in 2012.

The Bill Klawitter buck is one of the most unique-looking bucks you will ever see. The buck's typical five-by-five frame is not particularly large, grossing 155⅝ inches while netting only 145⁰/₈. However, the number, the sizes, and the shapes of the abnormal points are simply amazing. The drop tine off the left beam is one of the coolest ever, looking like a multipronged tongue of fire dripping off the antler. The drop tine on the right is equally impressive, measuring 11²/₈ inches. With eighteen non-typical points totaling 79⅛ inches, it is one of the greatest non-typicals ever shot in Nebraska, and the largest ever from Madison County.

27

Public Land

The Dave Oates Buck, 1985

- 214⁶/₈-inch non-typical
- Hitchcock County

It is fitting that someone who spent his entire professional career studying and protecting our public wildlife resources shot one of the largest whitetails ever killed on public land in Nebraska.

Dave Oates began his forty-year career as a public servant in 1969, working as an unpaid, temporary employee at the NGPC. "I just wanted to see what was going on and get my foot in the door," explains Oates. Although a chemist by training, Dave eventually founded and built the crime laboratory at NGPC, developing many of the scientific techniques used in solving wildlife poaching cases.[1] Over his long career he worked hundreds of cases in multiple states, serving as an expert witness for the Law Enforcement Division, resulting in the convictions of numerous wildlife poachers. A national expert in his field, Dave published books and numerous peer-reviewed articles on a variety of topics, including wildlife forensics, disease, and parasites.

Another one of Dave's many duties was working deer-check stations for the NGPC. Which meant his 1985 deer firearm season began like many others, with a drive from his home in Seward to check in other hunters' bucks. His check station of choice was in Hastings, allowing him to stay at home and enjoy his mom's home cooking. He also enjoyed spending time with his father, who was also a frequent volunteer at the check station.

Dave also liked to work the Hastings check station because it was closer to Swanson Reservoir State Recreation Area, a four-thousand-acre piece of public ground in Hitchcock County that was one of his favorite deer hunting spots. After working the first weekend of the 1985 season, he left Hastings on Monday morning and drove three hours west to meet up with his two hunting partners, Carl Wolfe and Steve O'Hare, who also worked for the NGPC. That afternoon they scouted Swanson, set up their tents, and settled into their sleeping bags in anticipation for the next morning's hunt.

Waking up well before sunrise, Dave made his way to his stand under a full moon. Reaching the big ash tree, Dave carefully crawled up the wooden steps nailed into the tree and settled in, as best he could, between the crotch of two limbs. "Back in those days we didn't have ladder stands, metal stands, we just crawled up and sat on a limb," remembers Dave.

His stand was located not far from the Republican River, near an old river channel thick with brush. As the sun rose Dave could see maybe a quarter mile to the west but considerably less in every other direction. His plan was to sit until noon. At about eight thirty a small fork horn whitetail appeared, passing directly beneath his stand. "In those days you could only have a buck permit, so I usually just killed any buck that came by," explains Dave. For some reason, perhaps since he had three days to hunt, he decided to let the small buck walk. It was a great decision.

An hour later Dave watched another hunter to his west climb down from his stand and walk away. Unfortunately for that hunter, thirty minutes later Dave watched as a giant buck and six does walked underneath the abandoned stand. "Even at that distance I knew it was the biggest buck I had ever seen," remembers Dave.

The buck and does made their way slowly toward Dave's stand, periodically disappearing and reappearing in the thick undergrowth. "All six of those does went right under my stand, and they all had smiles on their faces. I thought the buck would follow. I had it made," Dave says with a chuckle. But the buck had other ideas, veering off the trail and entering a dense plum thicket.

FIG. 41. Dave Oates shot this enormous public-land non-typical in 1985 while perched between two tree limbs. Photo courtesy of Dave Oates.

Noticing one small opening ahead of the buck, Dave settled the crosshairs of his Remington .30-06 on the spot and waited. As soon as hair appeared in his scope, Dave squeezed the trigger.

At the shot the massive buck bolted, disappearing quickly into the thick timber. After climbing down, Dave walked the one hundred yards to the plum thicket but found no blood or sign of a hit. Following the trail the buck ran down, Dave soon found a few drops of blood. After following the trail for another seventy-five yards, Dave spotted the biggest buck he had ever seen lying dead in the leaves.

The Dave Oates buck is unquestionably one of the largest public-land bucks ever shot in Nebraska. The buck's typical five-by-five frame grosses 191⅝ inches, with an inside spread of 22⅜ inches, main beams of 25⅝ and 27⅝ inches, and exceptional mass, including bladed, knifelike G2 points. The buck's ten abnormal points, including a drop tine off the left beam, total 36⅞ inches, resulting in a final score of 214⅝ inches. After all these years the buck still ranks in the top twenty-five in the Nebraska records book and is still the largest non-typical ever shot in Hitchcock County.

Visiting with Dave on his acreage south of Seward, he reminisces about his long career working for the NGPC, including all those days spent working deer-check stations. With a proud smile Dave explains, "During all those years I never saw a buck bigger than mine come through one of my check stations."

28

Working Man

The Jack Grevson Buck, 1962

· 212²/₈-inch non-typical

· Stanton County

By all accounts Jack Grevson never shied away from a hard day's work. His son, Tim, agrees: "Dad always wanted to work." After farming for forty years, owning and operating a grain elevator in Enola, Nebraska, and breeding and raising Simmental cattle, he finally "retired," moving off the farm into nearby Norfolk. Did he relax? Maybe take up golf, read, or travel more? Not Jack—he drove a cement truck for the next eighteen years. After a long working life, Jack passed away in 2015 at the age of eighty-six.

However, his life was not all work. Jack played and coached softball for thirty years, rode across Iowa during RAGBRAI, and flew his own airplane. Along with Audrey, his wife of sixty-five years, he raised three daughters, Brenda, Denise, and Julie, and a son, Tim, eventually enjoying eight grand-children and ten great-grandchildren.

He was also a lifelong outdoorsman, hunting, fishing, and trapping near his Stanton County farm. In the fall of 1962 Jack and his hunting partners gathered on a cold November day for a deer drive.

"It was Dad's turn to sit and block, the others were the drivers," explains Tim. Joining him that day were locals Phil Harsch, Ray Halsey, Duane Naithan, and Dan Bhrun. Arriving at their hunting ground along the south side of the Elkhorn River, they devised a plan. After allowing Jack time to walk in and get into position, the other four began walking toward him, weaving their way through the dense plum thickets and cottonwood groves.

After finding a small clearing, Jack stood holding his Remington .280, scanning the thick underbrush for any movement or sound. Spotting a blur of brown coming toward him, he raised his rifle, waiting for a clear shot. The next thing he saw was a mass of antlers pushing through the brush way too close. "The buck was facing Dad straight on, so he had to wait for an opening to shoot," shares Tim.

With the buck only a few yards away, Jack centered the crosshairs on the buck's neck, just above the chest, and squeezed the trigger. The massive non-typical dropped.

"It was a long, heavy drag to get that buck to the pickup," shares Tim. Once the buck was loaded, the small party of triumphant hunters drove proudly into nearby Stanton, where the buck tipped the meat locker scales at over three hundred pounds. Parked downtown in front of Hrabak's grocery store, the buck soon attracted a small crowd, with locals taking pictures and wanting to hear the story of the hunt.

FIG. 42. Young Tim Grevson posing with his dad's buck in front of Hrabak's grocery in downtown Stanton. Photo courtesy of the Boone and Crockett Club.

It must have been quite a sight along Ivy Street in downtown Stanton that cold November day. With deer hunting still relatively new to the area, big bucks like this were exciting events, often included in local newspapers. "A lot of photographs were taken. Lots of people came to see the deer," explains Tim. In the excitement someone lifted Tim into the bed of the truck, setting him directly behind the buck's incredibly wide rack and capturing the moment with a photograph.

"The buck was scored by a man who had just finished the class on how to score. It was his first buck, and I remember his hands shaking," remembers Tim. The Jack Grevson buck would make most hunters and scorers shake. The buck is a mainframe seven-by-seven grossing 187⅛ inches with an outside spread of nearly thirty inches. The thirteen abnormal points, five on the right and eight on the left, total 43⅝ inches, resulting in a final score of 212⅜ inches. The buck currently ranks as the twenty-fifth-largest nontypical whitetail killed with a firearm in the Nebraska records book. It still holds the record as the largest whitetail buck ever shot in Stanton County.

The lesson—work hard, but always make time to enjoy life and do what you love.

29

Spanky

The Spanky Greenville Collection

- Lincoln County ....
- Keya Paha County ....
- Knox County ....
- Hall County ....
- Washington County ....

There is something about antlers. The way they look: the endless variety of sizes, shapes, colors, and points. The way they feel: smooth and cool to the touch but with an abundance of bumps and curves and sharp edges. And what they represent: wild animals and wild places, adventure, stories, and successful hunts.

Antlers are also practical. For millennia people have used them in countless ways, as tools, utensils, buttons, potions, weapons, and especially for decoration. We festoon our caves, cabins, and homes with an assortment of antlers; we use them on lamps and chandeliers, knife handles, candelabra, wine holders; and then of course, there are big-game mounts.

For some the fascination evolves into something more; they become antler collectors. These individuals often spend vast amounts of time and money pursuing and purchasing the highest-scoring or most unique specimens. James "Spanky" Greenville was one such individual.

Spanky was born in 1944 in Beaumont, Texas, eventually becoming a successful entrepreneur, owning nightclubs, pubs, and a real estate company specializing in south Texas ranch land. He passed away in 2006, with his obituary stating, "He was a great musician, hunter, friend, son, and above all, a wonderful father."[1] He also acquired an affinity for antlers, tracking down and purchasing them from various states, including Nebraska.

His name first appeared while researching the 224⅛-inch non-typical white-tail Bill Klawitter shot in 1963 in Madison County. While interviewing Bill's son-in-law, Kevin Wingard, about that buck, he shared a letter postmarked July 26, 1985. Inside was a number of photographs of big bucks, Spanky's business card, and a handwritten letter from Spanky to Bill. The letter reads:

Bill,

Hope this little note finds you and your family doing OK.

These are just a few of the heads I display. I just received three from Nebraska and one from Iowa. I think all total I use nine whitetail, three mule deer, and one elk, ranking fifty-third in the B&C book.

I will be displaying the heads at the end of August at the Astro Hall in Houston (This really turned into an expensive hobby).

Anyhow, when you are through with the photo's please return them and also send a couple of your horns.

Sincerely Yours,
Spanky

Bill Klawitter never sold his records-book whitetail to Spanky. However, some of Nebraska's greatest whitetail bucks, spanning the years 1957 to 1969, did end up in his collection. One difference between the Nebraska records book and the B&C records book is the latter lists both the hunter and the owner. Spanky is listed as the owner of four Nebraska whitetails shot by Ray Liles, Alvin Zimmerman, and Albert Ohrt, and one where the hunter is unknown. Two other whitetails, shot by Roy Wullbrandt and Charles Babel, are only listed in the Nebraska records book. However, pictures of these two bucks are included in the aforementioned letter, so it can be safely assumed that Spanky purchased them as well.

The largest Nebraska buck in Spanky's collection, scoring 212⅜ inches, is the non-typical shot by Ray Liles in 1959 in Lincoln County. The official

FIG. 43. Ray Liles holding the largest non-typical from Lincoln County. Photo courtesy of Kevin Wingard.

scoresheet puts the location of the kill a half mile south and two miles west of Hershey. In the "Remarks" blank on the scoresheet it says: "This trophy occupies 3rd place in this class in 1961 Boone and Crockett competition." At the time, the B&C held biennial awards competitions, recognizing the largest trophies in each category, meaning the Ray Liles buck was the third-largest non-typical shot in North America in 1959 and 1960!

The Ray Liles buck sports an incredible seven-by-seven typical frame, grossing 203⅛ inches, including main beams of 29⁰⁄₈ and 28⁴⁄₈ inches and an inside spread of 24⅜ inches. The buck has eight abnormal points totaling 18⁰⁄₈ inches, resulting in a non-typical net score of 212⅜ inches. The buck currently ranks as the twenty-seventh-largest non-typical firearm buck in the Nebraska records book. Although the third-largest county by area in the state, Lincoln County has only twenty non-typical bucks in the records book, with the Liles buck topping them all.

Spanky also obtained the beautiful typical whitetail shot by Roy Wullbrandt in 1966 in Keya Paha County. The buck is one of the most impressive, clean five-by-five bucks ever shot in Nebraska. Grossing 195⁶⁄₈ inches, it has nearly matching main beams of 27²⁄₈ and 27⅜ inches and an inside spread of 21²⁄₈ inches. Extremely symmetrical for a rack this size, it has only 6²⁄₈ inches of total deductions. Mass is impressive as well, with all eight circumference

Roy Wullbrandt score 189½

FIG. 44. The extremely symmetrical Roy Wullbrandt buck still stands as the largest typical from Keya Paha County. Photo courtesy of Kevin Wingard.

measurements over five inches, totaling an incredible 45⅜ inches. Netting 189⅛ inches, the buck still ranks as the eighth-largest firearm typical in the Nebraska records book and the largest ever from Keya Paha County.

The unique shape of the five-by-five Alvin Zimmerman shot in 1966 in Knox County is perhaps what led Spanky to purchase this particular buck. The long upward flaring beams, both measuring over twenty-six inches, creates a distinctive heart-shaped rack. Unusually long G3 points of over twelve inches further accentuate the shape. Finally, it is amazingly symmetrical, with only 2⅛ inches of difference between the two sides, resulting in a buck that grosses 179⅞ inches and nets 176⅝.

Another difference between the B&C and the Nebraska records books is

FIG. 45. The distinct shape and over twenty-six-inch beams of the Alvin Zimmerman buck led Spanky Greenville to add it to his collection. Photo courtesy of the Boone and Crockett Club.

that the former requires photographs of each trophy along with an official scoresheet. The B&C archive therefore includes the wonderful vintage photograph of Alvin, bundled up against the Nebraska cold, proudly holding his unique trophy.

The collection also includes the buck shot by Charles "Chas" Babel on November 10, 1969. According to the scoresheet Chas shot the buck southwest of Wood River on Babel Island in the Platte River. An extensive search for a Babel Island in Nebraska, including searching the U.S. Board on Geographic Names (yes, there is such a thing), found no such island. Perhaps that is just what Chas or the locals called it.

Regardless, on that November day in Hall County, Chas shot a very nice typical whitetail buck scoring 177$\frac{3}{8}$ inches. A mainframe five-by-five with both main beams stretching over twenty-five inches, the buck grosses 184$\frac{5}{8}$. It still stands as the largest typical firearm buck in both the Nebraska and the B&C records books from Hall County.

The final buck in Spanky's collection is an amazing typical shot by Albert Ohrt in 1962 four miles west of Fort Calhoun in Washington County. The

FIG. 46. The 177⅜-inch Charles Babel buck is still the highest-scoring typical from Hall County. Photo courtesy of Kevin Wingard.

Charles Babel score 177 3/8

buck is a mainframe four-by-four typical with a forked brow tine on the right antler. This 3⅝-inch fork is the only abnormal point. The buck's inside spread is 25⅝ inches, while the main beams measure 28⅜ and 27⅜ inches. Tine length is exceptional, with both brow tines over ten inches, and the G2 points measuring 14⅜ on the right and 15⅝ inches on the left. The buck grosses 185⅝ inches and nets 174⅝.

To put this score in perspective, there is only one clean Nebraska eight-pointer in the B&C records book, the 160⅛-inch buck John Woloszyn shot in 1994. If the Albert Ohrt buck did not have its one abnormal point, it would score 179⅝ inches, making it the fourth-largest true four-by-four in the entire B&C records book! Indeed there are only four nine-pointers in the B&C records book from Nebraska, and the Ohrt buck is the largest.

FIG. 47. The impressive Albert Ohrt buck is one of only four nine-pointers from Nebraska in the B&C records book. Photo courtesy of Kevin Wingard.

30

Goliath

The Jacob Gipson Buck, 2017

- 239²⁄₈-inch non-typical
- Lancaster County

"It was a God thing. I just happened to be in the right place at the right time. That is how I know this buck was a blessing from God. It wasn't because of my hard work, it was just God's good will," Jacob Gipson said to his wife. "We should name him," was her reply. "Let's call him Goliath, since he was a giant that got slain," replied Jacob.

The story of Goliath starts years before with another blessing, growing up in a hunting family. "My mom, my dad, we all hunted together," remembers Jacob. For years his family has hunted deer on the same piece of ground in eastern Lancaster County. When Jacob was twelve he shot his first deer on the property, a rutting two-by-two buck hot on the hooves of a doe. In 2013 his mom, Julie, shot a beautiful double drop tine buck scoring 161⅝ inches.

However, trophy bucks are not what drives Jacob into the deer woods. "I wouldn't consider myself a hard-core deer hunter. I grew up on deer meat, it's a way to put meat in the freezer," Jacob explains. "We have taken just under ninety deer off that land. That's a lot of families fed."

Jacob's true passion is duck hunting. Like other waterfowlers, he has to make some hard decisions every fall, since deer rifle season is usually prime duck hunting. "It's always a battle to leave the duck blind and my buddies for a week to hunt deer. It's usually a joke among the guys—hurry up and shoot a deer so we can get back in the marsh!" laughs Jacob.

In 2017 the trail camera pictures on Jacob's cell phone made the "deer or ducks" dilemma a lot easier. Sent to him by his father, the pictures showed a massive non-typical, much larger than anything the family had ever shot, or even seen.

Opening morning of rifle season Jacob was in his deer stand, thinking about the big buck. After an uneventful morning he met up with some of his hunting buddies for breakfast at a local café. Swapping stories of the morning hunt, Jacob jokingly pulled out his smartphone and said, "I'm going to shoot this monster tomorrow morning."

Early the next morning Jacob was back in his stand, and soon after first light he caught movement behind him. Turning and peering through his binoculars, he spotted a doe cruising along the edge of the cornfield about one hundred yards away. Lifting his Remington 700, he found the plump doe in the crosshairs. Feeling the trigger against his finger, indecisive thoughts began swirling in his head. *Today is the last chance I have to hunt until next weekend. . . . If I don't shoot this one, the pressure will be on next week. . . . Being overly selective usually leaves me empty-handed. . . . I enjoy filling the freezer.*

While debating what to do, Jacob noticed the doe getting fidgety, looking back over her shoulder. Following the doe's gaze, Jacob spotted a big buck. "I knew within a half second that this was the buck from the trail camera photos," recalls Jacob. The surge of adrenaline hitting his bloodstream took Jacob by surprise, speeding everything up and making it difficult to focus on the buck's vitals.

Approaching the doe from behind, the giant non-typical paused, standing perfectly broadside. "I knew this was my opportunity. I put the crosshairs on him and didn't hesitate," remembers Jacob. The buck dropped at the shot. Standing up in his blind, Jacob whispered, "Thank You, Jesus."

After climbing down from his stand, Jacob realized that at ground level he could only see the tips of the buck's antlers. Walking toward the buck and cresting one final terrace, he was surprised to see the giant buck jump to its feet and limp away toward the creek bottom. Running after the buck,

FIG. 48. There are only fifteen bucks in the B&C records book with a longer combined beam length than the incredibly massive Jacob Gipson buck. Photo courtesy of Jacob Gipson.

Jacob watched it cross an old abandoned concrete bridge and turn, following the tree line on the opposite side. Seeing a small window through the brush, Jacob shouldered the rifle and put the buck down again. Taking no risks this time, Jacob put one final shot into the buck. Goliath was down for good.

The Jacob Gipson buck is worthy of the name Goliath. The main beams are mind-bogglingly long, measuring 31⅛ inches on the right side and 29⅛ inches on the left. To put this in perspective the B&C records book includes only fifteen bucks with a longer combined beam length. The typical five-by-five rack, despite missing a G4 point on the right side, still grosses 192⅞ inches while netting 180⅞. The brow tines are exceptional, with both over eight inches. The buck has fourteen abnormal points totaling 58⅜ inches, including a 12⅝-inch drop tine curling down off the G2 point on the right side. Netting 239⅜ inches, there are only two Nebraska non-typical firearm bucks scoring higher.

Seeing his buck up close for the first time, Jacob remembers being in disbelief but also feeling blessed. After sending his father a picture, he field dressed the buck and sat waiting, enjoying the natural high of a successful hunt. "After Dad arrived, that was a special moment for both of us. He said a prayer of thanksgiving for the harvest of such a beautiful deer."

31

Buck Jam

The Dan Boliver Buck, 1996

- 239⅝-inch non-typical
- Pawnee County

Hunting oftentimes comes down to luck, being in the right place at just the right moment. Just ask Dan Boliver.

Born in 1966, Dan grew up in Omaha, with his hunting experiences limited to some upland bird hunting. Eventually landing a job with the Omaha Public Power District, he began hanging out with some coworkers who were hunters. "One of the guys told me he hunted Pawnee Prairie, a piece of public ground in Pawnee County, just north of the Kansas border. I decided to go along," remembers Dan. In the fall of 1995, pushing thirty years old, Dan went deer hunting for the first time. "I saw a really nice buck that first year, he was chasing a doe. Seeing that buck hooked me."

Although he did not harvest a deer that first year, Dan's hopes were running high as the 1996 firearm season approached. Making a last-minute decision to purchase his own rifle, he went out and bought a "Walmart special," a Marlin lever-action .30-30 with a scope already attached. With no time to sight-in the rifle, he just removed the scope the evening before opening morning.

Following a short night's sleep Dan was on the road by three o'clock in the morning, driving south from Omaha to rendezvous with a friend. Arriving in Pawnee City at their prearranged meeting spot, he realized his friend either was running late or was not coming. With daybreak approaching Dan sped south toward the Pawnee Prairie Wildlife Management Area, the property he had hunted the year before. A one-thousand-acre block of public ground only a couple miles north of the Kansas border, it consists mainly of rolling, open prairie interspersed with narrow, wooded ravines.

Two pickup trucks were already sitting in the parking lot when Dan arrived, with neither belonging to his hunting companion. With the eastern sky already turning gray, Dan shouldered his pack and Marlin rifle and quickly covered the quarter mile to the same spot he had sat the year before. Finding a tree he sat down and leaned back, holding his new .30-30 across his lap.

He wouldn't sit for long. "I heard him coming down the tree line. I was thinking squirrels, but I could hear the sound getting closer. Then he just popped up out of the ravine fifty yards away, looking over his shoulder," remembers Dan. "I couldn't really see his rack, since he was standing under a tree and it was up in the branches. But at that time I really didn't care about antlers; I just wanted to shoot a deer with a big body to put meat in the freezer."

Lifting the Marlin, Dan lined up the iron sight on the buck's shoulder and sent the first bullet down the rifle's shiny new barrel. "At the recoil the buck dropped. I don't know if I had my eyes closed or what, but he just disappeared. Then I noticed the grass and brush thrashing around, and I knew he was down," remembers Dan. "I didn't know how big he was until I walked up on him. After seeing how big bodied he was, my first thought was, 'How the hell am I going to get him out of here?'" Dan was also trying to make sense of the massive tangle of antlers sitting atop the buck's head.

Having never gutted a deer before, Dan dug in. "I had bought one of those kits from Walmart, with the gloves that go all the way up your shoulder. I had no idea what I was doing, but I got it done." Tying a rope around the buck's massive antlers, he began dragging the buck across the prairie toward his truck. His hunting partner, who had finally arrived, saw Dan approaching from a distance, and wondered why he was dragging a tangle of branches behind him through the grass. When Dan arrived at the parking lot, his hunting partner and several other hunters stood staring down in disbelief.

After loading the buck into the bed of his pickup, Dan pulled out onto the highway, where the truck promptly died. In Yellowstone National Park cars often stop on the road to look at grizzly bears, causing cars to stack up into "bear jams." With his truck on the side of the road and a giant non-typical buck in the back, Dan caused a "buck jam" on Nebraska Highway 99. "There must have been forty guys that stopped to look at my buck and take pictures. I told the first guy that stopped that I was going to walk to Pawnee City to get an alternator. He told me not to leave that buck, or it will be gone when I get back. I'm glad he told me that," remembers Dan.

Dan instead called his stepfather in Omaha, who drove down with an alternator. After installing the alternator on the side of the highway, Dan drove to the check station in Pawnee City, causing yet another scene as a large crowd gathered, snapping photos and admiring the massive buck.

The Dan Boliver buck is definitely a traffic stopper. With 25-inch main beams, long tines, and good mass, the buck's typical rack grosses 194⅝ inches while netting 183⅝. With eleven abnormal points on the right and six on the left totaling 55⅞ inches, the buck nets 239⅝ inches. The buck stood as the second-largest firearm non-typical buck for over a decade, while currently ranking fifth. Not bad for your first deer.

"A week after I shot it, a guy calls me, asking if I wanted to sell it. I told

FIG. 49. Dan Boliver's brand-new Marlin .30-.30 rifle resting on the first deer he ever shot. Photo courtesy of Dan Boliver.

FIG. 50. Dan and his son, Cody, admiring his twenty-eight-point Pawnee County buck. Photo courtesy of Dan Boliver.

him, 'Are you crazy?'" laughs Dan. The buck still hangs above the staircase in his home. His son, Cody, who was only two years old when the buck was shot, grew up admiring his dad's buck. "When I was coming down the stairs every morning from my room, I was eye to eye with it," remembers Cody.

It made an impression. Turning around, Cody shows off the tattoo on his calf—a striking reproduction of his dad's buck.

PART 3

Typical American Elk

32

That Guy

The Russell Coffey Bull, 2018

- 378⅝-inch typical
- Sheridan County

Russell Coffey dreamed of being "that guy." That guy—hauling ass east on I-80, elk rack ratchet-strapped to his flatbed trailer, Rocky Mountain snow still clinging to the hood. That guy—standing at Casey's with the small crowd ogling the horns sticking up above his truck bed. That guy—stock trailer full of white coolers, red gas cans, four-wheelers, and a blue tarp flapping in the wind providing brief glimpses of ivory-tipped antlers.

In 2018 his dreams became a reality. "I remember looking in the rearview mirror, seeing those antlers sticking out the back of my truck. That day I was that guy," shares Russell.

Russell's elk hunting journey began like most Nebraskans', with his first whitetail buck. "My father took me hunting for the first time when I was fourteen. I remember it vividly. After passing on one buck, I decided to shoot the next one I saw. After I missed the next buck standing broadside, I kept shooting, dropping him on my fifth and final shot," remembers Russell. Quickly hooked on big-game hunting, he and his father, Glen, began building a lifetime of hunting memories.

Like many hunters Russell and Glen often talked about going elk hunting. With the years slipping by they finally quit talking and in 2014 went on a five-day hunt in Colorado. Russell shot a nice six-by-seven on the last day of the hunt. "As we drove home, laughing and talking about our hunt, I also thought that this would probably be my only elk hunt with my dad," remembers Russell.

Although it would take four years, Russell and Glen would get to go elk hunting together again. In July of 2018 Russell was just laying down for a nap before his night shift as a police sergeant in York. Hearing an email come through his cell phone, he decided to check it. He had pulled a bull elk tag in the Bordeaux unit! "I was overcome with joy that I would be given one more opportunity to elk hunt with my dad."

Having never hunted the Nebraska Panhandle, they did their homework, contacting landowners, making arrangements, and working up hand loads for Russell's .300 Winchester Short Magnum. "During this process we met some great people, including locals Justin Simmons and Jeremy Adkins," says Russell.

Opening weekend of the 2018 season found Russell and Glen hunting elk together in the Pine Ridge. The first couple days went well, with Russell passing on a nice bull elk. When they met up with Jeremy, he told them about a big bull they called Ghost. This bull earned his name by disappearing each year from his normal haunt near the South Dakota border, sometimes traveling over twenty miles south with his harem of cows. His destination—unharvested corn.

Russell, Jeremy, and Glen set up that evening overlooking four pivots of unharvested corn, with the goal of seeing the Ghost. After sitting awhile, "Jeremy turns to me and says, 'Want me to call in a bull?'" remembers Russell. "I just looked at him with a smirk, and told him to go for it."

Jeremy began chirping on his cow call. As promised a bull elk came running in, bugling and scraping the ground, throwing grass over his shoulders. Russell and his dad then watched in amazement as a second bull came running in, challenging the first. Both bulls sent numerous bugles back toward the cornfields. Soon a cow emerged, moving toward the bulls. Then the cornstalks parted again and out stepped a much larger bull. "It's Ghost," whispered Jeremy.

FIG. 51. Russell (*kneeling*) and his father, Glen Coffey, pose with the elusive bull called Ghost. Photo courtesy of Russell Coffey.

The massive six-by-six, with beautiful matching royals, made his way toward the cow, attempting to herd her back into the corn with the rest of his harem. With the bull now at one hundred fifty yards, Russell shouldered his Browning, found the elk's shoulder in his scope, and squeezed the trigger. The Ghost was down.

The Russell Coffey bull currently ranks as the seventh-largest typical taken with a firearm. A basic six-by-six with a small abnormal point on the left antler, it grosses 394⅜ inches while netting 378⅝. From the front the rack does not look particularly large due to a narrow inside spread of only 36⅝ inches. However, look at it from the side and you notice the mass and especially the beam lengths of 51⅝ inches on the right and 55⅝ inches on the left. Point length is also exceptional, with six points measuring over twenty inches.

Russell realizes how fortunate he is. "This hunt was an experience of a lifetime. I met wonderful people, developed relationships that will last a lifetime, and most important of all, I got to elk hunt with my dad one more time."

33

Family Affair

The Dillon Mortensen Bull, 2017

- 407^{6}/$_{8}$-inch typical
- Lincoln County

Dillon Mortensen's family has made a living off their land north of Curtis, Nebraska, for five generations. Farming, ranching, and hunting on their land means knowing it well. If something changes, they notice it.

Dillon's father, Allen, and his grandfather, Ivan, remember when the stories began—complaints of straying cattle, reports of downed fences, patches of flattened corn, strange noises. No one knows for sure when, perhaps in the early 1980s, a small band of migrating elk, working their way eastward down the Platte River valley, moved south into the rugged canyon country of southeastern Lincoln County. This small seed herd grew, splintered, and grew some more, eventually moving onto Mortensen land.

Lincoln County, encompassing the city of North Platte and covering over twenty-five hundred square miles, is the third-largest county in the state. The northern half, lying north of the Platte River valley, is mainly sandhills, as is a good portion of the western quarter of the county lying south of the river. The southeastern quarter is much different, due mainly to the presence of loess soils. This wind-deposited glacial soil is highly erodible, and over time a landscape that geographers call "deeply dissected" emerged. On an aerial image these loess canyons look like veins, but instead of carrying red blood, they sustain thick green stands of eastern red cedar. With the flatter ridgetops often planted in row crops, it is perfect habitat for deer, elk, and other wildlife. This is where the Mortenson family lives, works, and hunts.

As the 2017 elk season approached, Dillon hoped the family's streak of elk hunting success would continue. The previous fall Dillon's brother Quenton shot a nice bull. The year before that, Dillon's grandfather, Ivan, who was ninety years old at the time, shot a good bull. Now both Dillon and his father, Allen, held bull tags, while Quenton had a cow tag.

"That summer guys started seeing elk ten miles to the east of us, but the elk in this area are funny; each year they move differently, especially depending on the corn. They love that corn," explains Dillon. Monitoring their own ground with trail cameras, they soon began capturing pictures of elk. "I've never seen so many elk calves, but we were also getting some nice bulls on camera." The week before elk season Dillon checked his cameras again. A giant typical bull was in the area.

Opening morning, September 30, dawned cool and foggy, with shooting light coming agonizingly slow. Not wanting to bump elk in the fog, the hunting party, consisting of Dillon, Allen, Quenton, and their friends Hezzy and Zach Brashears sat in their trucks, waiting. With the fog finally thinning and the sky brightening, the group clambered out of the trucks. "When we stepped out of the pickup they were just bugling everywhere that morning. I bet we heard at least six different bulls," remembers Dillon. Moving along the edge of an old Conservation Reserve Program (CRP) field toward the bugling bulls, Zach began chirping with a cow call and periodically bugling. Looking across the field the group spotted a six-by-six bull moving quickly toward them.

Squatting down in a low wash bordering the field, the group was now at ground level with the charging bull. "He just came right at us. I could hear his hooves hitting the ground. I was looking through my scope and decided I wasn't going to shoot him," remembers Dillon. With the bull now at sixty yards and closing fast, Allen raised his iron-sighted Browning .30-06 and cleanly dropped the bull with a shot through the center of the chest. The heavily palmated bull was later aged at twelve years old.

FIG. 52. The eight circumference measurements
on the Dillon Mortensen
state-record typical total
an incredible 71⅔ inches.
Photo courtesy of Dillon
Mortensen.

As the group celebrated, taking pictures and field dressing Allen's bull,
they could hear other bulls bugling. "My dad finally says, 'You better go
check that out.' I guess I'm glad I did," recalls Dillon, smiling. Following
the bugling bulls, Dillon and Zach trailed the herd for over a mile as they
meandered through a thick, cedar-choked canyon. "Every once in a while
we could see them move through the trees, but they weren't going to come
out of that thick stuff." Somewhere along the way Zach lost the reed to his
elk bugle. Pulling out his spare call, he realized that that one was missing
its reed as well! Down to only a cow call, they pushed on.

Looking down and across the draw, they caught fleeting glimpses of
moving bulls. Finally a particularly massive bull stepped broadside into a
small clearing, and Zach hit his cow call. "He just stopped and looked at us.
It happened really quickly," remembers Dillon. Lifting his .300 Winchester

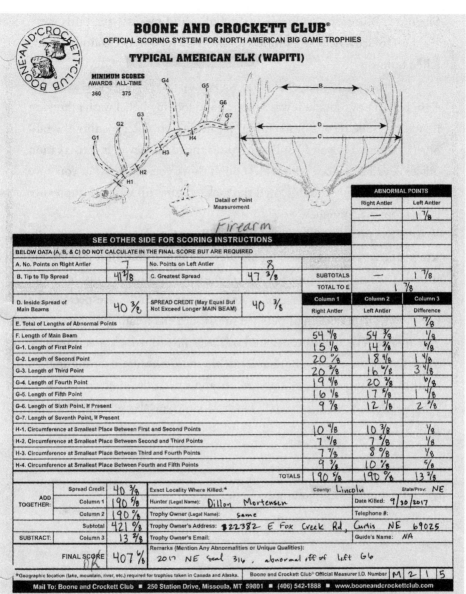

FIG. 53. Dillon Mortensen scoresheet. Note the nearly matching 190 inches of antler on each side of this immense rack. Courtesy of the Boone and Crockett Club.

Magnum, Dillon shot offhand at the bull standing over 250 yards away. The bull folded. Dropping prone, Dillon sent a reassurance round into the fallen bull.

After crossing the canyon, Dillon walked up on the enormous seven-by-eight bull. "I just thought it was a pretty good-looking bull. I wasn't thinking he was the state record or anything," recalls Dillon. After loading the bull onto a flatbed truck and hauling it out to the road, they met conservation officer Alex Hasenauer, who said, "I don't think you realize what you have here!" Alex quickly rough-scored the rack, coming up with an impressive gross score of 423 inches.

After the sixty-day drying period, the Dillon Mortensen bull was officially scored at 407⁶/₈ inches, smashing the previous state-record typical by over 17 inches. The rack is deceptively large, due mainly to a narrow inside spread of only 40³/₈ inches. However, everything else is exceptional, especially the mass, with the eight circumference measurements totaling an incredible 71²/₈ inches! The main beams are both over fifty-four inches and include long, symmetrical tines. Both sides of the rack measure over 190 inches, resulting in a gross score of 421⁰/₈ inches and a net score of 407⁶/₈. Not only a Nebraska state record; it is one of the largest typicals ever shot in North America, currently ranking thirty-third in the B&C records book.

34

Flip of the Coin

The Curtis James Bull, 2015

· 381⁴/₈-inch typical

· Dawes County

"I'll flip, you call," whispered Curtis. Calling heads, Ryan watched as the coin arced through the cool late-afternoon air, landing safely in Curtis's hand. "Tails—I shoot first," Curtis said with a grin. Climbing up onto the round bales, they settled in, hoping for another chance at the giant seven-by-seven.

Sometimes elk hunts start with a coin flip. Why? Because once you shoot an elk, you quickly realize the amount of work involved in field dressing, skinning, packing, and processing such a large animal. This is why most avoid hunting elk solo. It is also why buddy applications for elk tags are popular, with either both hunters drawing, or neither. Curtis James and Ryan Gilsdorf drew their 2015 bull elk tags using a buddy application, and thus the coin toss.

Curtis grew up in Wymore, Nebraska, hunting upland birds and trapping. "I was trapping rabbits when I was ten years old, just going out back and setting traps in brush piles," says Curtis. In 1997, at the age of fifteen, he became a big-game hunter, shooting his first whitetail. Soon after, he began making regular elk hunting trips to Colorado with his father. With two Colorado elk already to his name, he drew a coveted Nebraska bull tag. "We didn't know anything about hunting northwest Nebraska."

FIG. 54. Winning a flip of a coin led to Curtis James dropping this giant 381⅛-inch typical bull. Photo courtesy of Curtis James.

A linesman for the Omaha Public Power District, Curtis lives in Omaha, which meant his scouting trips began with a four-hundred-mile drive to the Bordeaux elk unit in Dawes County. "We decided to hunt public land, specifically the Metcalf Wildlife Management Area," shares Curtis. Located about twenty miles east of Chadron in Sheridan County, the Metcalf includes over three thousand acres of quality Pine Ridge elk habitat. "I was already planning on hunting Colorado during the bow season, so we decided to wait and hunt Nebraska during rifle season. We put up cameras on the Metcalf and had pictures of elk right up until bow season. Then nothing."

Arriving in Chadron for opening weekend, Curtis and Ryan hunted the Metcalf long and hard. They did not see an elk. "We were getting pretty frustrated, but then we ran into some guys hunting pronghorn, and they told us about seeing elk south of Chadron," remembers Curtis. "We drove down there, and there were elk everywhere."

After making contact with a landowner, Curtis and Ryan left their hotel the next morning, driving south through thick fog. "We got set up, but we couldn't see twenty feet," laughs Curtis. Again, no elk. The next morning their luck changed. Driving south to hunt the same property, they spotted a cow and a massive seven-by-seven bull standing in a field, only forty yards from public land. "We snuck in on the public ground and tried to call him in, but he wouldn't budge," recalls Curtis.

Later that afternoon, after the coin toss, Curtis and Ryan sat waiting, hoping the big bull might move their way. "We were sitting on the hay bales, and I see some bulls moving off to the west. Then I see a cow elk jump the fence, a long way off," remembers Curtis. Unbelievably, following the cow was the bull from that morning.

With his flat-shooting 7mm Magnum resting solidly on a hay bale, Curtis felt confident in taking the four-hundred-yard shot. At the recoil the bull disappeared from view. Climbing down, they made their way slowly across the field. Topping a small knoll, they saw the bull lying dead. "Oh my God, what did you do!" shouted Ryan.

What he did was shoot a bull grossing nearly four hundred inches! The Curtis James bull is a seven-by-seven with seven typical points on the left side, six on the right, and one small, 3-inch abnormal point coming off the right G5. Although having a relatively tight rack with an inside spread of only 39 4/8 inches, it has great tine length, with the G1 and G2 points all over twenty inches. The bull grosses 397 4/8 inches while netting 381 4/8. The bull currently ranks fourth in the typical firearm category in the Nebraska records book.

With no need for another coin toss, Ryan's hunt also ended well. The next evening, sitting on the same round bales, the two hunters watched twelve bulls saunter into the field. Ryan took home a nice 340-inch bull.

35

Imperial

The Jason Mosel Bull, 2015

· 380⁶/₈-inch typical
· Morrill County

Where in the world am I going to put it? Will my wife let me hang it in the house? If you ever have the good fortune of tying your tag on a trophy bull elk, these questions will come up. A shoulder-mounted trophy bull is a wall eater, making hanging it in a room with standard ceiling heights particularly tricky. And once you do get it on the wall, it will dominate the decor like it dominated satellite bulls!

For Jason Mosel of Scottsbluff, the issue came to a head, pun intended, after he shot a magnificent seven-by-seven bull. "My wife and I fought over it," recalls Jason. "It sat nose-down in the corner for like six months, until it finally replaced the piano in the corner of the living room."

Growing up near Orchard, Nebraska, Jason spent more time fishing than big-game hunting, until his father started deer hunting. After shooting his first whitetail doe at fourteen, he caught the big-game hunting bug, including the joy of processing and eating what he killed. Eventually attending Wesleyan University, he met his future wife, Lindsey, who was studying pre-medicine at Wayne State at the time. After Lindsey completed her studies and residency at the University of Nebraska Medical Center in Omaha, the young couple headed west to live, work, and hunt in the Scottsbluff area.

After pulling an elk tag in July of 2015, Jason began calling local land-owners. In this area hunters with an elk tag need to reach out quickly since ranches holding elk often get numerous requests to hunt. The landowners also often have landowner tags they want to fill first, before opening up their property to others. Although sometimes charging a trespass or trophy fee to make extra income, most ranchers also want to manage the number of elk to reduce crop loss. After a few calls Jason secured access to a ranch south of Redington in Morrill County.

Jason would be hunting an area geologists call the Cheyenne Tablelands, or even better, the Gangplank. This wedge of land between the North and South Platte Rivers was tilted upward as tectonic forces built the Rocky Mountains. The Platte rivers and their tributaries then cut downward, eroding and transporting materials eastward, creating a rugged, beautiful landscape of pine-dotted bluffs and prairie-covered valleys. Where more resistant cap rock protected underlying materials, ridges like the Wildcat Hills and land-marks like Chimney Rock, Jail Rock, and Scotts Bluff formed.

The first morning of the 2015 archery elk season found Jason sitting atop one of these bluffs, overlooking a valley south of Chimney Rock. In some places the valley was just wide enough to allow the turning of a center pivot, with the irrigated corn attracting and holding elk. Jason soon spotted eight nice bulls, and grabbing his bow he dropped down into the valley. Reaching the field, Jason began stalking along the edge of the cornfield. An adolescent bull walked past at twelve yards, while four rows over a much larger six-by-six bull sent cornstalk-rattling bugles into the air. Drawing his bow Jason centered his pin behind the bull's shoulder, sending an arrow through the corn. "I couldn't quite get high enough over the corn and my arrow deflected, striking the bull's front shoulder and not penetrating," recalls Jason. "I watched him for over two miles, until he disappeared over a bluff. That's a hard moment." Confident the bull survived, Jason refocused, preparing for the upcoming rifle season.

With the landowner's nephew wanting to fill his tag, Jason sat out opening weekend. This was fine, since operating his own arborist business allowed Jason to hunt the less-pressured weekdays. On the Tuesday after the rifle

FIG. 55. Jason Mosel with his beautiful seven-by-seven imperial bull from Morrill County. Photo courtesy of Jason Mosel.

opener, Jason left work later than he wanted, speeding down the highway to meet Steve, his brother's father-in-law, who was coming along to help. "When we reached the property we saw combines in the cornfield. We were disappointed, and I told Steve that the first decent six-by-six I see I was going to take," remembers Jason. Hurrying up the bluff, Jason settled in behind his .300 Winchester Magnum, and as soon as he did, a bull stepped out from the corn. "Steve immediately says, 'That's the bull you want to shoot!'"

Laser ranging the bull at five hundred twenty yards, Jason knew he needed to close the distance for an ethical shot. Hurrying down the ridge Jason closed the distance to sixty yards and could see ivory antler tips moving up a draw paralleling his position. "I ease over the ridge expecting a shot, but I can't find him. I couldn't believe it!" Jason remembers. Moving back up the ridge to the top of the bluff, they began glassing feverishly for the massive bull. Nothing. Exasperated, Jason finally said, "Let's go and shoot a different bull."

Not a minute later they spotted the giant seven-by-seven standing still in the pine trees, now six hundred yards away. The bull again disappeared into the trees. "I was so amazed how an animal that size can just disappear in those pines," remembers Jason. Once again he scrambled down the bluff toward the bull. "I come over the ridge and look to my left and the bull is drinking water out of a cattle tank. We both just look at each other," he remembers. The bull bolted, and so did Jason. Running uphill and cresting a rise, Jason dropped prone and found the bull through his riflescope, standing broadside at two hundred yards. "That .300 Magnum is so loud, but I heard the thump of the bullet hitting him." The big bull dropped. Seeing the elk fall and with his adrenaline surging, Jason stood and yelled, "Yes!" Soon after, the bull stood up, forcing Jason to drop prone once again and make the final shot.

Elk hunters dream of shooting a six-by-six, a royal bull. The longest point on a royal bull is usually the fourth point, called the royal point since it juts skyward from the top of the rack. The Jason Mosel bull is even better, a clean seven-by-seven, sometimes called an imperial. The royal points on this bull are simply amazing, measuring 23⅛ and 23⅜ inches. The G5 points are impressive as well, measuring 19⅞ inches on the right side and 18⅝ inches on the left, making the top of the bull's rack visually stunning. It is also extremely symmetrical, grossing 389⅛ inches and netting 380⅝.

The year after shooting his bull, Jason drew and filled a cow elk tag. The next year his wife, Lindsey, also drew and filled a cow tag, her first big-game animal. Jason hopes she will someday draw a bighorn sheep tag, or better yet, a bull elk tag. "She is a really good shot," says Jason.

If Lindsey shoots a big bull, where will they hang it?

36

Wildcat Hills Wapiti

The KC Merrihew Bull, 2014

- 358⅛-inch typical
- Morrill County

As the evening sun sets, throwing long shadows across the Wildcat Hills of western Nebraska, the rutting bull elk pauses from raking the ponderosa pine tree with his massive six-by-six rack. Hearing the soft chirp of a cow elk, he whirls and begins slowly walking with legs stiff and head down across the small clearing. Tipping his head back and flaring his nostrils, he draws in the cool evening air with the hope of catching the odor of the cow, or perhaps a competing bull. However, the evening is dead calm with the air currents carrying little scent, so he continues scanning for movement as he enters the tree line on the opposite side of the clearing. Out of the corner of his eye he notices, senses something out of place, and freezes.

Ten yards away sits KC Merrihew, his compound bow at full draw, shoulders and arms burning, praying the bull takes one more step.

KC was born in 1978 and grew up on a Sandhills ranch south of Ashby, learning early on to appreciate the vastness and solitude of western Nebraska's expansive landscape. He also learned that hunting meant food. "We weren't rich by any means, and anything we shot ended up on the dinner plate. I grew up eating deer, pheasants, and lots and lots of geese. I can hardly eat a goose now," KC remembers.

Having already shot a lot of game with rifles and shotguns, he decided at the young age of twelve to become a bowhunter. "I grew up in an area where you could go out and shoot a deer anytime you wanted. I wanted more of a challenge," recalls KC. Completing his bowhunter safety course in the early 1990s, he began stalking deer, turkeys, and even pheasants with his bow. He learned quickly that bowhunting requires skill, patience, and especially the ability to keep quiet. However, KC's life was soon going to get considerably louder.

Making the decision to join the service in 1998, he found himself stationed in Virginia at the Joint Expeditionary Base–Little Creek. Trained as a combat medic and assigned to a Marine supply unit, he was one of the "first to go, last to know" after 9/11. And after spending several years in the chaos of the war in Iraq, he returned home to the family ranch near Ashby. "After my time in the military the quiet time was very welcome," shares KC.

After a couple years running the ranch with his grandfather, he returned again to the noise. Now a flight paramedic working out of North Platte, he flies into situations where noise and mayhem are the norm. "I have a very stressful job, very taxing, and one way for me to escape is to go hunting," explains KC.

When KC drew a Nebraska bull elk tag in the summer of 2014 he was ecstatic, since he knew where he would hunt—the Wildcat Hills. A forty-five-mile east-west-trending ridge transecting Banner, Morrill, and Scotts Bluff Counties, the area is most closely associated with iconic landmarks—Chimney Rock, Scotts Bluff, Courthouse and Jail Rocks. Consisting of sandstone, siltstone, volcanic ash, and limestone weathered over the millennia by wind and water into a rugged landscape of deep ravines and flat-topped bluffs, it is a beautiful landscape. It is also one of the most biologically unique areas of the state, supporting ponderosa pine, Rocky Mountain juniper, and mountain mahogany interspersed with clearings covered in short-grass prairie. Perfect elk habitat. The area KC planned on hunting is an area he knows well, since his mother, Deb, and his stepfather live on the property. "I've been over that place numerous times on horseback. We find sheds; we know where the elk hang out," explains KC.

The first two days of the archery season were uneventful, with KC sitting immobile in a ground blind, hunting a big bull known to be in the area.

With his frustration growing he made the decision to change tactics on the third day of the hunt, waking up particularly early and packing everything necessary for a solo spot-and-stalk hunt.

With the weather unusually warm, he spent the morning walking the ridges and peering into the deep draws, calling periodically with his cow call. With no sightings or responding bugles, he decided to take a midday nap, laying down in the shade on a bed of pine needles. After waking, with the sun sliding low in the west, he made another set, calling softly. "I finally see this bull come over a knoll about one hundred fifty yards away. He hadn't bugled back, and when I called at him again, he turned and walked away," remembers KC. Puzzled by the bull's reaction, he watched as the bull began thrashing a tree with his antlers.

With the bull busy mauling the tree, KC moved quickly, closing the distance. When he arrived where he thought the bull was, it was gone. Looking to the north he saw another tree shaking violently above the brush. Sneaking to within fifty yards across a small clearing, he set up behind a chest-high bush and blew into his cow call. The bull whirled and headed directly toward him, and that is when KC drew his bow.

After crossing the clearing, "I could see his eye staring at me. He was uncomfortably close. You don't realize how large an elk is until he is standing that close," remembers KC. With his arms and shoulders burning and shaking from holding the bow back, he scanned the brush, looking for a window through it. Spotting two cedars stripped bare by rubbing elk, KC thought, *If he takes one more step, I can put it between those trees. It's not the best, but I can't hold it any longer.* The bull stepped, and KC released the arrow, watching it sink to the fletching behind the shoulder. "It couldn't have been a better shot. Thank God, because I had been at full draw for a long time."

At the shot the bull bolted, crashing through the brush and disappearing. Following the bull's path KC found half the arrow, covered in blood. Not wanting to jump the bull and send it running, he left his bow and pack hanging on a tree and hiked the four miles back to the house to get help. After returning with his mom and stepdad, they found the bull piled up only seventy-five yards from where he was arrowed. Working well past midnight,

FIG. 56. This massive six-by-six bull was only ten yards away when KC Merrihew made a killing shot with his bow. Photo courtesy of KC Merrihew.

they finished quartering the bull and hauling him home. "I had hunted all day, running on adrenaline, and was tired, bloody, and just exhausted," remembers KC.

Aged at twelve years old, the KC Merrihew bull was at the end of his prime antler-growing years. A classic royal bull, with six symmetrical points on each side, it has exceptional beam length, with the right side measuring 54⅜ inches and the left 55⅛. With only 10⅜ inches of total deductions, the bull grosses 368⅜ while netting 358⅛, making it the third-largest typical archery entry in the Nebraska records book.

Reminiscing on the experience KC reminds people to "find a balance between the chaos and busyness in their lives, and serenity. In my work I have a very fine-tuned perspective on life. People need to take care of themselves and find time to enjoy life."

37

Bull with a Bow

The John Rickard Bull, 2017

- 359⅞-inch typical
- Sheridan County

Arrowing a bull elk is exceptionally difficult. In most states elk hunting success rates, even when including rifle hunters, are oftentimes under 20 percent, and even lower on public-land, do-it-yourself hunts. For archers, success rates often dip into the single digits, especially when pursuing mature bulls.

Just getting into bow range of a bull is challenging enough, but factor in weather, tough terrain, the prying eyes of cow elk, adrenaline, good shot placement, and then actually recovering an animal notorious for its toughness, and it is rather amazing when a bowhunter actually closes the deal. No wonder there are fewer than twenty archery bulls in the Nebraska state records book.

So why bowhunt? John Rickard's story is typical among archers. Growing up in Kearney, his hunting experience was limited to pheasants, until a college roommate took him deer hunting. "I went deer hunting for the first time when I was twenty, and I was hooked," recalls John. Over the next decade he hunted deer exclusively with firearms. "I shot a lot of deer with a rifle and it was fun, but after a while taking a deer at three hundred yards became less interesting. I wanted more of a challenge, more time in a tree stand, and more time with nature."

By 2017 John was an experienced archer, having taken multiple deer and an Ontario, Canada, black bear. When he drew his Nebraska elk tag, he made the decision to hunt with his bow. "The landowner who gave me permission to hunt was surprised when I told him I wanted to bowhunt. Most just bring their rifles," shares John.

John made his first scouting trip to his hunting area in Sheridan County in July. It was beautiful Pine Ridge elk country. With summer waning the landowner began sending trail camera pictures of numerous elk, including images of a gorgeous six-by-six bull.

Driving up to the Bordeaux elk unit that September with his good friend Rob Muirhead, their anticipation was palpable. After settling into their Chadron motel, they met the landowner to do some scouting the evening before the opener. "We didn't see anything in the areas we thought would hold elk, and we also discovered a truck-filled camp of other hunters we weren't expecting to see. I was getting nervous," remembers John. With darkness approaching the trio drove to one last spot, parked on the road, and listened. In the distance they heard the unmistakable sound of bugling elk.

Arriving back at that same area the next morning, they drove the two miles off the main road to a pop-up blind the landowner had previously set up. After crawling in and organizing their gear, John and Rob sat quietly, waiting for shooting light. Soon a herd of elk meandered through in the darkness with several bulls bugling and the cows chirping. "I thought to myself that this was going to be a short hunt," recalls John. However, by the time shooting light arrived, they were gone.

Having never seen their surroundings in daylight, they soon realized they were sitting in an abandoned farmstead. To the north, about seventy-five yards away, sat an old graying farmhouse with a tree line and cornfield behind it. Thirty yards in front was a water tank, while seventy-five yards to the south squatted another outbuilding.

Besides a short break to stretch their legs, they sat all day. At sunset, not wanting to spook any nearby elk, they decided to wait until it was fully dark before heading back to the main road. Just before they were going to leave, elk came through again, encircling the blind, bugling, and making all kinds of strange noises. The next day, after checking the trail camera overlooking the water tank, they would discover pictures of the giant six-by-six breeding a cow.

The next morning they were back in the blind by four thirty. At dawn, with temperatures in the mid-sixties, they heard a bull raking trees behind the farmhouse. Thinking they may try a stalk by using the farmhouse as cover, they instead decided to try cow calling first. After hitting the call a second time, John spotted a cow coming from the left, and pointing, whispered, "Don't move." Rob looked up and said, "No, it's right there!" John hadn't noticed a giant six-by-six trailing the cow.

With an arrow nocked and ready, John estimated the distance at about thirty-five yards. Leaning forward Rob attempted to pull down the mesh screen covering the blind's window. It wouldn't budge. Pulling harder the mesh gave way with an audible pop, causing the bull to look right at them, spin, and start moving away. Being a deer hunter John instinctually used his mouth to grunt at the bull, stopping it. Leaning forward to avoid hitting one of the blind's support poles, he released the arrow from his Mathews bow. "He was quartering away, so the arrow entered farther back than I wanted, but I thought I caught the opposite lung," remembers John. At the shot the bull just walked into the nearby tree line.

Shaking with adrenaline and already worried about the shot, they heard the worst sound possible—raindrops hitting the blind. After sitting an hour in the pouring rain, their worst fears were confirmed: no arrow and no blood trail. Deciding to back out and give the bull time to bed down, they made their way toward the truck. Incredibly, they spotted the bull, bedded down in a field two hundred yards from the blind. After watching through binoculars for a half hour, they saw the bull stand and with blood streaming down both sides, walk away into the heavy timber.

Sick with worry John returned to town and turned on the Husker game to pass the time. Returning several hours later to where they last spotted the bull, they found nothing. "I was heartbroken; I was even contemplating selling my bow," John explains. After looking fruitlessly for several hours,

FIG. 57. John Rickard's beautiful 359⅞-inch typical bull missed beating the archery state record by a mere three inches. Photo courtesy of John Rickard.

they decided to split up and start walking the rugged ravine the bull was last seen entering.

After several hours walking up the drainage, John spotted the bull slowly moving through the timber toward him! Scrambling, he closed the distance to sixty yards and sent two arrows through the bull's lungs. The bull went down and John's hunt was finally over. Walking up on his bull, John remembers thinking, *Oh my gosh, this thing is huge, and oh my gosh, it's a long way up that hill!*

The John Rickard bull is a beautiful example of a typical elk. The five-year-old bull is a clean six-by-six with an inside spread of over forty-four inches and long beams measuring 53⅝ inches on the right and 52⅘ inches on the left. Although it also has good tine length and mass, symmetry is what makes it exceptional. The bull grosses 364⅞ inches with a mere five inches of total deductions, resulting in a net score of 359⅞. It missed breaking the current typical state archery record by only three inches.

Although the bull elk mount now adorns the wall of his home, John also has a family to feed, including three young daughters. So before returning home with the deboned meat in the bed of his truck, John stopped at the grain elevator in Amherst. "I pulled in and said to the guy, 'Hey, I have a bunch of elk meat in my truck, can I weigh it?'" Three hundred eight pounds of lean, healthy, and tasty Nebraska venison.

38

Thank God He Made It

The Doug Correll Bull, 2014

· 362⅞-inch typical
· Banner County

Doug Correll wrote it all down. From his first scouting trip, to hanging his state-record archery bull on the wall of his Scottsbluff home. The following are excerpts from his handwritten (cursive nonetheless) story about his massive state-record Banner County bull. It begins with the supporting cast:

Nate Luehrs—son-in-law, drew elk tag for me, guide, scout

Kerry Keane—experienced professional guide & elk caller from Gering NE

Roger Luehrs—Nate's father, scout, professional field dresser (Roger is a veterinarian, so he has gutted lots of critters)

Doug Correll—extremely lucky archer (with lots of practice), retired owner of Correll Refrigeration Inc. of Ogallala NE. Has hunted mule deer, antelope, wild turkeys with bow. Used Diamond by Bowtech bow with Cabela's carbon arrows and Muzzy 3 blade broadheads

August 22

Roger saw a 5 or 6 point bull, cow, and calf cross north of windmill on section 18 north of Rd 74.

August 27

Marlene (my wife) and I saw 2 cows and 1 calf from hill north of windmill. Marlene looked really great all camouflaged up and de-scented. Took camper down to Broadwater RV Park and set it up....

September 13

Saw a five-by-five between grain bins west of Rd 133 on Andy Co. in the morning.

September 14

Saw cows and bull on the alfalfa west of Rd 133.

September 15

After a mile hike into Andy Co. on opening archery morning, Kerry and I set up on a 6x6 bull on NW corner of section 18. I could not see, but Kerry said he was within 35–40 yds from me, but I could not see him to get a shot due to corn being in the way (imagine that!).

Had a 6x6 at about 60 yards on south end of alfalfa in SW corner section 7 that evening but no shot.

September 16

Small 6x6 bull encounter near pivot point on alfalfa. It was too far to shoot—about 60 yards and yes, corn was in my way!

September 17

Roger & I scouted in morning at Andy Co. and heard bulls in all directions. Saw 3 bulls at Newkirk's—one nice 6x6 on south side of middle pivot just north of wheat pivot. He jumped 4 or 5 feet in the air and bolted into the corn. Roger & I lunched on meat loaf, mashed potatoes with Marlene's apple crisp, vanilla ice cream & oatmeal with raisin cookies.

That evening at Andy Co. alfalfa a 6x6 bull chased a cow from the SW corner mud wallow to east of Rd 133. Another big 6x6 herd bull came out to center of alfalfa field & bugled but no shot, left after shooting time.

When I was leaving had a 6x6 at 10 yds. I stepped into the corn so he would leave but he followed behind me at 15–20 yds for 200 yds & grunted at me. I won't lie, I was scared. I was glad when his grunts got further away. Finally, I got back to my pickup & called Nate to give him the story. Whew!

September 18

Thursday morning big 6x6 herd bull chased 6 or 7 cows across the alfalfa field from the east until he drove them in the corn. No shot. Nate joined me for evening hunt & we had a 6x6 bull come from the north in the alfalfa field but he turned & went east across road at their crossing point north of the alfalfa bales along road 133.

September 19

Nate & I picked up Kerry Keane early in the morning and went to Art Olsen's ground. Heard bugling so we decided to make a set with a cow decoy & Kerry calling. Had a large 6x6 monster bull come by me at 30–35 yds but I screwed up & didn't get him stopped for a shot. I was at full draw when he went north. I thought he was about 40 yds and by that time I was starting to weaken & was shaking. I let an arrow fly but missed badly.

While looking for my arrow I looked back at where I shot from & decided it was 60–70 yds. He was so big I thought he was closer. I didn't take my range finder with me but that was the last time I did that! I was mad at myself & felt embarrassed that I had let Kerry & Nate down. Kerry did a great job of calling him by me but it was all on me. I looked for a hole to crawl into but couldn't find one.

We got back to Nate's truck and it had a flat right rear tire. I jacked up the truck but had to saw the cable holding the spare tire to get it out to put on. Only cost Nate $280 for new spare tire lift! His new tires look good!

September 20

Took the day off to go to the Farm & Ranch Museum with Marlene . . . and watch Carter play soccer at soccer fields north of Scottsbluff cemetery.

September 21

I went out to Olsen's about 6:00 pm to see where elk were going. A large bull took 8 cows southwest out of east half circle of corn over to pivot of corn as there were about 150 Angus cows out on Olsen's beet field on the west end of our hunting area. The bull elk held the cows from going to the beets where they really eat well. They love beets. There was a lot of commotion at the sugar beet field with cowboys, four wheelers, dogs & pickups going every which way. That was still going on at dark thirty so I went home.

September 22

Kerry & I went out early & set up on the northeast edge of the west cornfield quarter circle pivot. Had cows running past us & a small 6x6 was about 25–30 yds east of me but I did not shoot. We heard a big bull bugling and after he 360'd us to try to wind us, he stepped out in the grassy area north of us. He came to about 70 yds north of us but did not like something & went west to the quarter corn circle. Kerry wanted to kick the monster 6x6 (same one I missed last Friday) in the face for being so smart and walking through the corn & completely circling us with no shot. Damn it!

Monday evening we set up at the northeast corner of the quarter corn circle next to the beets. This time Kerry used his new bugle & my new different decoy and we spread apart about 75 yds to change things up.

Kerry got the big boy, the monster 6x6 to come from the south along the corn. He was walking north in the sugar beets and when he got 50 yds south of me he started moving away to the northeast. I had ranged some weeds at 38 yds to familiarize myself with the distances this time. When the 6x6 bull got beyond those weeds, he stopped & was approximately 50 yds from me. I quickly got my 50 yard sight pin on his rib cage & touched my arrow off. It smacked him in the right ribs halfway up his side but it was about 4–6 inches back of where I wanted it.

He turned & faced south so Kerry & I couldn't see the exact shot placement. He stood there approximately 6 minutes & was really sick & wobbly. He got in the corn. Kerry ranged him going into the corn at 150 yards so we had a starting point.

FIG. 58. Doug Correll (*left*) and guide Kerry Keane pose with the current typical archery state record. Photo courtesy of Doug Correll.

It was really hard to sleep that night. We called Nate & he called Roger to meet at Kerry's house at 6:00 am for what we hoped was a big 6x6 bull recovery.

September 23

With trailer & mule in tow Roger, Nate, & I met at Kerry's at 6:00 am to head out to Olsen's to see if we could find an elk. Kerry ranged us down 150 yds south in the beet field to find about where he entered the corn. There was blood on every corn stalk on the bull's right side. About 40 yds he got out of the pivot track and broke off the fletching of the arrow. Nate went ahead about another 15 yards & found where he laid down & bled. He got up and went 20 more feet east to his final stopping point.

I don't know who was more excited, Nate, Roger, or me. For once there was no ground shrinkage as he was bigger than we thought. After pictures, high fives, handshakes, & yes, hugs I asked Roger to gut him.

Eventually we got him on the trailer, out of the cornfield, and across the beet field. Whew! Kerry got up in the trailer & pretended to kick him in the face so I took a picture of his redemption.

September 24

Got up at 5:30 am to head to Mom & Dad's to show them the "horns." They were up when I got there about 8:00 am. Dad put on his cap & coat and came out to join Mom & I. Dad thought he looked pretty good. He was more impressed than Mom.

I headed to Barry Johnson's. Barry thought he looked good so he did a "Green Score" which was unofficial and came up with 375⅛ inches gross and 361⅝ net inches after deductions. I helped hold the head while he caped him out. I have to wait 60 days before the rack can be officially scored. I am patiently waiting.

September 25

Went to Broadwater to recover camper & pay the owner at Mitchell's Guns and Ammo. I only slept in the camper 4 nights but paid for 10 nights. It was worth it to keep from driving an hour each way. It also was handy for midday naps!

Undated

Barry Johnson got Brad Wiese from Benkelman to score the rack. He grossed 376½ inches and netted out 362⅞ after deductions. The elk was a new state archery record by a little over 10 inches.

Nate came over to help me hang him above the stairs as that was the only place he would be safe. Marlene had made a deal with me that if he was the new state archery record that he could hang above the stairs.

Thank God he made it!

39

First Bull

The Warren Chapin Bull, 1986

- 319⁴⁄₈-inch typical
- Dawes County

Looking at a map of the Great Plains you find an abundance of cartographic elk sign. Towns like Elk City, Oklahoma; Elk Horn, Iowa; Elkhart, Texas; and Elk Point, South Dakota. Rivers like the Elkhorn in Nebraska, the Big Elkhorn in Texas, and Elk Creek in North Dakota. Lakes named Elk Lake in Minnesota and Elkhorn Prairie in Oklahoma. If you go to the United States Board of Geographic Names online and conduct a search for "elk" you find thousands of places with "elk" in the name. When humans, from Native Americans to westward-moving pioneers, sought to name a feature on the landscape, they often used what they saw. And what they saw were huge numbers of elk grazing across the Great Plains.

Before the arrival of Euro-American settlers in North America, elk (*Cervus elaphus*) were the most widely distributed deer species on the continent.[1] Their range stretched from the Atlantic to the Pacific, north into southern Canada and south into northern Mexico. An extremely adaptable ungulate, elk inhabited a wide range of biomes, including the vast prairie of the Great Plains and all of present-day Nebraska.

The first recorded sightings of elk in Nebraska were by the Lewis and Clark expedition of 1804–6, when the expedition began seeing elk upon arriving in the far southeastern corner of the future state of Nebraska. On July 14, 1804, William Clark made the following journal entry: "Observed two Elk on a[n] I[sl]and in the river, in attempting to get near those elk obse[r]ved one near us. I Shot one."[2] Although they had killed elk earlier in their journey, in present-day Missouri, this was the first recorded kill in present-day Nebraska, most likely near the Richardson and Nemaha County line.

Within a few decades thousands of settlers, fur traders, and military personnel were following the Oregon, Mormon, and Deadwood Trails westward along the Platte River, shooting elk along the way. With no game regulations and market-hunting commonplace, elk populations followed a similar downward trajectory as the bison. With the completion of the Transcontinental Railroad two years after statehood, Nebraska's human population grew rapidly, placing even more pressure on wildlife populations. Sometime during the 1880s both elk and bison went extinct in the area. In 1907 the Nebraska legislature made it illegal to kill an elk anywhere within the state.

With the passage of game laws and the advent of modern wildlife management practices, elk slowly began migrating back into the state from eastern Wyoming. During the 1950s and into the 1960s elk sightings increased across the Pine Ridge of northwestern Nebraska. By the 1970s elk were using the Bordeaux Creek drainage in Dawes County, with the herd expanding to approximately seventy-five by 1985.

After a seventy-nine-year hiatus, the NGPC decided it was time to once again hunt elk in Nebraska. This is where Warren Chapin enters the story of elk hunting in the state.

Born in 1938 in Cozad, Warren grew up in small towns in western Nebraska and Colorado. Similar to others of his generation, he began hunting at an early age, pursuing small game. Eventually settling in the Scottsbluff area, he married his wife, Wauneta, in 1960. Three years after they were married, Wauneta shot a 164⅛-inch records book mule deer in Garden County. Warren meanwhile took up bowhunting, eventually shooting thirty-nine deer with his bow and several elk in Montana and Colorado.

In the summer of 1986 Warren put his name into the drawing for one of only seventy-four permits issued for the first modern-day elk season in

Nebraska. Sitting with eighty-year-old Warren and Wauneta in their home in Gering, I could tell that the memories are still vivid. "I was really lucky to draw a tag, since two thousand five hundred people put in," remembers Warren.

Soon Warren and Wauneta were packing up their gear and loading their camper for what they didn't realize would be a historic hunt. Arriving north of Chadron, along Bordeaux Creek, they set up camp and prepared for opening day.

On September 20 they headed out in their 1981 Jeep Cherokee to a location they knew held elk. "When we arrived we saw trucks already parked in our spot, so we made the decision to try our second choice spot, but when we arrived the fog was so thick you couldn't see nothing," remembers Warren. Not wanting to risk spooking elk in the dense fog, they sat waiting in the dark, with Wauneta rolling down the Jeep window, listening for elk bugles. "I said, 'Warren, did you hear that!' He was hard of hearing so he couldn't hear anything," remembers Wauneta, laughing.

With the sky turning gray Warren whispered to Wauneta, "That's my bull." Walking slowly through the fog toward the back of the meadow was an elk. Climbing quietly out of the Jeep, Warren crept about forty yards to a fence and took a rest against a post. "I could see the bull walking across the meadow with his head tilted back into the air. I couldn't see his rack, but I could tell by the way he was walking that it was a bull."

Miraculously, not five minutes after legal shooting time, the fog lifted, providing Warren a clear look at the bull. "I pulled my rifle up and I was just shaking. I told myself 'You're never going to hit him doing that,'" Warren recalls. After taking a couple deep breaths, he settled the crosshairs on the bull and squeezed the trigger. After hearing the bullet hit he saw the elk drop. Wauneta climbed out of the Jeep and running over, exclaimed, "I thought you were just going to sit there and let him get away!"

As they were celebrating, the bull stood and began walking away. Warren hurriedly chambered another round, and shooting offhand dropped the bull for good with another three-hundred-fifty-yard shot. Nebraska elk hunting

FIG. 59. Warren and Wauneta Chapin posing proudly with the first elk shot during the first modern-day elk season in 1986. Photo courtesy of *Nebraskaland* magazine/ Nebraska Game and Parks Commission.

was back! The NGPC later officially confirmed that Warren's bull was the first harvested in the state during modern times.

With the help of some other hunters, the Chapins slid the bull into the back of their Jeep. "We slid that bull in until his hind feet were sticking between the two front seats. His brow tines poked holes into the headliner," remembers Warren. When they arrived back on the road, a photographer from the NGPC captured the historic moment with a wonderful picture of Warren and Wauneta standing proudly with their bull elk, rifle resting across the rack.

Although far from the largest elk in the records book, the Warren Chapin bull is arguably the most historic. A clean and symmetrical six-by-six, it grosses 331²⁄₈ inches while netting 319⁴⁄₈. On the scoresheet, in the blank titled "*Remarks*," the official measurer typed: "First Nebraska Season." The bull hangs prominently on the wall in the Chapin home, a constant reminder of their hunt and the role they played in the history of elk hunting in Nebraska.

Records of North American
Big Game

BOONE AND CROCKETT CLUB

205 South Patrick Street
Alexandria, Virginia 22314

Minimum Score:
Roosevelt 290
American 375

ENTERED
#4

WAPITI

Kind of Wapiti __American__

DETAIL OF POINT
MEASUREMENT

	Abnormal Points	
	Right	Left

				Total to E			
SEE OTHER SIDE FOR INSTRUCTIONS				Column 1	Column 2	Column 3	Column 4
A. Number of Points on Each Antler	R. 6	L. 6		Spread Credit	Right Antler	Left Antler	Difference
B. Tip to Tip Spread	36 3/8						
C. Greatest Spread	47 7/8						
D. Inside Spread 45 of Main Beams 2/8	Credit may equal but not exceed length of longer antler			45 2/8			
IF Spread exceeds longer antler, enter difference.							
E. Total of Lengths of all Abnormal Points							
F. Length of Main Beam					48 6/8	51 3/8	2 5/8
G-1. Length of First Point					15 2/8	16 0/8	6/8
G-2. Length of Second Point					14 0/8	16 6/8	2 6/8
G-3. Length of Third Point					11 4/8	10 3/8	1 1/8
G-4. Length of Fourth (Royal) Point					14 3/8	16 1/8	1 6/8
G-5. Length of Fifth Point					12 4/8	10 3/8	2 1/8
G-6. Length of Sixth Point, if present							
G-7. Length of Seventh Point, if present							
H-1. Circumference at Smallest Place Between First and Second Points					6 6/8	7 1/8	3/8
H-2. Circumference at Smallest Place Between Second and Third Points					5 6/8	5 5/8	1/8
H-3. Circumference at Smallest Place Between Third and Fourth Points					6 2/8	6 1/8	1/8
H-4. Circumference at Smallest Place Between Fourth and Fifth Points					5 4/8	5 4/8	------
TOTALS				45 2/8	140 5/8	145 3/8	11 6/8

ADD	Column 1	45 2/8	Exact locality where killed NE corner of Pasture #43 DAWES CO NEBR.
	Column 2	140 5/8	Date killed 9-20-86 By whom killed Warren R. Chapin
	Column 3	145 3/8	Present owner Same
Total		331 2/8	Address Box 55, Melbeta, NE 69355
SUBTRACT Column 4		11 6/8	Guide's Name and Address N/A
FINAL SCORE		319 4/8	Remarks: (Mention any abnormalities or unique qualities) First Nebraska Season Rifle

FIG. 60. Warren Chapin scoresheet. Courtesy of the Boone and Crockett Club.

40

Pine Ridge

The Robert Marsteller Bull, 2004

- 390 3/8-inch typical
- Sioux County

Standing atop Pleasant Ridge on his ranch in Sioux County, Bob Marsteller takes in the majestic view. Forty-five miles north looms the dark southern edge of the Black Hills, what the Lakota Sioux call Paha Sapa, "the center of their universe."[1] Turning east, the western edge of the Pine Ridge begins its sweeping, coniferous-laden, one-hundred-mile arc across Sioux, Dawes, and Sheridan Counties before trailing off into the Pine Ridge Reservation in South Dakota. South is rolling short-grass prairie, dissected by the Niobrara River meandering into Nebraska from its headwaters near Lusk, Wyoming. Thirty miles westward into Wyoming are the Rawhide Buttes, and fifty miles beyond that, jutting up from the Laramie Range, is 10,275-foot Laramie Peak. Not a bad spot to spend a day hunting.

Born in 1957 in Harrison, Nebraska, Bob grew up in Sioux County, working on local ranches and hunting deer and ducks. "We rode around in that country in an old Willys Jeep," he recalls with a grin. "In those days we had big herds of mule deer, while seeing a whitetail was a novelty." He doesn't remember seeing elk, or hearing about mountain lions. Eventually moving to Alliance and beginning a forty-year career working for the railroad, he never stopped making trips north to the ranch.

During his lifetime Bob witnessed elk repopulating the Pine Ridge, including his land north of Harrison. Although drawing a tag for and having previously taken a cow elk, Bob drew a landowner bull tag for the 2004 elk season. Having seen elk on his land and in the nearby Gilbert Baker Wildlife Management Area, Bob and his son Ryan decided to try hunting public land. "The day before I shot my big one, we bugled in a nice bull in the Gilbert Baker, but it was straight down, rough country, and we looked at each other and decided we didn't want to shoot him," remembers Bob. Later that evening he called a neighbor to the west who had mentioned that elk were feeding on one of his oat fields. He agreed to let them hunt.

The next morning found Bob, his good friend Rick Deans, and Ryan, who was playing hooky from school, looking through their binoculars at an oat field covered with thirty elk, including ten bulls. "There were a number of really nice six-by-six bulls out there, but one was clearly bigger than the rest," remembers Bob. The giant bull's rack stood high above the other bulls as he swaggered among the herd, trying to control his harem of cows. Having positioned himself on a timbered ridge about a mile from the oat field, Bob began bugling, hoping the herd would move toward the timber to bed down.

The elk had other ideas. As the sun rose higher, the smaller bulls began drifting off in twos and threes, heading toward the timber in different directions. Keeping his eye on the herd bull, Bob moved several times, trying to guess where the bull would enter the timber with his cows and calves. Unexpectedly the bull moved away from the timber, bedding down with his harem on an open hillside. "We couldn't believe it. Eventually we gave up, since they were out in the open, and drove up to the next ranch. But we could still see that herd bedded down up in the hills, out in the open, really close to Wyoming," recalls Bob.

Eventually the herd rose to its feet and began moving toward the timber. Bob hurriedly drove to another spot, thinking they might still intercept the elk before they made it to cover. "In a lot of ways it was more like a pronghorn hunt than an elk hunt. It was wide-open country," explains Bob. Moving into position on an open hillside, Bob readied his .300 Weatherby

FIG. 61. Bob Marsteller (*right*) and his son, Ryan, pose with his 390⅜-inch bull that stood as the state record for thirteen years. Photo courtesy of Bob Marsteller.

Magnum. Finally the giant bull came strolling over the hill, giving Bob a clear three-hundred-eighty-yard shot. "The first shot hit him kind of far back, but two more shots put him down."

"When we walked up on him, I just couldn't say anything. I knew he was big when I saw him, but I was just amazed at how big he actually was. He just kept getting bigger," remembers Bob. Friends and family soon gathered on the open prairie, marveling at the magnificent bull, taking pictures and enjoying the memories. "We were out there for a long time, just enjoying the experience and a magnificent animal."

The Bob Marsteller bull is an amazing typical elk. A six-by-seven, with a missing G6 point on the right side, it has it all, including an inside spread of 50⅛ inches and exceptional beams of 58⅝ and 57⅝ inches. The fronts are outstanding, with both brow tines over eighteen inches, while the G2s both measure slightly over sixteen. However, symmetry is what makes this a truly remarkable bull. There are only 8⅝ inches of deductions between the two sides, and 3⅛ inches of that is the unmatched point on the left antler! Grossing 399⅛ inches and netting 390⅜ inches, it is no wonder this bull stood as the state record for thirteen years.

Bob continues visiting, hunting, and enjoying his ground north of Harrison. His basement is full of hunting pictures and memorabilia, including framed trail camera pictures of elk. However, it is the beautiful trail camera pictures of mountain lions that really catch your attention. Although Bob has never seen one, he takes joy in knowing these cats, and the elk they pursue, are roaming his property. "A lot of people think Nebraska ends at North Platte," he says with a chuckle. "But this land out here, it is truly special."

41

Center Pivot

The Chuck Anderson Bull, 2016

- 379⅛-inch typical
- Banner County

Every year Nebraska hunters mutter, "I hope the corn is out by rifle season." Millions of acres of corn create a vast, protective green blanket of ten-foot-tall grass. Through late summer and into fall, whitetail bucks use cornfields as sanctuaries, sauntering deep inside these fields to bed down in the shady rows, knowing they can hear the rustling of anything moving their way through the cornhusks, which of course rarely happens. If you wound a buck near standing corn, that is where he will go. Few indeed are the Nebraska hunters who have not followed a blood trail smeared and dribbled across dry cornstalks.

In the eastern third of the state corn is often on dryland and found in rectangular fields. Move westward, over the vast Ogallala aquifer, and you encounter center pivot irrigation, corn in the round. A Nebraska invention, there are now over one hundred thousand pivots circling the landscape. Corn in pivots is often taller and thicker than dryland corn due to the availability of water. In the western part of the state elk and center pivots coexist, and elk, being the opportunistic animals they are, use cornfields much like whitetail.

Born in 1979 and growing up only seven miles from the Canadian border near Rolla, North Dakota, Chuck Anderson knew little of center pivots. What he did know was that he loved the outdoors. Cutting his hunting teeth on vast flocks of snow geese and other waterfowl using the nearby Rock Lake National Wildlife Refuge, he eventually developed an appetite for all types of hunting and fishing. "I have a passion for chasing about everything. I don't concentrate on anything in particular, although when I have a chance to waterfowl hunt or upland bird hunt, I'm in," shares Chuck.

After attending one year of college, Chuck noticed an advertisement for the opening of Cabela's fifth store in East Grand Forks, Minnesota. After making the long drive to Minnesota to apply for a job at the new store, he found they had already hired their entire crew. Not giving up, he told them he would do anything they wanted, if they would just give him the opportunity to work. "My first job was actually driving buses from the overflow parking lots to the new store." After working at a variety of Cabela's stores, he transferred to the Sidney headquarters in 2009 and began hunting Nebraska.

Drawing a bull elk tag in July 2016, Chuck quickly reached out to a number of outfitters and landowners he knew in the North Platte elk unit. No luck. Recalling that he had seen a couple cow elk on some center pivots in western Banner County near Bushnell, he gave the landowner a call. "This landowner has the only pivots in the area, and elk began using them about seven years ago," Chuck recalls. "It's really wide-open country, not what you would think of as elk country. But those center pivots attract and hold elk." On his subsequent scouting trips, perched high on a bluff overlooking the remote cluster of five center pivots, Chuck glassed a herd of at least thirty elk, including eighteen bulls. Two were true monsters.

Opening morning dawned cool and full of anticipation for Chuck and his hunting party. Joined by good friends Justin Carpenter, Brad Gerber, and Phil Dalrymple, the game plan called for Phil and Justin to stay up high on the bluff with the spotting scope, while Brad and Chuck made their way along the edge of the standing corn, hoping to catch the elk in the bordering wheat stubble. Chuck shouldered his .300 Remington Ultra Magnum and his pack, and he and Brad moved to the sound of bull elk bugling in the distance. With the eastern sky brightening, they could see dark shapes in the distance as the two crept along the corn. Lifting his range-finding binoculars, Chuck lasered several elk at two hundred yards.

With shooting light coming quickly, and still needing to cover about fifty yards to be in position for a shot, Chuck slipped off his backpack and binoculars and along with Brad began belly-crawling toward the drifting herd. Reaching the spot, he positioned his rifle on its bipod and waited. "Brad whispers that we have three minutes, then two, and finally, 'Okay, it's shooting time,'" recalls Chuck. Looking through the scope, he located the massive six-by-seven he had watched numerous times on his scouting trips. Settling the crosshairs on the tan hide behind the front shoulder, he slowly squeezed the trigger. At the shot the massive bull reared back on his hind legs. "I think I got him," hissed Chuck. Brad meanwhile exclaimed, "You shot the wrong one!" After a tense discussion they realized Brad had his binoculars on a different bull, a five-by-eight.

Settling down, Chuck shot again, with no perceivable reaction from the bull. Quickly racking another round, he shot again, this time dropping the bull. Unbelievably the bull got back to his feet, forcing Chuck to send his last round at the bull. Nothing. As Chuck was now out of ammo, Brad scurried back, retrieving Chuck's pack and binoculars. Digging through the pack, Chuck pulled out a box of ammo, only to find it was full of spent brass! Lifting his binoculars he again ranged the bull. Four hundred yards—much farther than he had thought. His bullets had been hitting low. The giant bull walked slowly away into the tall, irrigated corn.

Moving back up to the bluff to rejoin the rest of the group, the four hunters spent the next several hours peering through their spotting scopes, periodically watching the bull stand, move, and then bed down again in the cornfield. "This bull and the five-by-eight were the only bulls with racks big enough that you could see them above the corn," explains Chuck.

The landowner soon arrived with some of his family members, and the entire group entered the corn with the hope of finding the wounded bull. "You get inside one of those fields, and you just can't see anything. It's a little frightening to be that close, and even though you can hear elk, you can't see them. There were elk running all over in that cornfield, but we couldn't find him," says Chuck.

FIG. 62. Chuck Anderson poses with his 379⅛-inch bull, shot in a Banner County center pivot. Photo courtesy of Chuck Anderson.

Finally a couple hunters from an adjoining property told them they had seen the bull drop and pointed them in the right direction. Entering the corn once again, Chuck squatted down, and peering down a row, spotted the bull. This time the shot was true, and his records book bull was down for good.

The first thing you notice about the Chuck Anderson bull is the beams. Most trophy-class bulls have beams over fifty inches, with exceptional bulls pushing sixty inches. This bull's right beam is 57⅛ inches and the left is 56⅜. With good symmetry, mass, and tine length, including excellent fronts, it is a trophy elk by any standard, grossing 393⅝ inches and netting 379⅛. It currently ranks as the sixth-largest firearm typical in the Nebraska records book.

"It was great to experience this with three of my best friends. It meant a lot to have them with me," shares Chuck. Fittingly for Nebraska, this magnificent bull spent his last few breaths in a center pivot cornfield.

PART 4

Non-Typical American Elk

42

Perfect Hunt

The Hannah Helmer Bull, 2016

- 426 7/8-inch non-typical
- Sioux County

"Dad, I wouldn't change a thing about my hunt. It was perfect," Hannah said with a grin. From beating the long odds of drawing a coveted bull-elk tag on her second try. To gaining permission to hunt a beautiful Sioux County ranch with a shot-in-the-dark email. Having that property hold a world-class bull and then locating him bugling and chasing cows on opening morning. To making a perfect 214-yard shot with the bull bugling right at her. Perfect indeed.

Everything coming together just right on that beautiful autumn morning is the highlight of my hunting life. It was also the main motivation for researching and writing this book.

Hannah's hunt began as many other elk hunts do in Nebraska, with a long drive along Highway 2, across the scenic Sandhills to the Pine Ridge. After meeting up with family friend Lee Johanson, we unpacked our gear at the hotel and headed west to glass before nightfall. We talked briefly with the landowner and decided to try glassing from a high point overlooking a long valley ringed by pine-covered ridges.

We soon set out, and topping the rise we spotted a herd of elk about a half mile ahead grazing on a small alfalfa field. One animal clearly stood out from the others, and after finding him in the spotting scope Hannah whispered, "Dad, he's huge." As the sun set before opening day, we took turns glassing the majestic bull as he chased two satellite bulls attempting to steal away his small herd of cows. Later that evening in our hotel room Lee and I debated the bull's size. We were both so wrong.

The next morning Hannah, Lee, and I gathered around a kitchen table with the landowner, his wife, and their adult son eating warm egg sandwiches and sipping hot coffee. After discussing multiple options we made the decision to hike from the back of the house to the crest of the high north-south-running ridge bordering the eastern side of the ranch. With the wind light from the west our plan was to get above the herd and hope they fed up, out of the valley into the thick, pine-covered draws.

Hiking along the ridge in the dark, Hannah smiled up at me as multiple bugles floated up from the valley floor. We walked for a half hour and stopped directly west and above the alfalfa field where we had glassed the bull the evening before. After some indecision and backtracking we settled under a cluster of pine trees as the sky lightened behind our backs. Hannah sat waiting behind the Remington 7mm-08 resting on its bipod. The landowner and his son, who had a cow tag, set up a short distance away.

We soon heard several bulls bugling, and we could tell they were getting closer. I could feel Hannah shaking next to me and began wondering if she could make a good shot if one of these bulls appeared. Lee, sitting a few feet behind us, hit his bugle call and a bull responded immediately from the southwest. After waiting a few minutes Lee bugled again, and this time the responding bugle left no doubt—he was close. The five-by-five bull stepped out from the pine trees at fifty yards and stared right at us. Hannah tried repositioning her rifle for a shot, but one small pine tree blocked her view. The bull slipped over the crest of the ridge and was gone.

Our disappointment was short-lived as another bugle echoed from across the opposite ridge. Hannah nudged me and said, "There's an elk across from us." I crawled to our right and spotted the massive bull through my binoculars. My heart nearly exploded with the realization that this was the bull from the night before, and we had totally underestimated his size. Hannah

Fig. 63. Fourteen-year-old Hannah Helmer is all smiles after downing her 426⅞-inch state-record bull. Photo courtesy of the author.

crawled over and we watched the bull and his cows filter through the pines. With so many cows the thought crossed my mind to stay put and not risk blowing the herd out of the area. However, looking below us Hannah and I noticed a shallow wash leading to a trail and hopefully a closer, clear shot at the bull. I led the way, scrunching down the wash on my rear with Hannah and Lee close behind. We arrived unnoticed, and Hannah once again settled in behind the Remington.

Looking across to the opposite ridge there was one small opening of about a quarter acre that might offer a shot. The bull stepped out, tilting his massive rack back and letting out another long bugle. Lee whispered, "He's at about two hundred yards." The bull swiftly moved out of view, chasing a cow. A few minutes later he reappeared, crossing the opening again but

FIG. 64. The Hannah Helmer bull has amazing "fronts," with the G1 and G2 points all measuring over twenty inches. Photo courtesy of the author.

not presenting a shot to Hannah peering through the riflescope. I glanced back at Lee and said, "If he steps out again, bugle at him."

Soon after, the bull appeared on the right edge of the clearing and began walking across. At Lee's bugle the bull stopped, and looking across the canyon directly at us, he tilted his massive rack back and let loose a throaty bugle. Hannah sent the 140-grain Nosler Partition into his vitals. The giant bull hunched, running to our left and disappearing into the pines.

After the shot Hannah burst into tears. I held her tight as the adrenaline and excitement of the hunt left her sobbing and shaking. Holding her close I prayed that her shot was good and the bull was down. We soon noticed a cow elk standing in the clearing and began glassing the surrounding forest. The bull was standing broadside, thirty yards from the initial shot! Hannah composed herself and quickly shot again, placing the second shot about three inches from the first. The bull went down for good. It was the perfect ending to a perfect hunt.

The Hannah Helmer bull has it all, amazing symmetry, long tines and

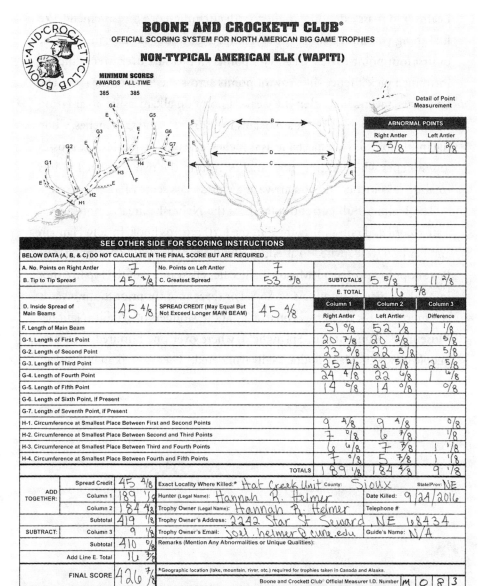

BOONE AND CROCKETT CLUB®
OFFICIAL SCORING SYSTEM FOR NORTH AMERICAN BIG GAME TROPHIES

NON-TYPICAL AMERICAN ELK (WAPITI)

MINIMUM SCORES
AWARDS ALL-TIME
385   385

Detail of Point Measurement

ABNORMAL POINTS	
Right Antler	Left Antler
5 5/8	11 2/8

SEE OTHER SIDE FOR SCORING INSTRUCTIONS

BELOW DATA (A, B, & C) DO NOT CALCULATE IN THE FINAL SCORE BUT ARE REQUIRED

A. No. Points on Right Antler	7	No. Points on Left Antler	7
B. Tip to Tip Spread	45 3/8	C. Greatest Spread	53 3/8

		SUBTOTALS	5 5/8	11 2/8
		E. TOTAL	16 7/8

			Column 1	Column 2	Column 3
D. Inside Spread of Main Beams	45 4/8	SPREAD CREDIT (May Equal But Not Exceed Longer MAIN BEAM)	45 4/8		
			Right Antler	Left Antler	Difference
F. Length of Main Beam			51 0/8	52 1/8	1/8
G-1. Length of First Point			20 7/8	20 2/8	5/8
G-2. Length of Second Point			23 2/8	22 5/8	5/8
G-3. Length of Third Point			25 2/8	22 5/8	2 5/8
G-4. Length of Fourth Point			24 4/8	22 6/8	1 6/8
G-5. Length of Fifth Point			14 0/8	14 0/8	0/8
G-6. Length of Sixth Point, If Present					
G-7. Length of Seventh Point, If Present					
H-1. Circumference at Smallest Place Between First and Second Points			9 4/8	9 4/8	0/8
H-2. Circumference at Smallest Place Between Second and Third Points			7 0/8	6 7/8	1/8
H-3. Circumference at Smallest Place Between Third and Fourth Points			6 4/8	7 7/8	1 1/8
H-4. Circumference at Smallest Place Between Fourth and Fifth Points			7 0/8	5 7/8	1 1/8
		TOTALS	189 1/8	184 4/8	9 1/8

ADD TOGETHER:	Spread Credit	45 4/8	Exact Locality Where Killed:* Hat Creek Unit	County: Sioux	State/Prov: NE
	Column 1	189 1/8	Hunter (Legal Name): Hannah R. Helmer	Date Killed: 9/24/2016	
	Column 2	184 4/8	Trophy Owner (Legal Name): Hannah R. Helmer	Telephone #	
	Subtotal	419 1/8	Trophy Owner's Address: 2242 Star St Seward, NE 68434		
SUBTRACT:	Column 3	9 1/8	Trophy Owner's Email: joel.helmer@cune.edu	Guide's Name: N/A	
	Subtotal	410 0/8	Remarks (Mention Any Abnormalities or Unique Qualities):		
	Add Line E. Total	16 7/8			
	FINAL SCORE	426 7/8	*Geographic location (lake, mountain, river, etc.) required for trophies taken in Canada and Alaska.		

Boone and Crockett Club® Official Measurer I.D. Number **M O 8 3**

Mail To: Boone and Crockett Club ■ 250 Station Drive, Missoula, MT 59801 ■ (406) 542-1888 ■ www.booneandcrockettclub.com

FIG. 65. Hannah Helmer scoresheet. This bull has eighty-five-plus inches of antler on just the G1 and G2 points. Courtesy of the Boone and Crockett Club.

beams, and mass extending to the fourth circumference measurement. The first thing you notice about the seven-by-seven rack is its amazing "fronts," or first four points. These G1 and G2 points all measure over twenty inches, forming a picket fence–like row of points across the front of the rack. The G3 points, meanwhile, often the weakest point on elk, measure an amazing 25⅛ and 22⅝ inches! The main beams measure 51⅜ and 52⅛ inches, while the inside spread is a respectable 45⅜ inches. The bull's typical frame grosses 419⅛ inches while netting 410⅜ inches. Add in the two abnormal points totaling 16⅞ inches and you arrive at a world-class score of 426⅞ inches.

The Helmer bull currently stands as the Nebraska firearm non-typical state record and ranks thirty-third in the B&C records book. In 2019 Hannah and her bull were invited to attend the B&C's 30th Big Game Awards at Bass Pro Shops in Springfield, Missouri, since her elk was one of the top five shot in North America from 2016 to 2018. For three months prior to the awards ceremony her elk mount was on display at the Wonders of Wildlife National Museum & Aquarium in Springfield, where over one hundred thousand people viewed it. Many undoubtedly wondered, "There are elk in Nebraska?"

43

Drought and Fire

The Casey Yada Bull, 2012

· 390²/₈-inch non-typical

· Dawes County

Where does the West begin? An interesting geographic question. Start any-where near the Missouri River and travel westward across Nebraska and you notice subtle changes. Vegetation becomes sparser, different, less green. Trees are shorter, more windblown, as if clinging on. Rectangular corn- and soybean fields increasingly give way to round center pivots, untidy prairie, sandhills, and grazing cattle. The air feels different, drier. The sky looks somehow bluer, clearer, more expansive, with a horizon visible for miles. Towns are few, and smaller, with wide streets and browning yards. You spot a pronghorn and notice a yucca. You are not sure when it happened, but you are in the West.

Geographers want a neater, cleaner demarcation—a line on the map. John Wesley Powell, the great river-runner and explorer of the American Southwest, in his 1879 *Report on the Lands of the Arid Region of the United States*, used the one-hundredth meridian of longitude as his line.[1] He believed it separated the humid East from the arid West, arguing that nonirrigated agriculture west of this line was precarious at best.

The one-hundredth meridian slices Nebraska roughly in half, passing through eight counties: Keya Paha, Brown, Blaine, Custer, Dawson, Gosper,

Frontier, and Furnas. Visit Cozad and you can peruse an entire museum dedicated to this imaginary line. And Powell was right in that the one-hundredth meridian does divide the wetter eastern half of the state from the drier western half. For example, Nebraska City, along the Missouri River, gets on average thirty-three inches of precipitation each year, while Scottsbluff in the panhandle gets maybe half as much.

Living and hunting in northwest Nebraska's Dawes County, Casey Yada knows firsthand how drought impacts life, and hunting. He drew his bull elk tag in summer 2012, the driest year on record in Nebraska. During an average year Crawford, in western Dawes County, receives about nineteen inches of precipitation. During the first six months of 2012, the weather station south of town did not record any precipitation, with the yearly total eventually reaching a scant two inches!

With the area in the grip of this historic drought, Casey began contacting landowners in the Bordeaux elk unit. Having helped his father, Lauren, harvest a nice bull in this unit in 2009, he thought he had a good idea of where to hunt. By the end of August, with the season only a month away and with numerous ranches to hunt, his confidence was running high. Then came the fires.

"Traveling to work on August 30, I watched the fires southeast of Crawford. Moments later I got a call from my parents, south of Chadron, telling me they were being evacuated and they needed my help. When I got there my father was cutting a fire line around his house with the tractor. We slung a garden hose with a sprinkler onto the roof and loaded the important things into the pickup, and headed for my house," remembers Casey. "Those fires changed everything."

The fires burned hundreds of thousands of acres across Nebraska but especially in the Pine Ridge. Wildlife, including elk must adapt quickly to such disturbances, or perish. "The tried-and-true areas and patterns I knew were out the window now. I struggled to find elk. The thought of eating this once in a lifetime tag was creeping into my mind." With the season fast approaching Casey spent evenings after work fruitlessly looking for elk. "I began to get desperate."

As they say, desperate times call for desperate measures. In an attempt to cover more ground, Casey purchased a mountain bike. He would use it only once. Starting on Bordeaux Road south of Chadron, he began a meandering path, peddling through the rugged Pine Ridge. Not bothering to follow trails, and carrying the bike as much as riding it, he scouted for elk sign. About midday, having run out of water and nearing exhaustion, he paused on a high overlook and pondered his predicament. Debating whether to wait for a few hours or try to call for help, he decided to take a different route back. "By the time I reached my truck it was dark, I was dehydrated, and I was using the stupid bike as a crutch," recalls Casey. And to top it off, all the elk sign he saw that day was weeks old.

With two weeks until opening day and the pressure mounting, Casey resorted to driving county roads, hoping to spot elk or at least fresh sign. Approaching the long driveway of a ranch he could hunt, he noticed a trail cutting through a cornfield. Turning in he spotted a small herd of elk feeding in a hay field. While looking over the herd from his pickup, a giant seven-by-eight bull suddenly appeared from behind a row of hay bales. "A fellow from work had told me I needed to hold out for at least a 360-inch bull," recalls Casey. "Up until that moment my scouting made that seem like only a pipe dream."

Each evening thereafter Casey was back at this same spot, scanning the fields with binoculars. Finally, after a week of watching and waiting, a string of elk again came into the field, this time on the opposite side of a nearby creek. Soon about one hundred elk filled the field, including numerous bulls, with one impressive six-by-six that Casey thought might score in the 370-inch range. However, the giant from the first evening was nowhere to be found.

Two nights before the opener Casey and his good friend Adam "Alabama" Strong, from, you guessed it, Alabama, made their way out for one last scouting trip. Splitting up, they scanned the fields, lingering until dusk. In the fading light Casey could hear, but not see, two bulls fighting. Soon Adam came walking up the path toward Casey with eyes wide. From his vantage he had seen the two large bulls fighting, with one being the giant seven-by-eight. Casey found it difficult to sleep the next couple nights before the season began.

On opening morning Casey and Adam sat waiting for dawn, listening intently for bugling bulls. At first light, with Casey cradling his Remington 700 in .300 Winchester Magnum, the two began their stalk by wading the creek bordering the field. Peering above the opposite bank they saw a huge group of elk, including several smaller bulls, moving near the property line to the south. Scanning the herd they spotted the giant bull trying to maintain control of his huge harem. "He looked ragged compared to the full-bellied, fat-from-summer's-loafing bull I had filmed two weeks earlier," remembers Casey.

Soon thereafter a 370-inch six-by-six showed up as well, herding his own harem of thirty cows, but with fewer pestering satellite bulls. With the cows attempting to merge, the two herd bulls squared off, standing tensely in the morning light. Charging simultaneously, they sidled away at the last moment, avoiding any contact. "They both backed away in a wincing manner . . . they had already played that game," remembers Casey.

Both bulls were about four hundred yards away as they continued across the field, parallel to Casey's position. With only open field between him and the bulls, there was no chance of closing the distance. But Casey came prepared. Waiting in his rifle's chamber was a hand-loaded cartridge, tipped with a 180-grain Nosler Accubond bullet. He knew from his time on the reloading bench and at the range, that he could make the shot.

Peering through the Zeiss scope, he found the giant bull standing rock still. The problem now was getting a clear shot among all the cows. "They were all around him, and traveling. They would clear his front, only to appear behind him," recalls Casey. Waiting patiently he noticed a "hole" in the herd, approaching from the rear. When this "hole" covered the bull, he would have a shot.

Compensating for a strong crosswind, Casey held just off the shoulder, knowing the drifting bullet would find the vitals. The recoil took him by surprise. Hearing the slap of the bullet, Casey found the bull in the cross-hairs again, preparing for a follow-up shot. No need, the giant buckled and

FIG. 66. With fifteen scoreable points, the Casey Yada bull is currently the fifth-largest non-typical in the Nebraska records book. Photo courtesy of Casey Yada.

fell. Walking across the field, with the bull getting slowly closer, Casey says, "There was no ground shrinkage."

For good reason. The Casey Yada bull is a beast of a non-typical, sporting fifteen total points, including unique matching "kickers" off the crown on each side. The dagger G2 on the left side is notable, measuring 24⅛ inches. The typical rack nets 353⅝ inches with only 10⅜ inches of deductions. Add in the three abnormal points totaling 37⅞ inches and you have a 390⅞-inch trophy bull.

44

400 Club

The Justin Misegadis Bull, 2017

· 400⅛-inch non-typical
· Dawes County

For whitetail deer hunters the ultimate goal is tagging a buck scoring over two hundred inches. Sheep hunters seek a full curl ram, while those pursuing pronghorns hope to break the magical eighty-inch mark. For elk hunters the pinnacle is bagging a bull with four hundred inches of sweeping, curling, ivory tips–shining, royal tine–soaring antler.

Don't get your hopes up too high. Since its inception in 1950 the B&C records book has accepted nearly eighteen hundred American elk. A scant 15 percent, two hundred non-typical and seventy-three typical bulls, have eclipsed four hundred inches. Nebraska hunters have entered only four such trophies: three non-typicals and one typical. A rare beast indeed.

Justin Misegadis knows this all too well. He has spent his working life surrounded by trophy big-game mounts. Apart from a brief hiatus during his college days at Chadron State College, he has worked at Cabela's in Sidney since turning sixteen. Returning after college to his hometown of Lodgepole, he landed a full-time job with Cabela's as a purchasing specialist. His job is to purchase trophy taxidermy for new Cabela's stores opening around the country. "It was really fun to see what was out there and see what trophies people were willing to part with. I was basically a glorified interior decorator for Cabela's," Justin shares with a laugh. Although he later moved into a different position, the time he spent evaluating and purchasing big-game mounts influenced his hunting. "It actually made my hunting life a lot harder. When you are buying one-hundred-eighty-inch whitetails, and you have a one-hundred-fifty-inch buck come by your stand, you don't think it is that big. But it is!"

The 2017 hunting season gave Justin the opportunity to appraise Nebraska bull elk trophies on the hoof. After applying for thirteen years, he finally drew a bull elk tag in the Bordeaux unit. "The homework really starts when you draw a tag," explains Justin. Taking advantage of connections he made during college, he was soon scouting elk in the Pine Ridge near Chadron. "On our first scouting trip we saw thirty-two cows and a couple raghorn bulls. By opening weekend the area we were going to hunt had over ninety cows and nearly forty bulls. With that many elk I set a goal of taking a bull in the three-hundred-seventy-inch range," remembers Justin.

With a clear goal in mind, and his .300 Ultra Mag in hand, Justin hunted hard the first five days of the season. Despite seeing and hearing multiple bulls, he returned to work in Sidney empty-handed. While planning for the following weekend's hunt, he got a call from a friend, telling him that they could hunt the Isham Ranch, a sprawling twenty-five-thousand-acre property northeast of Chadron.

Hunting with good friends Chuck Anderson and Joe Wild, the trio were soon surrounded by bugling bulls. Six different bulls came swaggering into their calls on Saturday and a nice 300-inch five-by-five the following morning. By noon Sunday, with temperatures climbing into the sixties, they made the decision to move to an area known as the Marlboro pasture. With a high butte and a deep U-shaped drainage thick with trees and brush, it is the most rugged part of the ranch. Just the type of shady terrain an elk seeks when temperatures rise.

"Once we were in position, I let a bugle go and instantly five or six bulls answered. We were right in their bedroom," remembers Justin. A giant bull came sauntering in, rack swaying, facing Justin head-on. "I had my cross-hairs right on him, but I couldn't tell how big he was." Quickly catching

FIG. 67. Justin Misegadis holding his four-hundred-plus inches of elk antler. Photo courtesy of Justin Misegadis.

their scent in the swirling wind, the bull crashed away into the timber. "My heart sank when I saw him turn and realized he was a great bull, probably a three-hundred-seventy class."

Justin's regret was short-lived. With Chuck positioned behind and above him and Joe higher yet up the ridge, they chirped through their cow calls while scanning the trees. A raghorn ran in to sixty yards, pacing and looking for the source of the call. After the raghorn melted into the timber, Chuck again hit his cow call, with two bulls immediately screaming back. They could hear the closer of the two bulls moving toward them, raking trees and breaking branches. "The bull suddenly appears, looking right at me, but I could only make out his right antler and his brisket," recalls Justin. "I whisper back to Joe, asking him how far away he is, and Joe just says, 'It doesn't matter, just shoot!'" From his higher position Joe could see the bull's entire massive rack.

Given the green light, Justin centered the crosshairs eight inches below the bull's nose, compressing the trigger and sending the bullet deep into the center of the bull's chest. The bull barely flinched, dropping in his tracks.

Shivering with adrenaline Justin sat, peering through his binoculars at the fallen monarch a hundred yards away, trying to determine the size of the antlers. After waiting about fifteen minutes, and placing celebratory calls to his brother and father, Justin and his friends made their way down to the fallen bull. "Your heart kind of stops when you walk up on a bull like that. He just kept getting bigger," remembers Justin.

The Justin Misegadis bull is what you call world-class, breaking the four-hundred-inch mark by an eighth of an inch. The typical six-by-six rack includes main beams of over fifty inches, an inside spread of over forty-three inches, and G1 points of over nineteen inches. The G3 points, often the weakest on elk, are notable, measuring $15\frac{4}{8}$ inches on the right side and $19\frac{2}{8}$ inches on the left. The typical frame nets $372\frac{2}{8}$ inches, and after adding in four abnormal points totaling $27\frac{7}{8}$ inches, you arrive at $400\frac{1}{8}$ inches of antler.

Justin no longer needs to go to work to see a trophy elk; he just walks down into his basement. "Putting myself in that four-hundred-inch class of elk is really amazing. I've only purchased a couple that size, and there is only one that size in the Sidney Cabela's store," says Justin.

45

Elk Hunter

The Frank Meyers Bull, 2016

- 378⅞-inch non-typical
- Dawes County

There are big-game hunters, and then there are elk hunters. Once you experience hunting elk, it can turn quickly into an obsession. There is something about it, something that gets down deep in your blood. Maybe it's the sight of a herd of cow elk filtering through golden aspens on a cool Rocky Mountain morning. Or the moment you're still-hunting and you catch the unmistakable smell of a rutting bull, and you know he has to be close. Perhaps it's hearing that eerie, otherworldly sound of an elk bugle floating down through dark timber. In 1988 Frank Meyers made the mistake of going elk hunting, and he has never been the same since.

"I grew up in northern Iowa, hunting pheasants, rabbits, and whitetail deer," remembers Frank. After a stint in the military, he followed his parents to Nebraska in 1975, met his wife, and landed a job in Cozad at Tenneco Automotive, where he worked for the next thirty-seven years. The move farther west allowed him to start pursuing a variety of big game—antelope, mule deer, and especially elk. "I try to go elk hunting every year, sometimes to several states. I guess I've been on at least thirty hunts."

Chasing bulls in Colorado, New Mexico, and Wyoming, his success rate is impressive, having taken twelve elk, with several bulls worthy of space on his basement wall. Eventually Frank set a goal of getting a larger bull on each successive hunt. His 2016 bull would make this goal exponentially harder to attain in the future.

Frank's initial plan for the 2016 elk season was to hunt Utah, arguably the best state for trophy bulls. However, his plan changed when he discovered he drew a Nebraska tag in the Ash Creek unit. Knowing the trophy potential of the area, he began making plans for the upcoming season. Prior to opening morning he headed north from Cozad to the Pine Ridge in Dawes County, near the small village of Whitney. After checking the zero on his Remington 700 at the range, he was ready.

"That next morning, as soon as we stepped out of the truck, the bulls were just bugling all around," recalls Frank. Although multiple bulls responded eagerly to his calling, none presented an opportunity for a shot. Following a midday break back at camp, Frank set up in the same location but again, lots of bugling with no sightings. The next morning Frank and Melvin, the ranch owner, tried a new area, with the same results. "After that hunt Melvin says, 'You know, I've got this spot where I've seen elk coming off the neighbor's property and jumping the fence in the corner.'"

After arriving at this new spot for the evening hunt, they set up a ground blind near the corner, placing a cow decoy about forty yards into the field. With the sun casting long shadows, Frank sat in the blind watching the corner, while Melvin set up a bit farther down and began periodically calling. Suddenly a giant bull appeared from the timber, staring directly into Frank's blind. Sensing something out of place, the bull jumped the fence and walked toward the decoy while continuing to look intently into the blind. "My heart is just thumping, and I'm trying not to move. I'm just thinking about how I'm going to get my gun up without spooking him," remembers Frank. Unbelievably the massive seven-by-eight came within twenty yards of the blind then turned around and left, jumping the fence back to safety.

"I thought that I had blown a shot at a bull of a lifetime, just because I didn't have my gun ready," remembers Frank. Fortunately his anguish was short-lived. Twenty minutes later Frank again spotted the bull, this time farther down the fence line. "This time I got my rifle ready." Once the bull reached

FIG. 68. Frank Meyers holding up the rack of his gorgeous Dawes County nontypical. Photo courtesy of Frank Meyers.

the fence, he stopped, scanning the field for what seemed like an eternity. Frank thought to himself, *You jump that fence and you are getting cooked.*

The bull finally did, leaping the five strands with remarkable ease. Steadying his Remington, Frank wasted no time sending a bullet through the bull's lungs, dropping it on the spot. Walking up on the bull, Frank knew he had shot something special, something bigger than he had ever shot.

Frank Meyer's seven-year-old bull was a warrior, with scars down his neck and around his eyes. With only nine inches of deductions, the typical rack grosses 344⅝ inches while netting 335⅝. Both main beams are over fifty inches, with an inside spread of 46⅞ inches. The three long abnormal points add 43²⁄₈ inches, resulting in a final score of 378⅞ inches. The bull currently stands seventh in the non-typical firearm category in the Nebraska records book.

Having hunted multiple states and shot multiple bulls, Frank believes that "a three-hundred-inch bull is good anywhere. You get above three fifty, and that's a beast." Frank's Nebraska bull adorns his basement wall, a constant reminder that meeting his goal of always shooting a bigger bull is going to be a challenge. "My next bull needs to be over four hundred."

You can be certain that Frank will be hunting elk somewhere every fall, hoping to raise his bull elk bar just a little higher.

46

Meadow Monarch

The Dana Foster Bull, 2008

· 409⅞-inch non-typical

· Garden County

Walk into Nebraska bars, businesses, and homes and there is a good chance you will see deer, elk, fish, or fowl mounted on the wall. For hunters, these mounts preserve our memories while also honoring magnificent wildlife trophies. Regardless of why someone mounts a trophy, taxidermy is Americana, part of our heritage as a nation of hunters.

Although some make it a full-time career, many use taxidermy as a way to supplement their income while doing something they enjoy. Trevor Foster is one such person. His father dabbled in taxidermy, so he began mounting deer in the 1980s during high school. Now he is one of the most well-known taxidermists in western Nebraska, operating Foster's Taxidermy out of his garage in Ogallala. Like many taxidermists he is also a passionate hunter, having taken multiple species, including a Nebraska bull elk grossing 351⅛ inches.

For Dana Foster, marrying Trevor changed her life in many ways, including making her a hunter. "I must admit I never really had the desire to become a hunter until I met Trevor in 2003," admits Dana. Although having grown up in Ogallala in a hunting family, she never really had the opportunity to hunt much. "I hunted birds a few times with my dad, but I never hunted big game."

After they were married Trevor did not waste any time introducing Dana to his passion. Trevor called Dana's first large animal, a coyote, to within eighteen yards. "I must admit it was an adrenaline rush that I didn't even know existed," shares Dana. Nebraska turkey and deer soon followed, along with a trip to Africa where Dana would take a zebra. Quickly becoming an accomplished and ardent hunter, Dana had no idea what lay in store for her as the 2008 fall hunting season approached.

In July the Fosters noticed an unexpected charge on their Visa bill from the NGPC. Checking online they realized Dana had pulled a bull elk tag her first time entering the drawing! Trevor dug out his list of elk landowner contacts and began placing calls, quickly securing access to some prime real estate along the North Platte River near the town of Lewellen.

The couple began an evening ritual, driving west from Ogallala, around Lake McConaughy, to scout for elk. "I still remember the first day of scouting. There were two bulls in velvet, up to their chest in a cornfield bordering the river," remembers Dana. Throughout late summer the two glassed from the bordering hillsides above the river bottoms, being very careful not to pressure the elk.

They were particularly cautious since their hunting area bordered the Garden County Wildlife Refuge, which stretches along the entire length of the North Platte River in Garden County. The refuge limits access to within one hundred ten yards of the riverbank, allowing pressured elk an easy escape to the safety of the river's islands. Through their glassing and game camera footage, Trevor and Dana identified two monster four-hundred-inch bulls they intended to hunt, one a wide seven-by-eight and the other an enormous, elusive non-typical they named the Meadow Bull. Having only seen this bull three times, Trevor told Dana, "This is the bull that will make you famous!"

With the two massive bulls on her mind, the anticipation for opening day was nearly unbearable. "I felt like the whole world was on my shoulders because we had promised so many that something special was about to happen. So many people, friends and family, were counting on me to make a quick and ethical shot. For three months all I had heard was, 'Good luck on the hunt, Dana. Don't miss!'" she remembers, smiling. Adding to her anxiety, Trevor sprung the news that Cabela's was going to video the hunt for a television show.

Opening morning, September 27, found the Fosters and a Cabela's video crew crouching in a meadow along the river, waiting for the fog to lift. The videographer then realized he had forgotten the DVD to record the hunt, forcing Trevor to make a quick return trip to the truck. Returning to the group Trevor set out a Montana cow elk decoy and with the cameras now rolling, began calling, scanning the river bottoms for movement while listening for bugles. After several setups with no responses, they decided to move several miles east where they had first seen one of the four-hundred-inch monsters.

Once in position again Trevor began calling, and within seconds multiple bugles rose up from across the river. Hearing splashing, they knew the bulls were coming quickly. "You can't shoot until they jump the fence from the refuge," whispered Trevor. The two three-hundred-fifty-class bulls emerged from the river, bugling and dripping wet at thirty yards. "Don't shoot, they're not big enough," hissed Trevor, as the two beautiful bulls walked slowly away. Exasperated, the Cabela's videographer exclaimed, "I know this isn't my hunt or my business, but I hope you know what you're passing!" Trevor's response, "That was awesome; let's go find a big one."

The next several days were a roller coaster of emotion and adrenaline, with multiple close encounters, just not with the big bulls. With the Cabela's crew off on another assignment, Trevor and Dana began the fourth day of the hunt, back in the river bottom. "We had elk bugling on all sides of us. You couldn't move your head in any direction without seeing a bull," remembers Dana. After the morning hunt they sat second-guessing having passed again on some great bulls, including a seven-by-seven that came to within ten yards.

Deciding to move west a few hundred yards, they jumped the giant seven-by-eight and his small harem of cows. Knowing this was one of the shooter bulls, Dana readied her Remington 700, hoping for a clear shot through the thick undergrowth. "At one time he was less than thirty-five yards away, but the cover was so thick I didn't have a shot. It was like he was taunting us, bugling and grunting right in front of us, but we couldn't do anything," shares Dana. Deciding to be aggressive they quickly circled the thicket, hoping to spot the bull. "It didn't work, and I passed on a one-hundred-yard running shot."

By the fifth day of the hunt Dana was mentally and physically exhausted. Her parents had been shuffling children to and from school and sporting events, while the clock was ticking down on her hunt. In three days, elk or no elk, she and Trever were going to depart for a previously booked British Columbia moose hunt.

As the sun rose Dana and Trevor made their way through a mile of waist-high wet grass to an area they called the Honey Hole. With elk bugling ahead of them, they decided to hunt more aggressively and try to cut off the elk before they left the meadows for the safety of the islands on the North Platte River. "We were almost trotting, and Trevor was working the cow calls while carrying the camera and tripod. We were giving them everything we had," recalls Dana.

With their lungs bursting, they heard a throaty bugle from a thicket to their left. "Trevor looked straight into my eyes and told me to get my shooting sticks up fast and get ready. I am thinking I can hardly breathe, let alone shoot," remembers Dana. A Russian olive tree about fifty yards away began shaking violently, as Trevor scrambled to get the camera tripod set up. Looking up they could see the massive bull coming at them, silver tips above some cattails.

"When he gets in the open, if I think he's big enough, I'll cow call to stop him," whispered Trevor. After finally seeing the bull's whole rack, there was no doubt. Trevor hit the cow call. "I can honestly say I do not remember the cow call or much about the first shot. . . . I swear the world stopped for a moment," shares Dana, grinning. With Trevor yelling, "Hit him again, hit him again," Dana sent another and final 7mm-08 round into the bull.

"The emotions were instant. . . . I was overwhelmed. I didn't realize what I had done until actually getting my hands on him for the first time. I just kept asking Trevor 'Is it bigger than your Nebraska elk? I must have asked him that ten times," remembers Dana. With elk bugling all around them, Trevor and Dana sat silently, taking it all in, savoring the moment.

FIG. 69. Dana Foster's massive Meadow Bull stood as the non-typical state record for eight years. Photo courtesy of Dana Foster.

The Dana Foster bull sports a typical six-by-six rack that grosses 393⅜ inches and nets 378⅜, with main beams of over fifty inches and an inside spread of 49⅛ inches. The rack is massive, with over sixty-eight inches of antler in the eight circumference measurements, including a first circumference measurement on the left antler of 12⅝ inches. The five abnormal points total 31⅛ inches, equating to a final score of 409⅞ inches. Dana's bull stood as the Nebraska firearm state-record non-typical for eight years.

Dana is thankful for the memories and especially to the people who made it all possible. "Thanks to my parents for shuttling kids. Thanks to my dad for countless hours of practice shooting prairie dogs. Thanks to my children for their patience. Thanks to Trevor for applying for the tag, for being my guide, and for keeping his cool at crunch time. Finally, this hunt could not have happened without the generosity and kindness of the landowners."

PART 5

Typical Mule Deer

47

Houdini

The Michael Dickerson Buck, 2018

· 197⁴/₈-inch typical

· Sioux County

Just because you see a buck doesn't mean you can kill it. This is particularly true when archery hunting mule deer in the wide-open expanses of north-western Nebraska.

Sitting on a hill at dawn in the Badlands of northern Sioux County, Michael Dickerson knows this all too well. Although the early September air is cool now, it won't be for long, as the day warms up. Mike feels the pressure, the anticipation, building, since he knows he doesn't have much time. His plan is always the same: spot a shooter buck moving in the early morning, glass him to his mid-morning bed, and then, if possible, stalk to within bow range. Although an exciting way to hunt, it requires extreme patience, excellent stalking skills, and a good bit of luck.

Growing up in Michigan, Mike learned to deer hunt in a much different way and in a very different landscape. "I grew up hunting whitetail deer in northern Michigan with my father, grandfather, and my uncles," he shares. In this thickly forested area most deer hunting is done from tree stands, although deer drives and still-hunting are also common. After catching the deer-hunting bug when he was twelve, Mike has pursued big game in Canada and multiple U.S. states, including Alaska. The opportunity to spot

FIG. 70. Michael Dickerson with his wide and high 197⅞-inch state-record typical from Sioux County. Photo courtesy of Michael Dickerson.

and stalk big mule deer is what pushes him to make the long drive from Michigan to western Nebraska.

On the morning of September 10, 2018, the first part of Mike's plan suddenly appears on the horizon. Houdini, the unbelievably wide and tall typical buck he has been hunting the last several years is on the move. As his name implies, this buck has an uncanny knack for disappearing in a landscape where you would think this would be difficult. A skill that has helped him live through multiple hunting seasons and grow some impressive headgear. For the next several hours Mike and his hunting partner watch intently through their binoculars, hoping Houdini beds down in a spot they can stalk.

"We watched him bed down in a spot we thought we could sneak into. We decided to go back to the house, regroup, and return in the afternoon to start our stalk," shares Mike. Arriving back at their vantage point at two o'clock, they found the buck bedded about eighty yards from where they had last seen him. Unfortunately three other bucks were bedded nearby.

Carefully studying the terrain and the position of the four bucks, they began their stalk. What you think you see while glassing is never what you encounter when you begin stalking. Hidden draws and washes are often deeper and more complex than expected, making it easy to lose your bearings

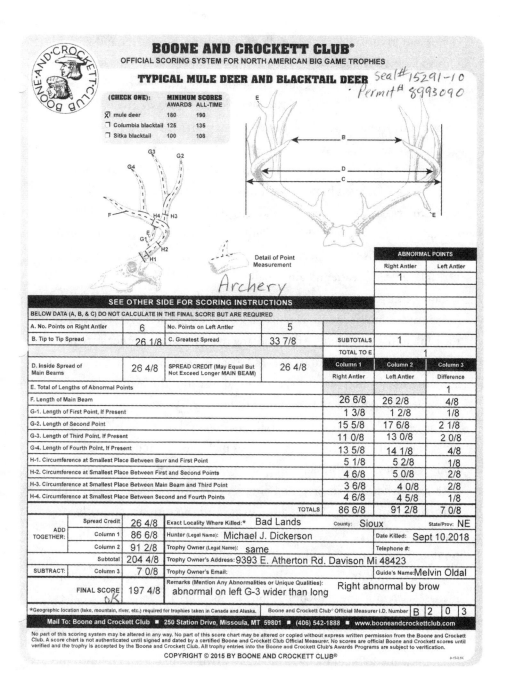

BOONE AND CROCKETT CLUB®

OFFICIAL SCORING SYSTEM FOR NORTH AMERICAN BIG GAME TROPHIES

TYPICAL MULE DEER AND BLACKTAIL DEER

Seal# 15291-10
Permit# 8993090

(CHECK ONE):	MINIMUM SCORES	
	AWARDS	ALL-TIME
☒ mule deer	180	190
☐ Columbia blacktail	125	135
☐ Sitka blacktail	100	108

Detail of Point Measurement

Archery

ABNORMAL POINTS	
Right Antler	Left Antler
	1

SEE OTHER SIDE FOR SCORING INSTRUCTIONS

BELOW DATA (A, B, & C) DO NOT CALCULATE IN THE FINAL SCORE BUT ARE REQUIRED

A. No. Points on Right Antler	6	No. Points on Left Antler	5		
B. Tip to Tip Spread	26 1/8	C. Greatest Spread	33 7/8	SUBTOTALS	1
				TOTAL TO E	1

				Column 1	Column 2	Column 3
D. Inside Spread of Main Beams	26 4/8	SPREAD CREDIT (May Equal But Not Exceed Longer MAIN BEAM)	26 4/8	Right Antler	Left Antler	Difference
E. Total of Lengths of Abnormal Points						1
F. Length of Main Beam				26 6/8	26 2/8	4/8
G-1. Length of First Point, If Present				1 3/8	1 2/8	1/8
G-2. Length of Second Point				15 5/8	17 6/8	2 1/8
G-3. Length of Third Point, If Present				11 0/8	13 0/8	2 0/8
G-4. Length of Fourth Point, If Present				13 5/8	14 1/8	4/8
H-1. Circumference at Smallest Place Between Burr and First Point				5 1/8	5 2/8	1/8
H-2. Circumference at Smallest Place Between First and Second Points				4 6/8	5 0/8	2/8
H-3. Circumference at Smallest Place Between Main Beam and Third Point				3 6/8	4 0/8	2/8
H-4. Circumference at Smallest Place Between Second and Fourth Points				4 6/8	4 5/8	1/8
			TOTALS	86 6/8	91 2/8	7 0/8

ADD TOGETHER:	Spread Credit	26 4/8	Exact Locality Where Killed:* Bad Lands		County: Sioux		State/Prov: NE
	Column 1	86 6/8	Hunter (Legal Name): Michael J. Dickerson			Date Killed: Sept 10, 2018	
	Column 2	91 2/8	Trophy Owner (Legal Name): same			Telephone #:	
	Subtotal	204 4/8	Trophy Owner's Address: 9393 E. Atherton Rd. Davison Mi 48423				
SUBTRACT:	Column 3	7 0/8	Trophy Owner's Email:			Guide's Name: Melvin Oldal	
	FINAL SCORE	197 4/8	Remarks (Mention Any Abnormalities or Unique Qualities): abnormal on left G-3 wider than long	Right abnormal by brow			

*Geographic location (lake, mountain, river, etc.) required for trophies taken in Canada and Alaska. | Boone and Crockett Club® Official Measurer I.D. Number | B | 2 | 0 | 3

Mail To: Boone and Crockett Club ■ 250 Station Drive, Missoula, MT 59801 ■ (406) 542-1888 ■ www.booneandcrockettclub.com

FIG. 71. Michael Dickerson scoresheet. Notice the "Exact Locality Where Killed": "Bad Lands." Courtesy of the Boone and Crockett Club.

in relation to the buck you are stalking. Jump an unseen deer and you risk blowing out your buck. Mike knows this, so over the next three hours they "played a careful game of chess, checking each drainage carefully while quietly sneaking into position. At about five thirty, we see the bucks stand up and start feeding, which played to our advantage."

The four bucks fed slowly up a valley, eventually moving behind a hill and into a small bowl. "We crawled into position behind the hill, and peaking over the crest I ranged him at fifty-seven yards," recalls Mike. Drawing back his Mathews bow, Mike stood up and settled the pin behind the buck's front shoulder. "The buck lifted his head and looked in my direction. I thought to myself, 'This is the opportunity you have been waiting for your whole life. Take a deep breath and aim small.'"

Squeezing the trigger on the release, he watched his Easton arrow disappear into the buck's vitals. "He kicked his back legs and began running up the bank to higher ground. After reaching the top he ran another sixty yards, looked back my way, and fell over." Mike did the same. "I fell to the ground as a wave of emotions came over me. I had just shot the biggest mule deer of my life and it made all those failed stalks worth it."

The Michael Dickerson buck would make most hunters fall over. Scoring $197\frac{4}{8}$ inches it broke Kirk Peters's $187\frac{2}{8}$-inch typical archery state record from 1989, one of Nebraska's longest-standing records. The buck is wide, with an outside spread of $33\frac{7}{8}$ inches and an inside spread of $26\frac{4}{8}$. The main beams measure $26\frac{6}{8}$ and $26\frac{2}{8}$ inches and support exceptionally long points. The deeply forked G2 points measure $15\frac{5}{8}$ and $17\frac{6}{8}$ inches, while the G3 points measure $11\frac{0}{8}$ and $13\frac{0}{8}$ inches. Oftentimes rather short on mule deer, the G4 points on this buck are impressive, measuring $13\frac{5}{8}$ and $14\frac{1}{8}$ inches. With only seven inches of total deductions, the buck grosses $204\frac{4}{8}$ inches and nets $197\frac{4}{8}$.

"The opportunity to harvest great bucks in a spot-and-stalk situation is what drew me to Nebraska. It truly was a privilege to have an opportunity at such a great animal," says Mike.

48

Brow Tines

The Terry Sandstrom Buck, 1968

· 196²⁄₈-inch typical
· Dawes County

Many historians contend that 1968 was the most important, transformative year in modern American history. That year saw the assassinations of Martin Luther King Jr. and Robert Kennedy, the election of Richard Nixon, humans orbiting the moon, an escalating war in Vietnam, urban riots, the passage of the Civil Rights Act, and the debut of the Big Mac, the 747 airplane, and Mr. Rogers.

It was also a historic year for deer hunter Terry Sandstrom, although it would take him twenty years to realize it.

During the fall of 1968 Terry was a long way from the historic changes shaking the country. A junior at Chadron State College, he kept busy attending classes and working full-time for the Chicago and Northwestern Railroad. He also found time to pursue his passion for hunting deer in the Pine Ridge of northwest Nebraska.

Reminiscing about his early years, he shares, "I grew up in the panhandle of Nebraska, on a place right next to Chadron State Park. The area reminds me of the Black Hills of South Dakota, rolling hills covered in pine trees. There were big groups of mule deer roaming the area during those years, before whitetails moved in and pushed the mule deer out. There was also

FIG. 72. Terry Sandstrom with his long-standing typical state record from 1968. Photo courtesy of the Boone and Crockett Club.

great pheasant hunting. It was a beautiful area, rich in history, and a great place to live."

During the several years leading up to the 1968 deer rifle season, Terry had been seeing a particularly impressive typical mule deer. He was thinking about that particular buck when he made the decision to squeeze in a quick morning hunt. "I didn't have any classes until later in the morning and didn't have to work until late afternoon, so I drove up to what I call the Table," remembers Terry. The Table was about five miles from his home in Dawes County and was a transition area where the pine forests gave slowly away to wheat fields and high buttes.

Arriving well before sunrise Terry climbed in the dark to the top of a butte, sat down, and waited patiently for dawn. As the sun rose over the fog-draped Pine Ridge he spotted five mule deer does on a small meadow below him. "I was about to head out and check some other spots, when I saw some movement in the trees past the creek," remembers Terry. While Terry watched and waited, the movement materialized into a buck, which

Mule Deer
Nebraska State Record
196 2/8 Typical
1968

stood still in a clearing about two hundred yards away. "He was a nice four-point buck so I was lining up for a shot. All of a sudden he took off like he had seen a bogeyman."

Scanning the trees Terry searched for whatever it was that caused the buck to bolt. "Out of the trees came this beautiful monster buck, bigger than anything I had ever seen. The first thing I noticed were his brow tines," remembers Terry. Quickly shouldering his .270 Ruger, he found the buck through the wide-angle scope. Settling the crosshairs on the buck's vitals, he squeezed the trigger. The buck went down. After waiting twenty minutes Terry climbed down the butte and walked toward the dead buck. "It was all I could do to get him loaded into the pickup before taking him to the check station. I was so excited that I was almost late for class."

After cutting off the antlers Terry put them in a shed at his parents' home, where they would stay for the next twelve years. "In those days taxidermy was just for rich folks, so that left me out," shares Terry. After getting married and moving to Wyoming, Terry did not think too much about the rack. "One day my father showed up with a pickup load of my belongings and simply said, 'Here you go,' handing me the antlers."

By 1988 Terry had become friends with a taxidermist from Casper, Wyoming. Upon seeing the impressive and still unmounted rack, he asked Terry if anyone had ever officially measured it. After finding out no one had, he arranged for a Wyoming game warden to do the measuring. After tallying the score Terry was surprised to find out that his buck from twenty years ago was now the new Nebraska state-record typical.

The first thing Terry Sandstrom noticed, as does anyone who knows anything about mule deer, about the buck is its brow tines. Most G1 points on mule deer bucks are short or nonexistent, but not on this buck, with each brow tine measuring an impressive 5⅜ inches. The rest of the buck's rack is also symmetrical, grossing 199⅛ inches while netting 196⅔. The inside spread, which measuring rules stipulate cannot be longer than the longest main beam, is 26⅝ inches, while the main beams are 26⅝ and 26⅛ inches. A tribute to its size, it has stood as the firearm typical state record for over thirty years.

After its certification as the state record, Cabela's periodically contacted Terry about purchasing the buck. "I finally decided that Cabela's was a good spot for him, allowing others who love to hunt to enjoy him," shares Terry. The buck now hangs in their Kearney store, with its brow tines still catching the eye of discerning mule deer hunters.

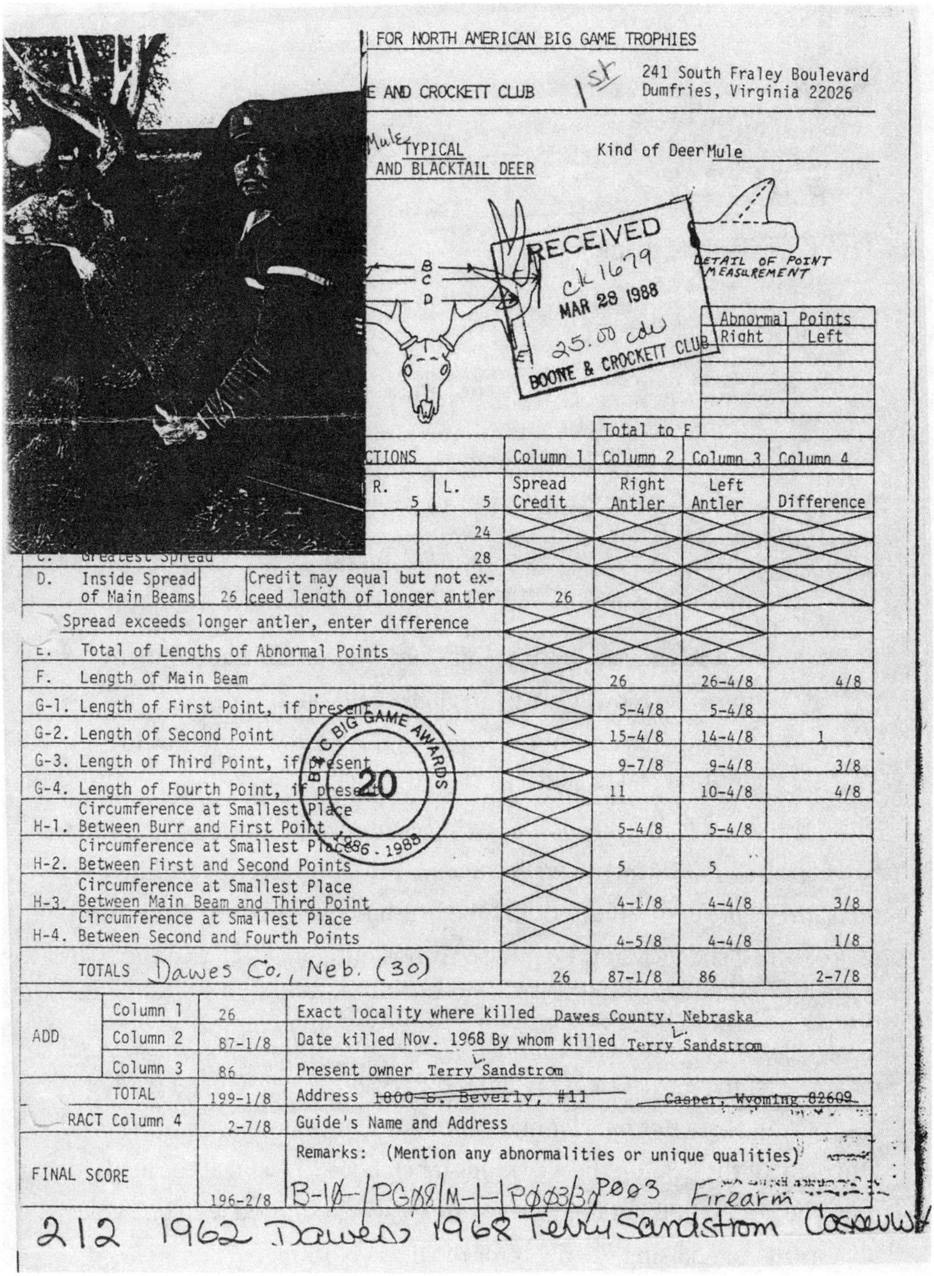

			FOR NORTH AMERICAN BIG GAME TROPHIES

E AND CROCKETT CLUB — 1st — 241 South Fraley Boulevard, Dumfries, Virginia 22026

Mule TYPICAL AND BLACKTAIL DEER — Kind of Deer Mule

RECEIVED
ck 1679
MAR 28 1988
25.00 cdw
BOONE & CROCKETT CLUB

DETAIL OF POINT MEASUREMENT

Abnormal Points	
Right	Left

Total to E

SECTIONS	R. 5	L. 5	Column 1 Spread Credit	Column 2 Right Antler	Column 3 Left Antler	Column 4 Difference
C. Greatest Spread		24 / 28				
D. Inside Spread of Main Beams	26	Credit may equal but not exceed length of longer antler	26			
Spread exceeds longer antler, enter difference						
E. Total of Lengths of Abnormal Points						
F. Length of Main Beam				26	26-4/8	4/8
G-1. Length of First Point, if present				5-4/8	5-4/8	
G-2. Length of Second Point				15-4/8	14-4/8	1
G-3. Length of Third Point, if present				9-7/8	9-4/8	3/8
G-4. Length of Fourth Point, if present				11	10-4/8	4/8
H-1. Circumference at Smallest Place Between Burr and First Point				5-4/8	5-4/8	
H-2. Circumference at Smallest Place Between First and Second Points				5	5	
H-3. Circumference at Smallest Place Between Main Beam and Third Point				4-1/8	4-4/8	3/8
H-4. Circumference at Smallest Place Between Second and Fourth Points				4-5/8	4-4/8	1/8
TOTALS Dawes Co., Neb. (30)				26	87-1/8	86	2-7/8

ADD	Column 1	26	Exact locality where killed Dawes County, Nebraska
	Column 2	87-1/8	Date killed Nov. 1968 By whom killed Terry Sandstrom
	Column 3	86	Present owner Terry Sandstrom
	TOTAL	199-1/8	Address 1800 S. Beverly, #11 Casper, Wyoming 82609
SUBTRACT Column 4		2-7/8	Guide's Name and Address
FINAL SCORE		196-2/8	Remarks: (Mention any abnormalities or unique qualities)

BIG GAME AWARDS 20

B-10 /PG08/M-1 /P003/30 P003 Firearm

212 1962 Dawes 1968 Terry Sandstrom Casper Wy

FIG. 74. Terry Sandstrom scoresheet. Note the matching five-inch-plus brow tines. Courtesy of the Boone and Crockett Club.

49

The Stalk

The Kirk Peters Buck, 1989

Kirk Peters

- 187²⁄₈-inch typical
- Dawes County

As I drove my truck toward work in Crawford, Nebraska, I glanced to my left and saw a group of deer feeding in an alfalfa field on the edge of a shallow brushy draw. I had seen several deer there in the last few days; mostly mule deer does and their fawns. Looking them over I suddenly thought, *That is either two deer standing one behind the other, or that is one huge-bodied deer.* Still too dark to see antlers well, it seemed that this deer had something substantial above his head. Could it be brush behind him? As I continued on, the angle changed and I could see it was only one deer, and the body was huge.

The sign near the property was clear—*No Trespassing.* But I couldn't get the image of that buck out of my mind the rest of the day. When I got home that evening, I got out my plat maps and found the name of the landowner. Driving past the field on the way to his ranch house, I scanned the fields for deer. The rancher was not home, but before leaving I stopped with binoculars on a small rise, glassing the fields for the buck. Nothing.

The next day I went to work a little later, stopping on the same rise and glassing the field and the two brushy draws that formed a "Y" between patches of hay field on each side. After ten minutes or so I spied the upper fork of one antler, and it was massive. I could not see the rest of the deer, but I had seen enough.

After work I again drove to the rancher's house. No one came to the door. I drove home, stopping again to glass but saw nothing. That was the pattern for the next week. In either the morning or evening I would see a tine, or a fork of antler, in one of the brushy draws. Other times an ear, or a portion of the deer's neck or face. Even though I would change my position on the road, I could never see a whole antler.

The next Monday after work I stopped at the ranch house again, and finally the rancher was in his shop. Having met him once before, I reintroduced myself and asked if that piece of land belonged to him and if I could bow-hunt it for deer. He chuckled and asked me if I realized how small a piece of ground it was. "Yes, I do," I replied. "Suit yourself," he said. I was thrilled, trying my best not to spin my tires as I drove out the driveway.

Reaching the spot where I had seen the buck, I noticed the gate was open. Looking down into the bottom of the draw, I saw the rancher's son bent over the hood of his truck, pointing his rifle at a target one hundred yards down the east fork of the draw. Hearing the report of the rifle, I could not believe it. Certainly he was doing nothing wrong, but I still could not believe he was shooting so close to where the buck was bedding.

On the way home the next afternoon I stopped at my usual spot and put up the binoculars. I was stunned. The giant buck was bedded in some low brush, up to his ears, with a small tree covering his left antler. However, I could see over half of the right side, and it was huge! I scrambled to the truck and headed for home, only three miles away.

Mumbling something to my wife about going to shoot a deer, I quickly changed clothes and grabbed my Damon Howatt recurve. Jumping into our Jeep Cherokee I drove past the property and behind a small knoll, easing the Jeep down into the ditch to keep from the buck's view. Staying low I made it to the draw where it crossed the road. Needing to be on the other side to start my stalk, I belly-crawled across the gravel and into the ditch on the same side of the road as the giant buck.

My plan was to make my way to the bottom of the main draw, where I could use the topography and vegetation to stalk within bow range. The buck was bedded facing west into the wind, but I needed to get below him while keeping the wind in my favor. The dry conditions of late October in western Nebraska made each step sound like I was walking on cornflakes as I began my stalk. Sitting down I removed my boots, continuing the stalk in my wool socks.

Reaching a barbed-wire fence, I tried slipping between, but when I pushed the middle wire down, it screeched against the staple holding it to the post. Luckily I found a low spot I could squeeze under, and I made it under the fence without too much noise. But after picking up my bow, I flushed a sharp-tailed grouse, sending it clucking into a nearby willow tree. My heart was in my throat. I so wanted to take the blunt-tipped arrow from my quiver and shoot that grouse!

Easing up on my toes I could see the buck's antler through my binoculars. He was still bedded, facing west. The next one hundred yards was slow going, step by step through dry grass, willow leaves, and cockleburs. Moving to the east side of the buck to gain better wind, I finally got to within thirty yards, only to see the buck suddenly stand and walk toward the hay field to the west. Amazingly the buck did not spot me, and after walking just a few steps he laid down again.

Taking an arrow from my quiver, I inched forward an agonizingly slow half step at a time. I could feel my lower legs and back tightening up. After closing the distance to eighteen yards, I stopped, waiting for the buck to stand. Just the week before I had blown a stalk on a four-by-four buck by tossing a rock to get him to stand. That buck immediately went from lying down to full speed!

I could see the sun dipping behind the buttes west of Crawford, so I was confident the buck would soon stand to feed. A few minutes later the buck rocked forward, lifting his rear end to stand. As he did, I drew my bow. The buck caught my movement, turning to look over his shoulder and providing me with a slim quartering shot. My eyes went to the last rib and I released the arrow. The buck exploded, running hard to the east, right through a large, dense chokecherry thicket.

FIG. 75. Kirk Peters shortly after his long stocking-foot stalk for his archery state-record typical. Photo courtesy of Kirk Peters.

Running to the corner of the thicket, I saw the buck thirty yards away, his head level with his body, walking slowly south. After walking twenty yards, he lay down. Looking across the nearby property line, I could see open hay field for nearly a mile and then the timber of the Pine Ridge. This was comforting, since if he left the property I would have him in sight for a long distance.

The giant typical stood again, walking a few steps to the south before bedding down. I decided to crawl after him through the sparse cover. He moved several more times, finally bedding down next to the fence marking the end of the property. Crawling to within twenty-five yards, I decided that if he stood again I would shoot.

A few minutes later the buck started to rise, and as he did, I drew. The buck spotted me, jumping the fence and running along the edge of the property on the neighbor's hay field. I thought, *He's still got steam!* But after one hundred yards his hindquarters dipped, and he fell to the ground for good.

Since I knew the owners of the hay field well, I crossed the fence and slowly walked over to the buck. I was stunned at the size of his body and the frame of his five-by-five rack. Standing next to him I felt a little shiver, and my heart started pounding. Sitting down next to the buck I looked at my stocking feet. They were at least twice their normal size from all the cockleburs!

I dug out my tag, canceled it, and finished field dressing the buck. As the sun set I retraced my stalk, back along the draw toward my vehicle, cockleburs making every step painful. Failing to locate my boots, I walked to the road, got into my Jeep, and drove home, shaking my head.

At home I changed into fresh socks and boots, then I drove back to load up the buck. After gaining permission from the landowner, I drove out onto the hay field to retrieve the buck.

Backing up to the buck and dropping the tailgate to its lowest possible position, I realized I should have brought help. I moved the buck until his antlers were resting on the tailgate, then I crawled past them into the truck bed. On sheer adrenaline I pulled the buck into the truck.

The buck hung for a few days in my garage, but warmer weather forced me to move him to the butcher shop to keep the meat cool. Unbeknownst to me, the butcher scored the buck, calling me on the telephone and asking, "Do you know how big he is?"

Later scored at 187⅞ inches, it broke M. R. Buchtel's 176⅝-inch state record from 1959. This was thirty years before I shot mine, and I broke his record by a bit over ten inches. In 2018, about thirty years after I shot my state record, Michael Dickerson broke my record by a bit over ten inches.

50

Symmetry

The Brent Klein Buck, 1984

· 195³⁄₈-inch typical
· Frontier County

Do you remember using mirrors in math class to determine whether a shape was symmetrical? You would move the mirror around on your worksheet, searching for the line of symmetry, that sweet spot dividing the shape into two perfect mirror-image halves. Standing in front of the buck hanging in Brent Klein's living room in McCook makes you want to put a mirror between the brow tines and find the line of symmetry!

Fortunately for Brent the B&C system for measuring North American big-game animals places a premium on symmetry. This was not always the case. In 1932 B&C member Prentiss N. Grey published the first records book based only on measurements of each animal's skull or longer antler or horn, and only one basal circumference.[1] It was soon obvious that this simplistic system needed improvement, so in 1949 a committee assembled to devise a better scoring system.

In 1950 the B&C adopted this committee's new scoring system, which is still in use today. According to the B&C, the "system places heavy emphasis on symmetry, penalizing those portions of the measured material that are non-symmetrical. This results in even, well-matched trophies scoring better and placing higher in the rankings than equally developed but mismatched trophies, a result that most people readily agree with and accept."[2] The P&Y uses this same scoring system, although with different minimum scores, as does the Nebraska Big Game Trophy Records Program.

Seven years after the B&C adopted this scoring system, Brent Klein was born. Growing up in southwest Nebraska, he learned to love the land and hunting. "My father taught all us kids how to shoot and hunt. He would take us along even before we could hunt ourselves, instilling a desire in us to hunt. I enjoy the thrill of the hunt but also spending time with my family," explains Brent. "I hunt to help feed my family but also to pass the desire to hunt to my children."

In early fall of 1984, when Brent was twenty-seven years old, he first spotted his uniquely symmetrical buck in Frontier County. "The area he was in was great habitat, deep canyons and hay pockets. I went around to neighboring farmers and got permission. I spent a good amount of time preseason scouting, trying to have a good game plan for opening morning," remembers Brent.

On November 9, the day before the rifle opener, Brent and his four-year-old son, Steve, drove from McCook to the family farm south of Farnam. Along with his younger brother, Jeff, who was still in high school, and his father, Raymond, they spent the evening reminiscing about past hunts. Outside a nasty cold front was dumping fresh snow across southwest Nebraska. "I was already pumped for opening morning. But with fresh snow falling and knowing that buck was out there, I didn't know if I would even be able to get to sleep," remembers Brent.

Up well before his alarm clock, Brent walked outside into the fresh snow. With Steve, Jeff, and Raymond joining him, they all loaded up and headed out, leaving tire tracks in the newly fallen snow. Based on his preseason scouting, Brent was confident he knew where the buck would be. Dawn was gorgeous, with clear skies and the sun turning the countryside into a sparkling white blanket. Driving into their hunting land southwest of Farnam, they noticed fresh deer tracks crossing near the head of a draw. Following the tracks with their eyes, they spotted a herd of does and a small two-point buck.

Continuing on they reached a gate where Brent noticed two sets of tracks heading south. "They were fresh tracks, with one set looking like a large

FIG. 76. Brent Klein (*far right*) with his young son, Steve, and brother, Jeff, posing with his state-record typical. Photo courtesy of Brent Klein.

buck track, so I took off following them," recalls Brent. Moving slowly, while periodically pausing to glass the canyons to his east, he followed the trail for nearly a mile. "I finally spotted the buck and a doe standing on the east bank. It was an awesome sight in the morning light, with that giant buck standing there against a snowy background."

With the buck still a half mile away, Brent watched carefully, trying to determine what the buck was going to do. "The doe started to stir and I wasn't sure if she got my scent in the breeze. She was getting antsy," remembers Brent. Fortunately the massive buck and doe moved westward, up a draw

FIG. 77. Brent Klein with his stunningly symmetrical buck, thirty-five years after the hunt. Photo courtesy of the author.

Brent had seen countless deer take over the years. "It was a God-given gift that they moved in the direction I was hoping for."

Knowing right where the deer were heading, Brent made his way quickly to the head of the draw and got ready. "I lost sight of them for a little bit, but I knew I would be in the right spot if they kept going up that draw. It wasn't long and here comes that buck following the doe right where I thought they would be," Brent shares. With the buck now trotting after the doe, Brent shouldered his father's Browning 7mm Mag semiautomatic and fired. The buck dropped dead into the snow.

The Brent Klein buck is exceptionally symmetrical, grossing 197⅜ inches while netting 195⅜, equating to a measly 2⅛ inches of total deductions. When measuring a typical mule deer there are nine opportunities for deductions—length of the main beams, the four points, and the four circumferences. On this buck four of the nine match perfectly, while the other five have differences of less than an inch! Two of the matching points are the incredibly long 13²/₈-inch G4 points. All but one of the circumference measurements match, and the one that does not has only one-eighth inch of difference. The buck stood as the state record for four years until the Terry Sandstrom buck scoring 196²/₈ inches eclipsed it by seven-eighths of an inch. It currently ranks third.

"I didn't know how awesome this deer was until I was actually able to get my hands on his antlers. It was definitely a deer of a lifetime. But the best thing about it was that I got to share it with my father and son. I'm truly blessed," shares Brent.

51

Deer Hunting Comes to Frontier County

The Henry Koch Buck, 1960

· 189⅝-inch typical

· Frontier County

"On the basis of present knowledge, there are no indications that the deer population of Nebraska will reach numbers great enough to warrant a statewide open season. . . . Local situations, however, where herds exceed the carrying capacity of the range, may necessitate harvests such as that conducted in 1945 on the National Forest area."[1]

Eleven years after this report from the Game, Forestation, and Parks Commission, "local situations" in Frontier County warranted a deer season. After hunting pheasants, squirrels, and rabbits their entire lives, hunters in southwest Nebraska were finally going big-game hunting. Can you imagine the excitement? Eighty-five-year-old Henry Koch can; he was there and remembers it well. Not only did he hunt that first season in 1960; he shot one of Nebraska's greatest mule deer.

Sitting with his wife Anita in their comfortable home north of McCook, they reminisce about life, family, and hunting. Born in 1934, Henry joined the army and married Anita right after graduating with the McCook High School class of 1952. The young couple soon found themselves living a long way from Nebraska. "I was stationed at Fort Hamilton, in New York City. I enjoyed it," remembers Henry. Shaking her head, Anita disagrees: "I was

FIG. 78. Henry Koch (*middle*) holds his young son, Eugene, while his state-record typical lies on the far left of the picture. Photo courtesy of Henry Koch.

scared to death. A country girl in New York, I don't know." Henry chuckles and says, "She didn't leave me anyway."

Returning home to Nebraska after serving two years in the military, Henry began farming in the McCook and Cambridge area. It was during this time, in the mid- to late 1950s, that people began seeing deer in Frontier County. Henry explains, "I never saw a deer growing up in this area, so I was really excited about getting to go deer hunting in 1960. It was something we had never done before. We all just kind of got together and went hunting, scattering out to where we thought there might be deer."

Henry decided to hunt some of his farm ground near Medicine Creek Reservoir, north of Cambridge. Arriving at the property he drove down the east side of the dam along a fence line separating his land from public land. Parking the truck and grabbing his Winchester Model 88 in .308, Henry began still-hunting the deep draws, hoping to surprise a buck. "I walked over this hill and I saw him standing down in the bottom of the canyon. He was quite a ways off, but he was big. In those days I was a good shot. I didn't have a scope or anything, just iron sights," remembers Henry.

Shouldering his Winchester, he settled the front bead into the rear notch of the iron sights, aligning it with the buck's vitals. After squeezing the trigger he watched the giant buck drop in his tracks. Scrambling down into the canyon Henry was more excited about shooting his first deer than about the buck's massive rack. "I didn't have any idea what a Boone and Crockett score was or any of that. I was just excited that I got one."

Henry wasn't the only successful deer hunter that morning. "We all got deer that opening morning. It took us about three hours," remembers Henry. Loading all five bucks into the back of a truck, the proud group of deer hunters posed for a photograph. Henry is kneeling in the middle holding his Winchester, with his giant typical buck on the far left, tines stretching off the edge of the photograph. Sitting in front of Henry is his young son, Eugene, holding what appears to be a toy gun.

When the local game warden saw the buck, he encouraged Henry to get it officially measured. His first buck was a new state record.

The Henry Koch buck is a clean, symmetrical five-by-five with only 6⅛ inches of total deductions. Both G2 points measure exactly 16⅝ inches and are deeply forked, with both G3 points stretching over eleven inches. The buck's inside spread is a respectable 24⅝ inches, while all eight circumference measurements surpass four inches. Grossing 195⅛ inches and netting an even 189⅝ inches, it is a beautiful typical rack. The buck stood as the typical state record for five years, while currently ranking eighth.

Henry has only missed one deer season since 1960. "That year I didn't get a tag because I thought there weren't enough deer around. The first hour of the season I saw a big buck," says Henry. Passing along the hunting tradition to his sons, Eugene and Kirk, his extended family now fills as many as fifteen tags a year. "I've got twenty-one great-grandchildren and they are all shooting deer now." However, their great-grandpa still has bragging rights.

52

Forgotten

The Clarence Dout Buck, 1949

· 195⅞-inch typical
· Sioux County

Clarence H. Dout was born in 1902, just south of the Pine Ridge in Harrison, Nebraska. Over the course of his seventy-one years of life, Clarence and others of his generation were witnesses to greater change than arguably any other generation. From horse and buggies to landing on the moon. From wood-burning stoves to electric ranges. From telegraphs to computers. They also witnessed the slow repopulation of the state by mule deer and whitetail.

The year Clarence was born the NGPC estimated in their biennial report that only fifty deer remained in the entire state, along the Dismal River in Thomas County. It is probable that small numbers of deer survived in other remote areas, such as the Niobrara River valley and the Pine Ridge, but in very small numbers. Regardless, in response to these low deer numbers, in 1907 the state legislature closed deer hunting across the entire state.

Clarence graduated from Sioux County High School in 1920 and five years later married Leona Pullen in Harrison. Working his family's ranch in northern Sioux County, Clarence undoubtedly noticed the mule deer population growing and expanding their range. A survey done in the winter of 1939–40 estimated that the Pine Ridge held approximately two to three thousand deer.[1]

FIG. 79. After lying unscored in a grain shed for fifty years, the Clarence Dout buck now ranks as the second-largest firearm typical. Photo courtesy of the Boone and Crockett Club.

In 1945 Nebraska held its first modern deer season on the Nebraska National Forest near Halsey, with three hundred sixty-one deer taken. Four years later the deer population in the panhandle warranted a second Nebraska deer season. The NGPC issued fifteen hundred buck-only permits for Sioux, Dawes, Scotts Bluff, Banner, and Morrill Counties.

Clarence, now forty-seven years old, purchased one of these permits. His great-grandson, Heath Serres, shares the family lore surrounding his hunt. "The story goes that while my grandfather and his crew were putting up hay, Clarence came to the ranch in northern Sioux County and borrowed my grandfather's .45-70 rifle. Clarence went to the creek because he knew from experience that there were deer there, and shot this buck. I don't think he had a very detailed hunting plan."

Regardless, on that early December day in 1949, Clarence shot one of Nebraska's most impressive typical mule deer bucks. Although he certainly appreciated the buck's exceptional antlers, he never had them scored or even mounted. "After the buck was shot, the head and neck were put in a grain shed on my great-grandfather's ranch," shares Heath. The rack and slowly mummifying head stayed there, largely forgotten, for the next half century!

In 1999 Heath decided to take the rack and head to a taxidermist and have a European mount done. "[The taxidermist] said it was pretty gross; there was even a mouse nest in the neck," recalls Heath. Four years later Heath finally had the rack officially measured and the scoresheet submitted to the B&C. Scoring 195⅞ inches, the Clarence Dout buck fell short of beating Terry Sandstrom's state record from 1968 by less than an inch. Although not especially wide, with an inside spread of 22⅝ inches, the rack is exceptionally tall. Both G2 points measure 19⅛ inches and are deeply forked, with nearly matching G3 points of 12⅜ and 12⅝ inches. Although overall very symmetrical, the 3⅝-inch abnormal point sprouting off the left G3 is what prevents the rack from being a state record. Grossing 202⅛ inches with 6⅛ inches of total deductions, the buck nets 195⅞ inches.

Although never entered into the Nebraska records book, the buck currently ranks as the second-largest typical shot in Nebraska. Unfortunately Clarence passed away in 1973, never knowing the true size of the buck he shot.

53

Western Adventure

The James Skorzewski Buck, 1965

· 192⅛-inch typical
· Keya Paha County

Ohio officially became the Buckeye State in 1953 when the state legislature declared the Ohio buckeye the state tree. The tree is so named because its nut resembles the shape and color of a whitetail deer's eye. The whitetail deer is also the official state mammal, with over six hundred thousand now roaming the state. Ohio is unquestionably a deer-hunting-crazed state and a top destination for trophy bucks.

Like many other midwestern states, this was not always the case. When James Skorzewski was born in 1932 there were few deer and there was no deer season. Growing up in northern Ohio, James remembers small game being plentiful while whitetail deer were scarce. "I could take my German shorthair out and have a limit of pheasants and bunnies in no time," he remembers. A true dog man, James would sometimes own as many as nine German shorthair pointers at once. To hunt deer James would sometimes travel to other states, including Pennsylvania and Wisconsin.

Like many in the Cleveland metro area, James began working for General Motors in the 1950s, the heyday of the U.S. automobile industry. Eventually working his way into management at the Chevrolet metal plant in Parma, Ohio, he saw countless cars roll off the assembly line. "In those days there were quite a few deer hunters working at the plant. One day one of the guys at the plant says to me, 'You want to go with us and hunt deer in Nebraska?'" recalls James. "I had never even been to Nebraska, but soon five of us were driving west to go hunting." Although space was limited, James found room for one of his favorite German shorthairs. "I heard they had prairie chickens out there, so I brought along a dog. We did end up shooting a few of those too."

After their thousand-mile drive, the group settled into a hunting cabin nestled in a deep draw along the Niobrara River in Keya Paha County. November 8, opening morning of the firearm season, dawned unusually warm as the group piled into their pickup trucks to start the day's hunt. Driving south into the Sandhills with his two companions, James spotted a nice mule deer buck grazing on a distant hillside. Quickly climbing out of the truck he began stalking toward the giant buck, his first experience walking the Nebraska Sandhills. "Wow, those hills are tough," he remembers. "I lost eight pounds walking those hills. At the end of each day we were just beat."

With hunting adrenaline pushing him forward, James crested a dune and spotted the giant buck moving downhill toward a brushy draw. Quickly shouldering his .308 Sako, he cleanly dropped the buck with a sixty-yard heart shot. "It happened really quickly. I was just in the right spot."

As James approached the dead mule deer, he first noticed the buck's body size. It was massive. After struggling to load it into the truck, they made it back to camp and hung the gigantic buck by its antlers from a tree. With James wearing a black cowboy hat, he posed along with two of his hunting companions for a photograph. "It was such a nice warm day, that after the hunt I just laid down and took a nap on the side of a hill," remembers James.

After hauling the buck back to Ohio, James had it officially measured. The extremely symmetrical typical grossed 196⅛ inches and netted 192⅛ inches. Ohioan James Skorzewski now held the Nebraska firearm state record! A record he would hold until 1982.

The James Skorzewski buck is a clean typical, with only 4⅝ inches of total deductions between the two sides. The inside spread is 25⅝ inches with main beams of 26⅝ and 24⅝ inches. The brow tines are long for

FIG. 80. Ohioan James Skorzewski (*far right*) with his first Nebraska deer, a buck that held the state record for seventeen years. Photo courtesy of James Skorzewski.

a mule deer, measuring 4⅜ and 5⅝ inches, with the six other points all measuring over ten inches. Also noteworthy is the circumference symmetry, with only a one-eighth-inch difference between the four measurements. Attesting to its size, the buck still ranks fifth after the passage of over fifty hunting seasons.

No longer able to hunt, James remembers his Nebraska hunting adventure every time he walks into his garage in Strongsville, Ohio. "Guys still come by to look at the rack," shares James. "We just had a great time in Nebraska. I only hunted there one other time and shot another buck. Everyone was just so nice. It was quite an adventure."

54

In Memoriam

The James Pavelka Buck, 1957

- 184⅞-inch typical
- Custer County

Most people associate "barn finds" with classic cars. Those amazing stories where someone happens upon a rare low-mileage muscle car sitting for decades in an old barn, covered in dust and mouse droppings. The story of the James Pavelka buck from 1957 makes you wonder how many giant mule deer, whitetail, and elk racks are likewise hanging forgotten or unscored in Nebraska barns and basements.

Each time Candice "Candy" Johnson visited her grandmother Lillian's house in Milligan, Nebraska, she saw the antlers. They were a part of the house, part of visiting Grandma. For decades the rack from the buck her grandfather, James, shot in 1957 hung in the enclosed porch, sometimes a topic of conversation but mostly just part of the decor. When her grandmother passed away in 1991, Candy's father, Bernard, who was with James when he shot the buck, took the antlers to his home in Lincoln and hung them above a stairwell. The shiny, varnish-coated antlers hung there for the next eighteen years. When Bernie passed away in 2009, Candy hung the antlers in the basement of her home near Valparaiso.

Over the next decade the antlers became a fixture in the Johnson home. Candy's husband, Dave, a deer hunter himself, had no problem with adding the antlers to his own collection of mounts and other hunting memorabilia. "I had told Bernie for years that he should get those antlers measured, but he just never did," shares Dave. Neither did Dave. Finally, after shooting a nice whitetail buck in 2018, Candy told Dave he might as well take both of them to Lincoln and get them scored.

In January 2019, sixty-two years after James Pavelka shot it, his mule deer was officially measured by Randy Stutheit, the Nebraska Big Game Trophy Records coordinator. The typical rack grossed 198⅜ inches and netted 184⅞ inches, qualifying for both the Nebraska and B&C records books. It is a beautiful mule deer, with a 23⅝-inch inside spread, G2 points measuring 17⅛ and 18⅛ inches, and G3 and G4 points all over ten inches. It currently ranks in the top twenty-five in the typical firearm category, while in 1957 it was in the top five.

"I felt really bad when I found out what it scored. I wish my dad was alive so he could have known," says Candy. In memoriam to both James and Bernie, Dave and Candy shared everything they could recall about the hunt.

In the early 1900s, when James was very young, his family left Bohemia and came to the United States, settling in Milligan. Like other immigrant families, they worked hard carving out a new life in a new country, with James eventually becoming a jack of all trades, working at one time as both a plumber and as the sheriff of Milligan. Although never much for the outdoors, James and Lillian made extra money cleaning ducks and pheasants shot by local hunters. Keeping the duck down, Lillian made feather tick mattresses, called *peřina* in Czech.

The couple had one child, Bernie, born in 1931. Unlike his father, he became an avid outdoorsman. "He loved to hunt and fish," shares Candy. "He had two girls, myself and Deena, and although he didn't take us hunting, we did go fishing with him." Bernie spent a lifetime hunting and fishing in Nebraska, while also hunting elk, caribou in Alaska, and wild hogs in Tennessee.

In November 1957 twenty-six-year-old Bernie convinced his father to do something he would only do one time—go deer hunting. Not much is known about the actual hunt, not even the exact date. We do know that sometime in November James made the two-and-a-half-hour drive from his home in Milligan to Broken Bow, where Bernie was living and working for the local newspaper, the *Custer County Chief.*

FIG. 81. James (*left*) and Bernie Pavelka pose with their bucks after their successful Custer County hunt. Photo courtesy of Candice Johnson.

Bernie and James began their hunt somewhere in Custer County, probably east of Broken Bow near the Middle Loup River. James was carrying a Mauser rifle chambered in .308 while left-handed Bernie was carrying a right-handed bolt action. Sometime during their hunt Bernie shot a nice whitetail buck and James his giant mule deer. "Bernie shot the whitetail not too far from where James shot the mule deer, closer to the river," Dave remembers Bernie telling him. "He shot that whitetail buck through the head, breaking the skull plate in half. He had one of those antlers mounted at his house and the other one at his dad's house," continues Dave with a laugh. "My father told me that the mule deer field dressed at two hundred eighty-five pounds," adds Candy. After the hunt the two posed proudly in the driveway with their bucks.

So many unanswered questions. What was the weather like? Did they hunt together or split up? How many shots did they fire? How far away were the bucks? How did James react after shooting his giant buck? We will never know. In a weird way, it makes the story better.

PART 6

Non-Typical Mule Deer

55

Rearview Mirror

The Barry Johnson Buck, 1992

- 226⁶/₈-inch non-typical
- Chase County

"Where should I take it to get it mounted?" This is often the first question someone asks after shooting a trophy buck or bull. For decades the answer in Nebraska was oftentimes, "Barry Johnson."

Over the years thousands of successful hunters have left downtown North Platte and driven north on Highway 83, searching for Barry Johnson's taxidermy shop. After crossing the North Platte River floodplain they look ahead, noticing how the road rises and bends, climbing into the southern edge of the vast Sandhills. Rounding that bend they spot the sign—Johnson's Taxidermy.

Like all other taxidermy shops, it is a fascinating place to visit. Clearly visible in the back room are white forms, hides, rows of antlers, and unfamiliar tools. Mounts cover the walls—mule deer, whitetail, elk, bear, fish, waterfowl, bobcats, and turkeys. For a hunter it is sensory overload. However, in a room full of impressive trophy animals, one particular mule deer stands out. Hanging high above the room on a tree trunk that disappears into the ceiling is an incredibly wide-racked buck, with double drop tines stretching toward the floor.

Sitting down among his mounted work, Barry shares his story. "I began doing taxidermy in 1969 as kind of a hobby, just playing around with it. I read a lot and just taught myself. In 1983 I went full-time, averaging over one hundred deer a year but also lots of elk, antelope, bobcats, and all sorts of other animals too," shares Barry. Through hard work and dedication he built an expansive national clientele, eventually mounting exotic game animals from Asia, Europe, and Africa. "I'm one of those guys who worked until midnight and then got up to work some more. Taxidermy is a job; you have to get up and go to work every day."

After mounting thousands of Nebraska's greatest bucks and bulls, in the spring of 2019 Barry was preparing to sell his business and retire. "I've mounted nearly every state record there dang near was. But I'm burnt out. It's time," shares Barry.

Although obviously a hard worker, over the years Barry found time to hunt. Born in 1950 in Imperial, he shot his first deer in 1965 when he was fifteen. Over the next four decades he amassed one of the most impressive lists of big-game trophies in the Nebraska records book. Barry currently has seventeen records book trophies, including one whitetail, six antelope, and an incredible ten mule deer. And these aren't just ordinary mule deer. His 192⅘-inch firearm typical is the fourth largest ever shot in Nebraska, while another typical, scoring 178⅜ inches, ranks sixth for archery. What makes his list even more impressive is the fact that he shot ten of these trophies with a recurve bow! Including the aforementioned giant double drop tine buck.

The story of that incredible buck begins after rifle season in late November of 1992. "A guy told me about a big buck he was seeing while he was harvesting corn. This was on land my dad once owned, so I knew the area well," remembers Barry. Deciding to go after the buck, Barry loaded up his recurve and hunting gear and drove down to Chase County.

Arriving at the property he began looking for the buck. "The guy told me he had seen the buck the last three days, but I couldn't find him. I even rode the combine and the grain cart looking for him," recalls Barry. With only one evening left to hunt before he had to board a flight to Las Vegas, Barry was losing hope. As the afternoon sun was still high in the sky, he decided to lie down in his pickup for a nap. "I was asleep when the tractor and grain cart pulls up and honks. The driver tells me the buck is right behind me. I look in the rearview mirror and there he is!"

FIG. 82. Barry Johnson's huge non-typical killed with a longbow hanging in his taxidermy shop, only days before it closed. Photo courtesy of the author.

Scrambling out of his truck Barry watched as the massive buck and several does bounded off into the uncut corn. With the combine still cutting corn in the field, Barry knew that eventually the buck would have to come out. "I figured he would run toward either the pasture or the opposite way to another uncut cornfield. It was fifty-fifty," remembers Barry.

Watching and waiting, Barry eventually spotted the massive buck and the does leaving the corn and heading toward the pasture. He would need to move quickly to get a shot. Crossing the fence separating the cornfield from the pasture and using tall Kochia weeds for cover, Barry made his way toward a trail he thought the deer might use. "I was standing, waiting, when two does jumped the fence fifteen yards from me. Then the buck jumped the fence, followed by another doe. That doe pegged me, but for some reason she turned and looked back into the field. That is when I drew."

Wasting no time Barry released an arrow from his recurve at the slowly walking buck. The arrow hit too far back, with Barry watching helplessly as the buck ran and disappeared over a nearby hill. After waiting fifteen minutes Barry crested the hill and spotted the does, but no buck. Looking fruitlessly until dark, he had no choice but to leave, since he could not afford to miss his morning flight from Denver to Las Vegas. After calling some friends and explaining the situation, they agreed to look for the buck the next morning.

A few days later Barry got the call he was waiting for. "That buck had circled around that cornfield and made it to the other uncut cornfield a mile away. How he got there without me seeing him I'll never know," shares Barry with a shake of his head. A few days later, while combining the cornfield, the farmer spotted the buck lying dead in a center pivot track. After arriving back in Denver, Barry drove straight to see his buck. "It was quite a thrill. He was better than I expected. He had some stuff on him that I hadn't noticed."

The Barry Johnson buck definitely has some "stuff" on it. The buck's symmetrical typical rack has an inside spread of $28\frac{4}{8}$ inches, which is longer than the $23\frac{0}{8}$- and $23\frac{5}{8}$-inch main beams. Since regulation states the inside spread credit may equal but not exceed the length of the longer main beam, the buck loses $2\frac{7}{8}$ inches. Regardless, the typical rack still grosses $179\frac{5}{8}$ inches while netting $175\frac{5}{8}$. However, the $51\frac{1}{8}$ inches of abnormal points, especially the matching drop tines, make it an especially unique trophy. Scoring $226\frac{6}{8}$ inches, it currently ranks as the second-largest archery non-typical in the Nebraska records book.

No longer able to pull his recurve, Barry gave up bowhunting several years ago. He now spends more time hunting with his grandchildren, especially Jenna Kimberling, who at age twelve shot a $184\frac{2}{8}$-inch mule deer. Her buck mount joins the many thousands of other Nebraska bucks hanging on the wall, compliments of Barry Johnson.

56

Wrong Buck

The Eric Johnson Buck, 2017

- 219⅛-inch non-typical
- Dundy County

Humans are good at drawing borders and boundaries. Innumerable invisible lines dissect our landscape into a crazy patchwork of parcels. State and county lines, city boundaries, natural resource districts, hunting units, and property lines. Hunters are keenly aware of the latter two. Is this barbed-wire fence the ranch boundary? Is this road the border of my deer unit? Is this state land? Federal land?

Hunters living near state lines face a particularly unique challenge, since the border is a barrier to roaming and hunting freely in that direction. Crossing the state line means different regulations, tags, seasons, and costs. Eric Johnson, from Wray, Colorado, knows this all too well. His home sits ten miles west of the Nebraska state line.

But living near a state line can also work in your favor. Wanting to improve hunting while protecting mule deer populations impacted by brainworm disease and conversion of habitat into row crops, in 2010 the NGPC created the Mule Deer Conservation Area, encompassing much of southwest and southcentral Nebraska. The more restrictive harvest regulations in this area have allowed bucks to reach their prime, resulting in a trophy-hunting zone. Therefore living close to Nebraska allows Eric to purchase a nonresident archery deer tag and pursue his passion for spot-and-stalk hunting, a passion he developed while chasing elk in southwest Colorado. "I learned quickly that if you want to hunt elk during the rut, you have to do it with primitive weapons, so I bought a bow and muzzleloader and started learning how to get close. Elk hunting the rut and spot-and-stalk mule deer became my absolute favorite hunts," says Eric. His hard work and dedication has paid off, with three mule deer each over two hundred inches adorning his home. All three were shot at less than fifty yards.

After moving to northeast Colorado, Eric began scouting for mule deer hunting land across the border in Dundy County, Nebraska. His training and career in precision agriculture and Geographic Information Systems software helps. "I do a lot of digital scouting of the places I hunt, since I have the software and the know-how," shares Eric. After gaining permission on an eight-hundred-acre property, Eric began making regular trips across the state line in pursuit of trophy Nebraska mule deer.

In September of 2016, after hunting this property for five years, Eric decided to place a game camera on a stock tank in a pasture he normally only coyote hunts. Checking the camera a couple weeks later he found a picture of one of the largest non-typical mule deer he had ever seen. "I immediately logged in to the NGPC website and purchased an archery tag!" remembers Eric. Despite countless hours of glassing and hunting, he never saw the giant buck that season. After a long, anxious winter worrying the buck would not make it, he spent the spring walking miles in hopes of finding its sheds. Nothing.

That August he once again placed a camera on the stock tank. Several weeks later, after scrolling through countless pictures of cows, he saw what he was hoping for. The giant non-typical was even larger than the year before, with nearly thirty scorable points!

When bow season opened Eric began making the twenty-minute drive from his home to hunt the massive non-typical. "In late September I got bronchitis. I knew I couldn't spot-and-stalk since every few minutes I wanted to cough," recalls Eric. By mid-October, he was feeling better and began making regular trips into Nebraska, following the same routine. Arriving well before first light and carrying his Mathews Q2 bow, he would quietly climb to a high point. After setting up his spotting scope, he would glass the treeless yucca-and-cactus-covered pasture, hoping to catch the giant buck moving to his bed. "I learned quickly that the bucks came in very early, almost too dark to make out antlers. I saw deer every time I was there, but I rarely stayed out more than an hour. I didn't want to walk around and bump him off the property," explains Eric.

On the morning of October 25 Eric sat glassing the pasture once again. Seeing movement a quarter mile away, he pivoted the spotting scope and slowly turned the focus knob. It was the giant non-typical! Eric watched as the buck bedded down just below a hilltop, mentally marking the spot with some taller vegetation standing nearby. Keeping low, with the wind in his face, he closed the distance to a heart-thumping twenty yards. Sensing something wasn't right, the buck stood quickly and was gone. "I couldn't get the shot off. The biggest deer I have ever seen alive. He looked like a Brahman bull. I beat myself up," remembers Eric.

After glassing fruitlessly the rest of the evening, Eric returned home and barely slept. Returning the next morning to the same hilltop, he soon spotted a big-bodied buck moving through the pasture in the early morning light. Looking through his binoculars, he saw lots of points. Thinking it was the buck from the day before, Eric moved quickly to another ridge to get a better vantage point. He bumped a smaller buck along the way and watched it trot away toward the big buck. Both bucks soon bedded down.

After stalking to within one hundred yards of the bucks, Eric ditched his spotting scope and pack, and took off his boots. With an arrow nocked, he crept through the cactus and yucca in his stocking feet. At sixty yards he spotted the bigger buck's rack above the sage. It wasn't the giant non-typical from the day before!

Although it wasn't the buck Eric thought, this one was huge as well. After gathering himself, Eric studied the sixty yards of terrain separating him from the bedded buck. Noticing a large sage bush fifteen yards from the buck, he felt confident he could stay hidden behind it. With the wind steady in his face, he padded silently toward the buck. "I was about twenty yards away when he moved his head slightly. I saw all those points flash and

FIG. 83. Eric Johnson with the smaller of two bucks on the Dundy County ranch he was hunting. Photo courtesy of Eric Johnson.

my heart began pounding with the adrenaline rush. I made it to within a couple yards of that sage bush and he stood up, shook, and then put his head down. I drew my bow and stood up at the same time. I found him in my peep sight, and the shot felt perfect when I let it fly," remembers Eric.

The arrow disappeared behind the buck's front shoulder, and he whirled and ran, taking the smaller buck with him over a nearby ridge. Eric took off running as well. "I think I stepped on every cactus on my way up that ridge," remembers Eric. Arriving breathless at the ridgetop, he spotted the smaller buck looking back at him, but there was no sign of the big buck. Working carefully back down the ridge Eric found his pack and gear and spent a few minutes picking cactus needles from his feet.

With his boots back on Eric picked up the blood trail and began tracking the buck. After only one hundred yards he found the buck lying dead in the sagebrush. "I was blown away that it was a buck I had never seen before. I sat there for a long time just admiring his unique rack," shares Eric.

The Eric Johnson buck is currently the third-largest archery non-typical in the Nebraska records book. Although not particularly wide at 19⅝ inches, it has excellent point length and symmetry. Both brow tines measure 3⅝ inches while the G3 points nearly match as well, measuring 13⅛ and 13⅜ inches. The typical rack grosses 181⅞ inches and with only 4⅞ inches of deductions, nets 177⁰⁄₈. With ten abnormal points totaling 42⅛ inches, the buck nets 219⅛ inches.

Not bad considering it was the second-largest buck on the property!

57

Full Velvet

The Mike Lutt Buck, 2014

- 232²/₈-inch non-typical
- Sioux County

Sitting in his hastily constructed ground blind of sunflowers and sagebrush, Mike Lutt glances down again at his watch. After waiting patiently for nearly four hours, with legal shooting light fading fast, he is second-guessing his hunt plan. Looking once again up the ravine to the south, his heart jumps. The giant non-typical he has been hunting for a week is standing there with his velvet-covered rack silhouetted against the horizon. All Mike needs now is for the buck to turn north and walk down the ravine toward the waterhole behind him.

The buck, of course, has other plans. Instead of turning north the buck moves eastward, paralleling the fence line. Making a snap decision Mike grabs his bow, and crouching low, crosses over quickly to an adjacent ravine to the east. Now out of view of the buck, he runs quickly to the south, hoping to reach the fence line before the buck does. After reaching the fence he fights to catch his breath while squatting with his bow at the ready.

"Finally I see his rack appear, coming down the fence line, so I draw my bow. I was too close to the fence though, so he was coming right at me. He came to within eighteen yards and then pegged me. He knew something wasn't right," remembers Mike. At full draw, with the giant mule deer buck staring directly at him, Mike counts off the seconds in his head. He would get to two hundred sixty-five.

The long countdown to this hunt actually begins in the early 1970s when Mike began tagging along on deer hunts with his father and uncles near Butte, Nebraska. In Mike's mind those first deer hunts were somewhat chaotic events. The group would conduct deer drives, pushing running deer past posted blockers, shooting some but oftentimes running them onto adjoining properties, where other hunters would then push them back.

When Mike was fourteen years old he discovered another, more peaceful, challenging, and enjoyable way to deer hunt: bowhunting. "The first doe I shot had a hurt foot from being caught in a snare. I would see her every day and knew where she would bed down. I snuck up on her with my recurve and killed her," recalls Mike, grinning. His first six deer, all does, were shot with a recurve, as was his first buck. "That buck came feeding underneath me. I wasn't in a stand, just sitting up in a tree, and he came to within five yards."

These initial experiences and successes led Mike to become exclusively a bowhunter at a very early age. "I quit hunting with a rifle at fifteen. Although I liked the two tags you could get for bowhunting, I really liked that the animals were undisturbed. Bowhunting is different; the animals are acting natural, and you get to see a lot of other animals as well," explains Mike.

This early fascination with bowhunting developed into a lifelong obsession. "I've archery hunted in about twenty different states, every Canadian province but one, and also Mexico and Africa," shares Mike. His ultimate goal is to complete the North American Super Slam, which entails taking all twenty-eight species of big game recognized by P&Y. His progress toward the Super Slam adorn the walls of his impressive trophy room—brown and black bear, pronghorn antelope, American and Roosevelt elk, Rocky Mountain goat, Coues deer, Canada moose, whitetail, mule deer, and so on. Mike is arguably one of the most successful, in terms of records book animals, of any Nebraska bowhunter. He currently has thirty typical whitetails in the P&Y records book, more than any other Nebraska hunter!

Although he lives and hunts whitetail deer in the eastern part of Nebraska, Mike began hunting Sioux County in his early twenties. "I started hunting some ranches in Sioux County in the early 1980s with a big group of guys. Our equipment wasn't the best, and if we shot a doe or maybe a small buck we considered it a good hunt," recalls Mike. Those early hunts taught him a lot, including a knack for getting permission on private land. He soon began making solo trips to northwest Nebraska, mainly for pronghorn.

After his son Dustin was old enough, Mike began taking him along as well. For years leading up to the 2014 season, Mike and Dustin had been hunting one particular ranch for pronghorn, although they often spotted good mule deer bucks too. The problem—a group from Maryland had sole permission to deer hunt the first three weeks of the archery season. "I talked to the caretaker and asked him if I could hunt if the archery season opener ever moved earlier. He said yes," recalls Mike.

At the time Mike was president of the Nebraska Bowhunters Association, which for years had been lobbying the NGPC to move the archery opener from September 15 to September 1. The change would not only give archers an additional two weeks of hunting; it would also provide the unique opportunity to shoot bucks in velvet. The lobbying efforts finally paid off in 2014, when, after thirty-five years of opening on September 15, the archery season would open on September 1.

With two weeks to hunt before the Maryland hunters arrived, Mike and Dustin headed west to Sioux County. Arriving four days prior to the archery opener, they glassed the wide-open sagebrush flats and rolling hills, hoping to find and pattern a good buck. "I first saw the non-typical buck as he was walking away from me, and I knew right away he was a world-class buck," recalls Mike. "I watched him for a couple hours every morning, and again in the evening. We tried to figure out what he was doing since he was going back and forth on a couple different properties."

On the third day of the season Mike and Dustin watched the buck early in the morning as he moved toward his bed. After laying down in the shade on the north side of a small embankment, they could see the buck's rack sticking up above the brush. "We glassed him for hours from a mile away. He got up a couple times to move, staying in the shade. Dustin and I talked about it over lunch and decided that if the wind increased to fifteen miles

FIG. 84. Mike Lutt with his gigantic full-velvet Sioux County archery buck. Photo courtesy of Mike Lutt.

per hour, I would try a stalk, but it never got strong enough to conceal the noise of a stalk," recalls Mike.

Plan B involved the aforementioned ravine and waterhole. The buck was bedded about three hundred yards south of a waterhole where Mike had a ground blind to hunt pronghorn. His concern about sitting in the ground blind was that if the buck did indeed move his way it would be dark before he came within range. Wanting to shorten the distance between the buck and the water, Mike crept up the ravine and built a makeshift ground blind.

At full draw and the buck staring right at him, Mike continued counting... two hundred sixty-three, two hundred sixty-four, two hundred sixty-five... "I was shaking pretty bad, and when I tried to relax, the bow string would jump forward. When he finally turned, I just aimed for the middle of his body and released the arrow," remembers Mike.

At the shot the buck jumped the nearby fence and ran, eventually turning back, jumping the same fence again, and disappearing down a ravine.

"I knew the shot was a killing shot, but I know enough not to push a buck that's hit. I said some prayers and wiped the tears from my eyes. I was just a complete basket case after holding my bow for so long, and the fact that I had been watching and hunting that buck for seven days," shares Mike. After giving the buck some time, and meeting up with Dustin, the two made their way in the dark toward the fallen buck. "Let's just say, he didn't disappoint."

The Mike Lutt buck is magnificent on multiple levels. First is the velvet. Light in color and covering the entire rack, it not only makes the rack look larger but also gives it a soft, textured look that is striking. Second, the rack is massive, including a typical frame grossing 191²⁄₈ inches and netting 186⁰⁄₈. The eleven abnormal points total 47²⁄₈ inches and include kickers off both sides, giving the rack an impressive greatest-spread measurement of 34⁴⁄₈ inches. With a final score of 232²⁄₈ inches, it is undoubtedly one of the greatest mule deer ever shot in Nebraska.

However, ranking it among other bucks is problematic due to the velvet. The P&Y does accept velvet-covered antlers, with their official scoresheets including an additional checkbox for indicating velvet entries. Although eligible, the P&Y ranks velvet entries separate from non-velvet. The B&C meanwhile does not accept velvet antlers, requiring stripping of the velvet prior to measuring. The Nebraska records book does not have a separate category for velvet entries. If you rank the Mike Lutt buck with non-velvet bucks, it would be the second-largest archery non-typical, behind only the 245⁴⁄₈-inch Chase County buck shot in 1999 by Gavin McClintock.

58

HisStory

The Art Thomsen Buck, 1960

- 256⅞-inch non-typical
- Dawes County

Hunting is our story, our history. Hunting is a thread running through our lives, stitching together time, places, people, and events. The thread includes vivid images of wild places, distinct smells, nasty weather, bloody hands, good friends, children, musty motels, and long road trips. Toward the end of our thread, all we have left are memories.

Although Art Thomsen's hunting life is over, his memories are still sharp. Sitting in the living room of his small home in Alliance, Nebraska, I was amazed at how he remembers minute details about hunts from thirty, forty, even sixty years ago. Now eighty-eight years old, Art shares story after story—including that fateful day fifty-eight years ago when he shot one of his two state-record mule deer.

Art was born in 1931 on a farm near Oelrichs, South Dakota, a small town twelve miles from the Nebraska border and thirty miles north of Chadron, where he attended high school. Growing up with three brothers and a sister during the lean Dust Bowl years, hunting was a way to put food on the family table. "We were dependent on hunting for food. We ate a lot of jackrabbits, until disease came and wiped them out. After that my mother refused to cook them anymore," Art remembers, laughing.

While still in high school, Art became a deer hunter, shooting his first deer in 1946 in southwest South Dakota. A few years later, after moving to Chadron to work on a dairy farm and then in the police department, he began a lifetime love affair with hunting the Pine Ridge. Over the next few years Art became increasingly obsessed with hunting trophy big game, especially mule deer. When he was only twenty-two years old, Art crossed the state line to hunt his familiar stomping grounds in Fall River County, South Dakota. During that hunt in 1953 he shot a 190⅝-inch typical mule deer that would stand as the South Dakota state record for fifty years!

Soon after that successful hunt he was drafted into the army, serving in Germany as a Morse code operator for the 3rd Armored Division. After serving his country Art made his way back to Chadron, rejoining the police department. Following a short stint as a police officer he was hired by the Nebraska Brand Committee as a criminal investigator—a job that would prove perfect for a big-game hunter. Eventually becoming the executive director and chief criminal investigator, he traveled across Nebraska, inspecting brands, registering feedlots, and investigating missing or stolen cattle. Over the years he met countless ranchers, with many letting him hunt. "Those ranchers were some of the best people in the world to work with," shares Art.

In 1959 Art began hunting a ranch ten miles southeast of Chadron in Dawes County. "We spotted this giant buck several times, but when rifle season came he just disappeared. We couldn't find him," remembers Art. With no reports of anyone shooting a giant buck, Art was hopeful the buck made it through the season.

The first few days of the 1960 rifle season passed uneventfully, with unseasonably warm weather limiting deer movement. However, as is often the case in Nebraska, a November cold front moved in midweek, dropping the temperature and four inches of fresh snow. Perfect conditions for still-hunting.

The next morning, after meeting with the landowner for an early breakfast before the hunt, the two headed out into the snow-covered hills. They decided to split up to cover more ground, so Art made his way along the edge of a deep, narrow canyon. An hour after sunrise he spotted several does

FIG. 85. Art Thomsen simultaneously held the South Dakota typical and the Nebraska non-typical mule deer state records. Photo courtesy of *Nebraskaland* magazine/ Nebraska Game and Parks Commission.

bedded down below the opposite ridge. Sitting down in the snow he began glassing the surrounding terrain in hopes of spotting a buck.

After thoroughly checking the opposite ridge, Art was ready to stand up and move on. However, a slight movement farther up the ridge caught his attention. Lifting his rifle and peering through the scope, he saw the giant non-typical from the year before, bedded under a small pine tree! Wriggling forward to a small mound of dirt, Art found the buck in his Weaver 4x scope, centered the crosshairs, and pulled the trigger on his FN Mauser .30-06. "It was probably one of the easier shots I made in my life," Art confesses.

The Art Thomsen buck has it all—symmetry, length, mass, and numerous abnormal points. The typical frame has only 7⅛ inches of deductions, grossing 203⅛ inches while netting 196⅛. The forks are especially notable, with the G2 points measuring 15⅜ and 17⅛ inches, while the G3 points measure 11⅝ and 13⅛ inches. The mass is noteworthy as well, with all eight circumference measurements over five inches. However, it's the abnormal points that make this a truly magnificent buck and give it a unique cactuslike appearance. The right antler has fifteen abnormal points measuring 43²⁄₈ inches, while the left side has nine measuring 17⁵⁄₈ inches, for a total of 60⅞ inches and a net score of 256⅞ inches.

A tribute to its size, the buck stood as the Nebraska firearm non-typical state record for thirty-four years, until Charles Hogeland broke the record in 1994 with his 265⅛-inch buck. Incredibly, Art held the South Dakota typical mule deer state record and the Nebraska non-typical mule deer state record simultaneously!

Over the next decade Art would prove that these two bucks were not strokes of sheer luck by putting together an unbelievable string of trophy animals. In 1961 he shot a 165⅛-inch typical mule deer. Two years later he shot one measuring 163³⁄₈ inches. In 1965 he shot a 76²⁄₈-inch pronghorn and in 1966 a 150⁰⁄₈-inch typical mule deer. In 1967 he shot a 165⁵⁄₈-inch typical mule deer, and finally in 1971 he took a 77²⁄₈-inch pronghorn. Modest about his hunting success, Art says, "I hunted at a great time; there were a lot of big deer around in the 1950s and 1960s."

Art also ventured outside Nebraska, hunting many other states and Canadian provinces, taking trophy moose, mountain goats, mountain caribou, and pronghorn antelope. He eventually sold most of his trophy mounts to Cabela's. A self-professed gun nut, he traded his two state-record bucks to his brother for a rifle.

Although his trophy mounts no longer adorn his home, he still has the memories of a long and rewarding hunting life.

59

Making Headlines

The Bill Glenn Buck, 1963

· 227³⁄₈-inch non-typical

· Jefferson County

"Son, would you look at that!" exclaimed Wayne Glenn, looking out the driver-side window at the road. Scrambling out of the passenger-side seat of the pickup truck, young Bill Glenn peered down, shaking with excitement. Sure enough, a perfect set of tracks—muddy proof that deer were living near their home.

Born in 1944, Bill Glenn remembers when spotting deer, or even deer tracks, was newsworthy. "There wasn't a deer season in this area until I was in high school," remembers Bill. However, that did not stop him from becoming a hunter. Armed with a .410, he hunted birds, rabbits, and squirrels on his family's farm near Powell, in Jefferson County. "I was hunting as soon as my folks would let me. I would just walk out the door and go."

In 1960 a neighbor took him deer hunting for the first time. With still no open season in Jefferson County, they made the long drive to the Pine Ridge, near Crawford. "My neighbor cleaned up an old military rifle and let me borrow it. Being a farm kid from eastern Nebraska, those deep canyons and pine trees really impressed me. I shot my first deer on that trip, a young mule deer fawn," recalls Bill.

The following year there was no need to travel to the Pine Ridge, as deer season had finally come to Jefferson County. Now a senior in high school and nursing a football injury, Bill shot his first whitetail buck that fall. After graduating the next spring from Fairbury High School, he enrolled at Fairbury Junior College, studying agronomy and playing on the football team. Nevertheless, he always found time to hunt, shooting another small whitetail buck in the fall of 1962.

The following spring, while looking for whitetail sheds near his home, Bill bent down and wrapped his hands around a massive, odd-looking antler. He realized, based on the shape and position of the points, that he was holding the shed of the massive non-typical mule deer buck he had spotted several times over the past couple years. This was especially exciting since mule deer were extremely rare this far east in the state. "Once in a while I would see a small group of mule deer does, and maybe a buck with them, but not very often," remembers Bill. "I jumped that buck again that summer, and he just had a mass of antlers. His rack was even bigger than the year before."

On November 6, 1963, Bill eased out the door of his parents' farmhouse into the still, cold morning air. Walking in the dark while cradling his Model 721 Remington, he knew from years of experience where to go. Reaching his chosen hilltop he sat down and waited for the sun to rise. "I saw the buck soon after daylight, crossing a pasture and then a cornfield. He went into a narrow strip of trees in a drainage," remembers Bill. "The chances of me sneaking in on him were slim so I went back home and got my parents to help."

The three devised a plan. Bill went to the upper end of the drainage, near a thick hedgerow, positioning himself where he thought the buck might go if jumped. Meanwhile his father, Wayne, and his mother, Anita, began slowly walking down the drainage toward Bill, hoping to push the buck his way. "I could see my mom and dad a few hundred yards away, moving toward me, but I still hadn't seen any deer," recalls Bill.

Suddenly the giant buck appeared, running hard only a few yards from Bill. "When I put my rifle up all I could see in the scope was hair," remembers Bill. Swinging the rifle as if following a rabbit with his .410, Bill squeezed the trigger, sending a .270 bullet through the massive buck's rib cage. After a few more bounding leaps, the buck piled up.

"As soon as I saw him, I knew it was the buck that I had the shed from since he just had a mass of antlers on his head," Bill remembers. With the help of his parents, he field dressed the buck and hauled him the short distance back to the farmyard. Using a block and tackle they hung the buck from a tree a few feet from the house.

Even in those days word spread quickly, with a reporter from the *Fairbury Journal-News* coming to the house to get the story. The next day the headline shouted "Bill Glenn Gets Trophy Head as Well as Venison . . . Bats 1,000 in Deer Hunting League with Giant Buck . . . FC Sophomore Successful Third Straight Year."

The Bill Glenn buck is definitely headline worthy. Scoring 227⅜ inches, it ranked fifth in the state, at the time, in the non-typical firearms category, while still ranking today in the top fifteen. A truly unique mule deer rack,

FIG. 86. Bill Glenn posing with his distinctive 227⅜-inch buck, the only mule deer in the records book from Jefferson County. Photo courtesy of Bill Glenn.

FIG. 87. The Bill Glenn buck is amazingly tight racked for a mule deer, with an inside spread of only 12⅘ inches. Photo courtesy of Bill Glenn.

the inside spread is a mere 12⅘ inches, while the tip to tip spread is only 6⅜ inches. The buck's typical frame is not very large or symmetrical, grossing 154⅘ inches and netting only 138⅖ inches. However, the buck has eleven abnormal points on the right side and ten on the left totaling 89⅛ inches, creating an extremely narrow but tall tangle of antlers that is freakishly cool looking.

After working for most of his career as a soil scientist in western Wyoming, Bill and his wife, Mary, moved back to Jefferson County. Now living near where he shot his buck in 1963, Bill spends much of his free time outdoors, hunting upland birds over good dogs. "A lot of people around here still talk about that deer," shares Bill. And rightly so, since there is only one mule deer buck from Jefferson County in the Nebraska records book, and it hangs in Bill Glenn's living room.

60

A Hunting Tradition
The Charles Hogeland Buck, 1994

Charles J. Hogeland

· 265⅛-inch non-typical
· Hayes County

I am only a young man, but hunting is a family tradition that is already dear to my heart. I went on my first hunting trip with my father, mother, and six-year-old brother when I was three months old. Hunting is bred into me, as I come from at least five generations of hunters.

In 1994 I turned sixteen, which had its advantages. I now had my driver's license and could go out driving to scout for deer on my own. As a sophomore in high school, I participated in sports. As soon as practice was over, I would head out into the surrounding country to scout for deer. I had received my hunting permit for the Frenchman unit of southwest Nebraska, so I knew that I would be hunting deer that November. Many hours were spent in the months preceding deer season looking through binoculars and a spotting scope, glassing the countryside.

One particular evening will stay in my mind forever. It was just prior to a huge red sunset. It had been very hot that day, and as the sun dropped in the sky I caught a glimpse of a very large buck and several does heading for a water hole. Through my spotting scope I realized that this deer was something special. I had never before seen such a spectacular rack. I counted at least eight points on each side, and several smaller projections when the buck turned his head just right. I watched the deer until they walked down a draw and disappeared.

I was very excited and raced home to tell my parents. For a while only Mom would believe that such a trophy could actually exist. Dad and Grandpa had seen a large buck at the close of muzzleloader season the previous year, but I don't think Dad believed me about the size and the mass of this deer. Then one evening, a week or so later, my dad ran into the house with a big grin and exclaimed, "I saw him!" That meant he was real. However, my brother was still a nonbeliever.

Opening day was fast approaching, so we made our annual stops and phone calls to local landowners to get permission to hunt. Three days before the season, I had to attend the National FFA Convention in Kansas City. Several of us at the convention had licenses for deer, so it was my job to get the advisor to leave on Friday, early enough for us to get home. Our advisor was my dad, so I didn't have to work too hard to leave a few hours early.

Saturday, November 12, started out like a typical morning. We woke up early, got dressed, and had breakfast. The only thing different was that we were all more excited than usual, since we were loading the vehicles to go hunting. On this hunt, I was joined by my dad, who was our guide; my sixty-two-year-old grandma, who was looking for any buck; and my brother, who was just going along, not really believing my story. As for me, I was only looking for "The Buck."

Finally, the time had come, and we were now off to find the monster buck. The weather that morning was overcast and chilly, with only a slight breeze blowing out of the south. We carefully checked each pocket in every draw we came to. As we approached each draw, tension mounted until the draw would prove empty. Occasionally we would flush a few pheasants or have a covey of quail explode at our feet, momentarily stopping our hearts. At about 9 a.m., we saw a few does as we continued to check draws, but no bucks.

Dad was the first to spot a nice buck, but he was a long way out at five hundred yards. Looking through the spotting scope we could see that he was at least a six-by-seven, with good width and some mass, but it wasn't my buck. Dad tried rattling the buck closer for Grandma to shoot and got him to come within one hundred fifty yards, but it was still too far out for Gram. The buck did stop for a short time, looked toward the sound of the clanging antlers, then toward the two does he was leaving behind. This time the does won out, as the rut was in full swing. After the deer disappeared, my dad asked me if I would have shot that nice buck. I replied, "No, it is only the first day, and I am in no hurry. Besides, Grandma was in the best position for a good shot."

We moved to another set of draws and immediately started seeing more does. I also noticed that these deer appeared to be nervous. The next pocket produced the reason for the watchful deer. As we approached and were able to see more of the draw, I saw movement. My heart started pounding, only to see a woolly white coyote run over the hill. The time was now 11:30 a.m. and another two pockets were ruled out.

The next pocket started out the same. I didn't see anything at first. Then all of a sudden, I saw three deer. I quickly realized that one looked awfully big and awfully familiar. What probably took seconds seemed to take hours—like super slow motion. I looked at the antlers and my mind went on autopilot. "Damn, it's him!" I said to myself. Range? One hundred fifty yards. I knew that my .270 was sighted in for two hundred yards, so it was a dead-on hold. I felt this shot was a piece of cake, since I had taken hunter safety and practiced many hours for this shot. I flicked the safety off, took a deep breath, settled the crosshairs behind his front shoulder, and squeezed the trigger. I prayed that my shot would be accurate and the deer would not suffer. The majestic buck reared up on his back legs like a horse. I chambered another round as the deer came to the ground on all fours. He started to move, so I took aim and squeezed the trigger one final time. The big buck was down for good.

A new excitement now started as I approached the deer cautiously. My dad, brother, and grandma came up to me and my trophy; Dad let out a loud yell, and my brother shook his head and my hand at the same time. Grandma later said that by the time she reached the three of us, I was just sitting beside my buck stroking his soft coat and admiring his antlers. I guess

FIG. 88. Sixteen-year-old Charles Hogeland with his 265⅛-inch non-typical state record. Photo courtesy of the Boone and Crockett Club.

I was in a state of shock, both happy and sad at the same time. I had great respect for that splendid animal.

Grandma had come prepared, pulling out her camera for some quick picture taking. By then my smiles told it all. Dad asked if he could have the honor of field dressing my deer, and asked jokingly if I wanted this small thing mounted. Little did he know that I was shaking too much to handle the job myself.

We finally got the deer loaded, and headed first to the landowner's house to thank him and show him the buck that his land produced. He could not believe that a deer that size was taken a half mile from his house and he had never seen it before.

We headed for home where Mom and Grandpa shared in the excitement as we relived the story. We then took the deer to the check-in station, where a few successful hunters congratulated me and admired the massive buck. On the way back home we had the buck weighed. My buck tipped the scales at two hundred ninety pounds, field dressed.

The following days were filled with many well wishes and handshakes. We estimated that close to five hundred people stopped to see the buck the first week. Many people suggested we make sure to have the deer scored. I knew that the buck was an exceptional trophy, but little did I know how exceptional. A few days after the big hunt, Dad, Mom, and I took my trophy to North Platte. Arrangements were made with Barry Johnson of Johnson's Taxidermy to do the mounting. He was impressed with the mass of the buck and suggested that we make an appointment with George Nason. Mr. Nason is the district manager of the Programs Section with the Nebraska Game and Parks Commission and is an official measurer for the Boone and Crockett Club.

On January 13, 1995, we watched patiently as Mr. Nason measured and remeasured the antlers. After what seemed like several hours, the totals were added. "It's official," Mr. Nason proclaimed. "Congratulations, Charlie, you are now the proud owner of the new Nebraska state-record non-typical rifle mule deer. This head is the most perfect non-typical specimen I have ever seen," he continued. [Indeed, the typical frame on this buck is extremely symmetrical, grossing 205²⁄₈ inches while netting 201⁰⁄₈. Add in the ten abnormal points totaling 64¹⁄₈ inches and you arrive at a net score of 265¹⁄₈ inches. The buck stood as the state record until 2001, when the Leo Dwyer buck from 1959 was officially measured at 265²⁄₈ inches.]

From that moment on, the chain of events continued. My hunting idol, Ted Nugent, called and later mailed a letter to congratulate me on my deer. In August 1996 I had the pleasure of meeting him in person. Ted is a musician, an avid bowhunter, a strong supporter of family hunting, and an active member of numerous hunting organizations.

On April 30, 1995, my trophy was ready to be picked up from the taxidermist. Barry Johnson had a big surprise awaiting me. Art Thomsen, the previous record holder came to North Platte to meet me and see my deer. His state record had stood since 1960. We spent part of the day swapping hunting stories and getting to know each other. Before departing, Mr. Thomsen left me with these words, "Don't worry that your deer broke my record, records were made to be broken."

61

Tough as Nails

The Dave Davis Buck, 1961

· 205⅞-inch non-typical
· Custer County

"We called him Nails, because he was tough as nails," chuckles Dave Davis, reminiscing about his time playing football with Tom Osbourne. Dave and Tom played football together at Hastings College in the late 1950s, as did their fathers in the 1920s. "I beat Tom for class president our freshman year, before they found out who he was, and who I was," continues Dave. Thinking he had zero chance of winning that election, Dave went home for the weekend, not finding out the results until his return. What was he doing all weekend? Hunting.

Now eighty-two years old, Dave grew up on a ranch in Custer County, southwest of Broken Bow. "We didn't have deer on our land until after the blizzard of 1949 that pushed deer into our area," recalls Dave. "When deer season finally opened, there were a lot of big bucks in that country. It was a fun time," recalls Dave. "We had about thirteen hundred acres with corn, milo, and alfalfa—the perfect way to fatten up a deer."

Dave's 1961 deer season began with a drive to his hunting land a few miles east of Callaway, Nebraska. Hunting with his brothers-in-law, Joel and Dick, they spotted several bucks in a pasture bordering his property. "A little later it sounded like a war broke out, and three of the guys over there filled their permits right away. But nothing big. We hunted all weekend, from one end of the pasture to the other, but didn't see anything," explains Dave.

On Monday Dave's father decided they had better drain the water out of the stock tanks so they would not freeze and crack. "My dad was a worker, not much time for hunting and fishing, so I was surprised when he told me I might as well bring my rifle," remembers Dave. Loading up in their International pickup, with Dave's .270 resting between them on the bench seat, they drove toward the ranch. As they passed through the gate Dave caught a glimpse of a rack disappearing over a nearby hill. Grabbing his .270 he took off after the buck, heading toward Sugar Loaf Mountain, the highest point on the property. "You could land an airplane on it. It was flat on top, big and tall."

Making his way toward Sugar Loaf, Dave was not expecting much since they had hunted this same area all weekend without seeing a good buck. Reaching the base of Sugar Loaf, he began climbing up the steep hillside. "Whenever I come to a hilltop or ridge, I slow down. Some guys just march over, spooking deer on the other side," shares Dave. Reaching the top, Dave slowly eased over the ridgetop, scanning the valley below. Spotting a group of six does and then antlers, he dropped to his stomach.

Knowing right away that it was a shooter buck, Dave inched forward on his belly. "There was a soapweed in front of me, so I slid my rifle through an opening in it and found the buck in my scope," remembers Dave. "I shot, and he took off down the ridge and then stopped and looked back." Again finding the buck in his scope, Dave shot repeatedly as the giant buck bounded over a ridge. "I'm looking down at my scope, thinking it was off, when my dad comes up in the pickup."

After driving a short distance toward where the buck had run, the two got out to search on foot. Cresting a rise they spotted antlers sticking up above the grass. "My dad got so excited he yelled, 'My God, that is an elk!'" says Dave. After struggling to load the big-bodied buck into the pickup, they drove into Broken Bow. "We drove around the square, showing the dentist and my brother-in-law at Holcomb Drug store. That was really a fun time."

FIG. 89. Dave Davis hoisting up his $205\frac{7}{8}$-inch Custer County buck. Photo courtesy of Dave Davis.

Next they took the buck to the town elevator, where it tipped the scales at three hundred thirty pounds.

"I wasn't even going to do anything with the head and antlers, but the banker called me and told me I needed to get it mounted. We went back to the packing plant, found the head and antlers, and put it on dry ice. I shipped it out to Jonas Brothers Taxidermy in Denver. Cost me sixty-five dollars just to ship it," shares Dave, shaking his head.

It was worth the money. The Dave Davis buck is massive, with an inside spread of $24\frac{3}{8}$ inches and main beams of $27\frac{4}{8}$ and $26\frac{4}{8}$ inches. The four typical points are exceptional, with the G2 points measuring $14\frac{6}{8}$ and $16\frac{5}{8}$ inches. The G4 points, often much shorter than the G2 points, are exceptionally long, measuring $13\frac{4}{8}$ and $12\frac{6}{8}$ inches. With seven abnormal sticker points totaling twelve inches, the buck nets $205\frac{7}{8}$ inches non-typical. It currently stands as the third-largest non-typical firearm buck from Custer County.

After spending nearly an hour talking with Dave and his wife, Ladonna, in their small assisted-living apartment in Lincoln, a nurse enters delivering medication. Reaching down, Dave rubs his calf, explaining he needs to take medication to relieve the pain in his leg. "I nearly blew this leg off with my deer rifle," he shares with a grimace.

"I was getting out of my truck to shoot a coyote with my .270, and BOOM! I got on the CB and the fire chief picks up and I say, 'I'm over east, you got to hurry, I'm bleeding like a stuck hog!' I crawled into the back of the pickup, found a piece of barbed wire, and twisted it around my leg to keep from bleeding to death. I had to concentrate on not passing out. I spent a lot of time in the hospital that year, but I still went deer hunting."

Tough as nails.

62

The Little Girl with a Spoon

The Delman Tuller Buck, 1965

· 249⁶/₈-inch non-typical

· Red Willow County

In 1962 the NGPC began its Big Game Trophy Records Program, awarding citations for outstanding Nebraska big-game trophies, with the process for entering a trophy not changing much over the decades. After waiting the required sixty-day drying period, an official measurer, trained and certified by the B&C, measures the antlers or horns and fills out and signs an official scoresheet. If the trophy meets the minimum requirements for entry, the hunter submits a copy of the scoresheet to the NGPC. If everything is in order, the trophy is entered into the Big Game Trophy Records book under the appropriate category and the hunter issued an official citation.

The records book is housed at the NGPC headquarters in Lincoln. Every scoresheet submitted since 1962 has been three-hole punched and placed alphabetically by the hunter's last name into black three-ring binders. Each trophy category has a binder, or in some cases several binders. With thirty-two different categories in the records book, the binders take up some serious shelf space. Recently all this information was made available online in a searchable database.

The Big Game Trophy Records Program is essentially a historic archive of big-game hunting in Nebraska. The scoresheets contain not only the exact

FIG. 90. Barbara Anne (Tuller) DeBolt sits on her father's giant 249⅝-inch buck, holding a spoon. Photo courtesy of Barbara Anne DeBolt.

measurements of each animal and the county where they were killed but also each hunter's name, address, telephone number, and on newer entries, email addresses. This information proved indispensable in researching this book, especially in relation to contacting trophy owners. However, the additional information oftentimes included with the scoresheet is also fascinating. For example, correspondence between hunters and the NGPC explaining certain aspects of the trophy or entry process; hometown newspaper clippings stapled to the scoresheet; notes handwritten in the margins of the scoresheet or scrawled across the top of the page; and finally, wonderful historical photographs.

One particular black-and-white photograph from 1965 really caught my attention. The picture shows Delman Tuller squatting next to his giant 249⅝-inch non-typical mule deer, while another hunter, clad in overalls, cigarette dangling from his mouth, sits on a much smaller buck. In between the two hunters, and sitting on Delman's buck, is a cute little girl holding what appears to be a large spoon.

With only an out-of-date McCook address on the scoresheet, I searched online for information about Delman Tuller. Eventually finding an obituary for Delman's wife, Miriam, who passed away in 2017, I saw that it noted her husband had passed away in 1976. It also mentioned they had two children, a son Stephen and a daughter Barbara Anne DeBolt, who was now living in Oklahoma. Could this be the little girl in the photograph?

Using Facebook I found a Barbara Anne Debolt living in Oklahoma and sent her a message. Bingo—I had found the little girl in the photograph. "Yes, that's me, and for some reason I am holding a spoon and wearing one of my mother's hats backward," shares Barbara. "And who sits their little girl on top of a dead deer?" Apparently Delman Tuller.

Delman was born in 1925, near Lebanon, a small town southeast of McCook in Red Willow County. After graduating high school in May of 1943, he joined the navy, serving until 1946. Returning after the war he married Miriam in 1949, with the couple settling down in McCook. A plumber by trade, he later worked for the McCook school system. Sadly cancer ended his life in 1976, when he was only fifty-one and Barbara was only fourteen.

Barbara, who was three years old in the picture, does not remember posing for the photograph. Nevertheless, she does remember that her father loved the outdoors, especially hunting and fishing. "We had a cabin on Cambridge Lake (what locals call Henry Strunk Lake), and Dad would take me fishing there. He didn't take me hunting, but he loved to fish," remembers Barbara. "I remember Mom telling me that she married someone who always wanted to hunt and fish."

By all accounts Delman was not only a passionate outdoorsman but a successful one as well. Barbara shared numerous pictures of her father posing with mule deer and whitetail bucks he had shot over the years. However, it was the giant mule deer buck Delman shot in 1965 that etched his name into the Nebraska records book. Little is known about the actual hunt, except that it took place on November 6 in Red Willow County. We can assume

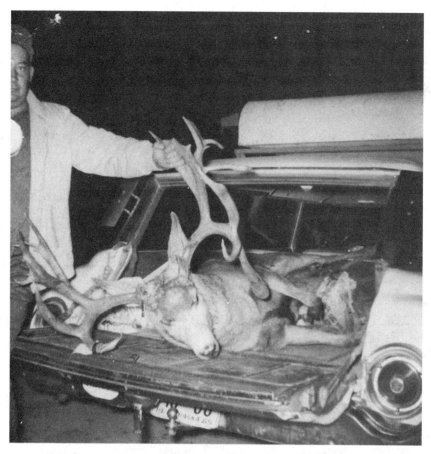

FIG. 91. Delman Tuller shows off his buck in the back of his station wagon. Photo courtesy of Barbara Anne DeBolt.

he was hunting with his neighbor, Tom Musgrave, who is the man posing with his buck in the photograph.

Fortunately the scoresheet survives, telling the mathematical story of one of the greatest mule deer ever shot in Nebraska. The first thing you notice about the Delman Tuller buck is the giant 10⅛-inch clublike drop tine stretching below the left beam. With eight additional abnormal points on the left side and five on the right, the buck has 57 total inches of abnormal points. The typical frame, grossing 197⅛ inches is massive, with both G2 points measuring over sixteen inches and all four G2 and G3 points over ten.

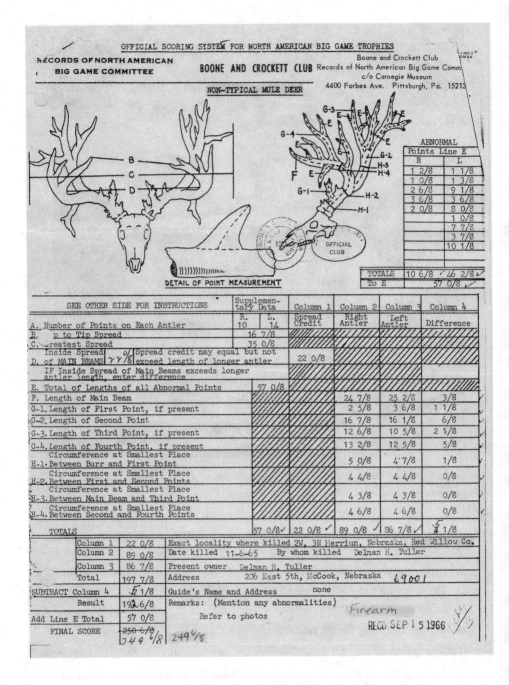

FIG. 92. Delman Tuller scoresheet. Note the 10⅛-inch drop tine off the left antler and the 57⅝ total inches of abnormal points. Courtesy of the Boone and Crockett Club.

Netting 249⅝ inches, it was the second-largest non-typical in the Nebraska records book for over thirty years, behind only the Art Thomsen buck from 1960. A testament to its size, it still currently ranks fourth after fifty-four years.

Barbara, although extremely excited I contacted her, wishes she had learned more from her parents while they were still alive. "I wish I would have talked with my mom more about Dad's hunting when she was still alive. We have a lot of pictures, but they aren't very organized. I hope others can learn from this and take the time to talk, share, and write things down," says Barbara.

63

Working Cattle

The Matthew Lake Buck, 2017

· 238⅛-inch non-typical
· Keith County

From 1956 to 1965 Nebraska license plates included the tagline "The Beef State." And rightly so, since raising cattle for beef spurred the settlement and development of the state and still accounts for a good portion of the economy. Nebraska has far more cattle than people, five million verses less than two million.[1] Nebraska leads the nation in the number of cattle on feed and cattle slaughtered, and contains the top three cattle-producing counties in the country: Cherry, Custer, and Holt.

Why does Nebraska produce so much beef? Its unique geography. The state contains over twenty-three million acres of rangeland, with half of this in the grass-covered and largely untillable Sandhills. Underlying most of the state is the High Plains aquifer, providing an abundance of water for cattle but also water to irrigate millions of acres of corn, more corn than all but two other states, Iowa and Illinois. This corn in turn fattens, or finishes, millions of cattle prior to slaughter.

Matthew Lake knows all this. He has spent his entire life working cattle. Born in 1983, he grew up in the mountains near Evergreen, Colorado, eventually working on cattle ranches in Colorado and Wyoming. In 2009 Matt and his wife, Alyssa, moved back to her home in Keith County, Nebraska, near Paxton, and began building their own cattle herd.

While growing up in Colorado, Matt also became a big-game hunter. "I shot my first elk, a cow, when I was thirteen. I grew up on elk meat," shares Matt. After moving to Nebraska his big-game hunting shifted to deer. "I've done less hunting since moving to Nebraska due to my workload, and having four small children, but I still get out some."

After living in Nebraska for eight years, Matt had shot some Nebraska whitetails, but no mule deer. That would change in dramatic fashion during the late fall of 2017. With less than two weeks before rifle season, Matt first spotted an incredibly large buck. "I was weaning cows, near the feedlot, and he showed up at dusk, trailing some does. I knew right away he was a special buck, and even though I had been grazing and rotating cattle all summer I had never seen him before," recalls Matt. Not seeing a particular buck is understandable considering the country. Sandwiched between the North and South Platte Rivers, Matt refers to this broken, rough country as the "hard hills." Consisting of clay and gravel, it is literally harder than the nearby Sandhills, containing deep draws and rugged canyons. "The whitetail stay down in the river valleys, while the mule deer tend to stay up in the hard hills."

Prior to opening day of rifle season Matt spotted the massive non-typical several more times. One morning just after dawn he saw the buck standing about one hundred fifty yards away. "He had torn off an entire limb of a cedar tree and was carrying it in his rack. He was all puffed up, and by the way he was carrying himself, he knew he was lord of the country," shares Matt. The evening before opening morning Matt had one more memorable encounter with the buck. "Another guy and I were riding on horseback, pushing cattle to the corral to pen them up. We spotted him about a quarter mile back on a ridgeline with some does. He was silhouetted against the sky, and the guy riding with me was just awestruck by his size."

Opening morning began with heavy fog, and for Matt, work. Heading out in his pickup to feed calves, he had mixed feelings. If he spotted the

FIG. 93. Matthew Lake holding his breathtaking 238⅛-inch Keith County buck. Photo courtesy of the author.

buck he would have a tough decision: go after the buck or uphold his work responsibilities. Sure enough he spotted the buck from his pickup. "I had the veterinarian and some help coming to pregnancy-test cows at seven thirty, so I knew I couldn't go after him," shares Matt. With all the trucks and ensuing commotion, Matt was certain they had blown the buck out of the area.

After completing his morning's work and eating lunch, Matt drove back to the area, arriving at about three thirty in the afternoon. With the sky now clear and the temperature mild, he glassed the surrounding draws from a hilltop. Unbelievably Matt soon spotted the big buck with a group of does, leaving a nearby well and moving slowly his way. Unfortunately the northwest wind was carrying his scent toward them. Taking off his spurs, Matt took off on foot, hoping to get the wind on the buck. "I went into the hills to try and get sideways of him so he wouldn't smell me, but I got caught in the open by a smaller buck. I backed out and went clear around through the canyons to try and get around them," remembers Matt.

Crawling under fences and periodically peeking over ridgetops, Matt eventually lost sight of the buck. Coming once again to the crest of a saddle, he finally spotted the buck chasing does about two hundred yards away. "I got a good rest in the prone position and took a shot. The buck dropped, disappearing into a patch of weeds. The does just stood there, so I decided to give him some time," shares Matt. With his heart still racing with adrenaline, Matt sat back and waited for a half hour before making his way toward the buck.

Reaching a flat about one hundred yards from the buck, Matt spotted the buck getting to his feet. Taking a rest on a fence post, Matt sent another round through his .30-06, dropping the buck for good. "I usually pride myself in one-shot kills, but I was really worked up and excited, so I probably rushed that first shot," Matt concedes. As he walked the final one hundred yards of the hunt, he was still uncertain as to how large the buck was. "I started pulling weeds out of his rack and more and more tines kept showing up. He was much more of a buck than I realized."

The Matthew Lake buck, scoring 238⅛ inches, currently ranks seventh in the non-typical firearm category in the Nebraska records book. With an inside spread of 22⅛ inches and an outside spread of 31⅛, the buck's typical frame grosses 201⅞ inches and nets 189⅞. The G2 points are particularly impressive, measuring 19⅝ inches on the right and 17⅞ inches on the left. With seven abnormal points on the right totaling 35⅞ inches and two on the left totaling 12⅜ inches, it is a magnificent-looking non-typical buck.

Despite the story and pictures of his buck spreading like wildfire and making him somewhat of a local deer-hunting celebrity, Matt speaks humbly, keeping it all in perspective. Sitting in his living room, with the mounted rack on the wall next to a large picture window, he shares his thoughts. "I like that it came off our place and that I get to enjoy hunting where I live and work. I can sit here, look out the window, and see where that buck lived, where he ate. I give the Lord credit for letting me shoot something like that. In the grand scheme of things, it's just a deer, but while we are here it is a blessing."

64

Nebraska's Oldest Trophy

The R. A. Wirz Buck, 1945

· 177⅞-inch non-typical

· Thomas County

Sometime in the early fall of 1945, R. A. Wirz walked out to his mailbox in Halsey, Nebraska, and peering inside, pulled out a letter from the Game, Forestation, and Parks Commission. He was going deer hunting! R.A. was one of the lucky few to draw a tag for the first Nebraska deer season since 1907.

R. A. Wirz was born in Nemaha County, Nebraska, on Christmas Day 1902. That same year University of Nebraska botany professor Dr. Charles E. Bessey, with the assistance of Gifford Pinchot, the first Forest Service chief, convinced President Theodore Roosevelt to set aside two treeless tracts of land in the Sandhills as "forest reserves."[1] The tract near Halsey, known initially as the Dismal River Forest Reserve and then later the Bessey Ranger District, also included the Charles E. Bessey Nursery for producing tree seedlings. In 1903 the first tree seedlings were planted into the sand, with the goal of creating the "World's Largest Man-made Forest." This forest, Dr. Bessey believed, would help offset an impending national shortage of timber.

In 1911, as some of the first large-scale plantings of jack and yellow pine were ongoing at the forest reserve, nine-year-old R.A. moved with his family to homestead land north of Halsey. After completing his schooling in Halsey,

R.A. began working odd jobs for neighbors before finding employment with the U.S. Forest Service.

After marrying Marie Rodocker, the couple purchased the general store in Halsey, which they would operate for the next thirty years. "He was very well known in and around Halsey because he owned Wirz Cash Store for many years. It was right across the street from the Double T bar," shares his son Bob. "From 1946 until 1986 he was also a rural mail carrier, traveling a fifty-five-mile route up through Purdum and Elsmere. It was often joked that ranchers could set their watch by the time he would come by with the mail."

Like most Nebraskans of his generation, R.A. hunted pheasant, waterfowl, and small game. It was his only option. After decades of unregulated sport and market hunting, deer in Nebraska were on the brink of extinction by the early 1900s. The year R.A. was born, the Game Commission's biennial report noted that about fifty deer remained in the state, along the Dismal River in Thomas County.[2] In 1912 one of these remaining mule deer was poached south of Thedford, with the hunter apprehended and the antlers subsequently mounted and put on display in a saloon in Falls City, Nebraska.[3] There were probably other small pockets of deer in the Pine Ridge, Wildcat Hills, and perhaps along some other river corridors, but no one knows for sure how many. Regardless, the population was too small and dispersed to withstand hunting pressure, so in 1907 the state legislature closed the season statewide.

Over the next few decades the herd along the Dismal River slowly grew, and taking advantage of the cover and habitat provided by the tree plantings, migrated north onto the national forest. By 1935 the population on the forest numbered nearly two hundred and by 1944, over eight hundred.[4] Forest personnel began noting damage to tree plantings and were becoming concerned about deer overpopulating the forest. In response, the Nebraska legislature authorized a special deer season on the forest from December 1 through 21, issuing five hundred permits.

Days before the 1945 opener, hunters from across the state began arriving at the forest for the first modern-day Nebraska deer season. The excitement was palpable, since most had never hunted deer and in many cases had never been to the national forest. R.A. described the scene to Jon Farrar in

FIG. 94. R. A. Wirz with the buck he shot during Nebraska's first modern-day deer season in 1945. Photo courtesy of Bob Wirz.

a *Nebraskaland* article from 1982, "A local man here set up a kitchen to feed people, and they housed them, too. Some stayed in those barracks, a few came with their own tents, and a few stayed with the hotel downtown and perhaps some at Thedford and Dunning. Anyhow, everyone was taken care of in nice shape and they had a lot of fun, I think."[5]

Many brought old military rifles or borrowed coyote guns—.30-30s, .35 calibers, and 30-40 Krags. Six hunters shot deer with shotguns. R.A., who did not own a rifle, borrowed a .30-06 military rifle from his brother-in-law. As you can imagine, keeping everyone safe was a major concern, so Game Commission employees set up a sighting-in range and held a pre-hunt briefing. R.A. explains, "The night before the hunt, they had a big meeting out there at the old CCC [Civilian Conservation Corp] camp, in one of the barracks. All the fellows gathered around and the warden from Nebraska gave a talk on safety . . . and how a fellow should always be sure you have a background to shoot into, because with these high-powered rifles, you know, why someone could get hurt. Fortunately everything worked out beautifully in spite of the fact that the next day, after that meeting, the first day of the hunt, we had the doggondest snowstorm you've ever seen. Visibility was at times almost nothing, and it was really a scary thing to be out there."[6]

Levi Mohler, a Game Commission biologist expresses similar sentiments in a 1946 article in *Outdoor Nebraska*: "Many of the December hunters saw the forest for the first time.[7] Seeing the forest was an eye-opener to many of them, and the chance to bag a Nebraska deer made the setup really attractive to the outdoorsmen, some of whom were taking their first outing since the war began. So from the time the first hunter checked in, until far into the night, the headquarters checking station, the mess hall, and the barracks were abuzz with hunting talk."

Over the course of that first deer season, hunters bagged three hundred sixty-one deer, of which only two were whitetails. Eighty-seven of these deer were over six and a half years old, equating to some outstanding bucks. Although short on details, we know that sometime during the season, R.A. used his borrowed .30-06 to down a trophy non-typical mule deer. Fortunately someone snapped a photograph of R.A. posing proudly with his buck, cigarette in his mouth and the car trunk open and ready for loading the deer.

According to Bob, this was the only deer his father ever shot. In 1982 R.A. had the buck officially measured at 170⅝ inches, which subsequently became the oldest entry in the Nebraska records book. He passed away in 1995 at the age of ninety-two and is buried in the Purdum Cemetery, near his old mail route. His historic mule deer hangs above a stairwell at NGPC headquarters in Lincoln, with a small gold plaque underneath stating: "This deer was taken in 1945 by R. A. Wirz at the Bessey Division of the Nebraska National Forest near Halsey during Nebraska's first modern-day firearm deer hunting season."

65

Better Late Than Never

The Leo Dwyer Buck, 1959

· 265²/₈-inch non-typical
· Wheeler County

Leo N. Dwyer claimed his hunting fame late in life. Born on a ranch on Beaver Creek, west of Elgin, Nebraska, in 1923, he would not go on his first Nebraska deer hunt until 1959. On that fateful hunt he would shoot an incredibly massive mule deer. However, Leo would wait forty-two years for it to become the current state record!

Much of the story of Leo's buck is unknown, including the exact date of the hunt. We do know that he was hunting on his ranch in Wheeler County with his ten-year-old son. When they came across a group of half-a-dozen big bucks, Leo picked one out and killed it at two hundred yards with his Winchester Model 88 chambered in .308.[1]

After getting the buck home Leo sawed the antlers off and hung them in his home, where they stayed unmounted and unscored for decades. Leo told his story to Joe Duggan, a *Lincoln Journal Star* reporter: "To be honest with you, I was pretty green and didn't know what I had or I would have had it mounted."[2] Leo eventually had the antlers officially measured and the scoresheet sent to the B&C for entry into the records book. Forty-two years after he shot it, Leo's buck was certified as the new Nebraska firearm

FIG. 95. The 265⅔-inch Leo Dwyer buck beat the old state record by one-eighth of an inch and is on display at the Cabela's store in Sidney. Photo courtesy of the author.

non-typical state record, eclipsing the Charles Hogeland buck from Hayes County by a mere one-eighth of an inch.

The Leo Dwyer buck has twenty-seven points, with nine abnormal points on the right side and eight on the left. The length of the seventeen abnormal points totals 74⅛ inches, giving the rack a unique serrated appearance. The typical frame is equally impressive, with an inside spread of 24⅝ inches and main beams of 25⅝ and 24⅝ inches. The four scorable typical points are long, with both G2 points over fourteen inches and both G4 points over eleven. The typical frame grosses just over two hundred inches and nets an impressive 191⅛ inches.

Leo eventually sold the antlers to Cabela's for an undisclosed amount. If

Records of
North American
Big Game

Drive
5980
1888

BOONE AND CROCKETT CLUB

OFFICIAL SCORING SYSTEM FOR NORTH AMERICAN BIG

NON-TYPICAL MULE DEER

MINIMUM SCORES
AWARDS   ALL-TIME
215   230

	Right Antler	Left Antler
	2 2/8	1 1/8
	2 2/8	3 4/8
	1 7/8	13 2/8
	2 2/8	8 1/8
	2 5/8	2 2/8
	4 1/8	3 3/8
	3 2/8	3 7/8
	11 7/8	3 7/8
	4 4/8	
SUBTOTALS	34 4/8	39 5/8
E. TOTAL		74 1/8

SEE OTHER SIDE FOR INSTRUCTIONS		COLUMN 1	COLUMN 2	COLUMN 3	COLUMN 4
		Spread Credit	Right Antler	Left Antler	Difference
A. No. Points on Right Antler	14	No. Points on Left Antler	13		
B. Tip to Tip Spread	21 3/8	C. Greatest Spread	32 7/8		
D. Inside Spread of Main Beams	24 5/8	SPREAD CREDIT MAY EQUAL BUT NOT EXCEED LONGER MAIN BEAM	24 5/8		
F. Length of Main Beam			25 5/8	24 5/8	1 0/8
G-1. Length of First Point, If Present			3 7/8	3 8/8	1/8
G-2. Length of Second Point			14 7/8	14 0/8	7/8
G-3. Length of Third Point, If Present			13 3/8	8 5/8	4 6/8
G-4. Length of Fourth Point, If Present			11 4/8	11 0/8	6/8
H-1. Circumference at Smallest Place Between Burr and First Point			6 2/8	5 6/8	4/8
H-2. Circumference at Smallest Place Between First and Second Points			5 6/8	5 5/8	1/8
H-3. Circumference at Smallest Place Between Main Beam and Third Point			4 2/8	4 7/8	3/8
H-4. Circumference at Smallest Place Between Second and Fourth Points			5 7/8	6 4/8	5/8
TOTALS		24 5/8	91 5/8	83 7/8	9 0/8

B & C BIG GAME AWARDS
24
1998 - 2000

ADD	Column 1	24 5/8	Exact Locality Where Killed:	5-2-01
	Column 2	91 5/8	Date Killed:	Hunter: Leo Dwyer
	Column 3	83 7/8	Owner:	Telephone #:
	Subtotal	200 1/8	Owner's Address:	
SUBTRACT Column 4		9 0/8	Guide's Name and Address:	
	Subtotal	191 1/8	Remarks: (Mention Any Abnormalities or Unique Qualities)	
ADD Line E Total		74 1/8		
FINAL SCORE		265 2/8	Ron Sherer Ab England	

FIG. 96. Leo Dwyer scoresheet. This buck has seventeen abnormal points totaling
74⅛ inches. Courtesy of the Boone and Crockett Club.

you visit the Cabela's store in Sidney, you can see the antlers on a full body mount, bedded behind a sign that says NEBRASKA STATE RECORD.

Leo passed away in 2015 at the age of ninety-one, leaving behind his first wife, five children, twenty-three grandchildren, and forty-seven great-grandchildren. Although his family is his most important legacy, his name and magnificent buck are part of the hunting legacy of Nebraska.

66

30 S 10 W

The Jack Kreycik Buck, 1963

· 227⅛-inch non-typical
· Cherry County

No one knows exactly where Jack S. Kreycik shot his giant non-typical mule deer. On the official scoresheet, in the blank after "Exact Locality Where Killed," the official measurer typed "30 S 10 W Valentine, Nebraska." Later, using a pencil, someone wrote, "Cherry." If we trust these directions, Jack shot his buck west of Highway 83 on the southern edge of the Valentine National Wildlife Refuge in eastern Cherry County. Jack's son David disagrees, thinking he most likely shot it on Fairfield Flats west of Wood Lake, Nebraska, since this was one of his favorite hunting spots.

In either location Jack was hunting in the Sandhills, one of the most beautiful areas in Nebraska and arguably the world. A deceptively expansive and rugged landscape, these grass-and-yucca-covered rolling sand dunes provide mule deer bucks room to roam and grow impressive headgear. But, as anyone who has ever hunted the Sandhills on foot for deer or grouse can attest, it is physically demanding. Shoot a deer where you cannot drive and it is going to be a brutal drag or pack out. This is why many deer hunts in the Sandhills entail driving ranch roads and glassing for distant bucks. Once a buck is spotted, the stalk begins. Or the deer is shot from the truck window or with the rifle resting across the hood. Although it is illegal to shoot from

FIG. 97. One of the most stunning bucks in the records book, the Jack Kreycik buck scores 227⅛ inches. Photo courtesy of the author.

a public road in Nebraska, you can shoot big game from a private road as long as the vehicle is not moving.

On November 3, 1963, Jack and his hunting buddy, Howard Miller, were driving a Sandhill ranch road, looking for a buck to shoot. According to Jack's nephew, Bob Cumwood, they spotted the buck laying in some buck brush and Jack shouted, "Stop the damn truck, that's my buck." They yelled at the buck to try to get it to stand up, but it wouldn't, so he just shot it laying down." David agrees, "It wasn't stalked or hunted. I think he just came upon it. Dad had never seen the buck before. Dad was shooting a 7mm Remington Magnum and he always shot deer in the neck, so as not to destroy any meat, and I'm sure this was no exception. He was an excellent shot."

Regardless of where or how it was shot, the Jack Kreycik buck is one of the most impressive mule deer ever shot in the Cornhusker State. The buck's typical frame is extremely symmetrical with only 2⅞ inches of deductions. Both G2 points measure exactly 16⅛ inches while the G4 points are 14⅖ and 14⅝ inches. With an inside spread of 25⅛ inches and both main beams over twenty-five inches, the typical frame grosses 198⅝ and nets 195⅛. With six abnormal points on the right and four on the left totaling 32⅝ inches, the buck's final score is 227⅛ inches.

The buck currently ranks as the fifteenth-largest firearm non-typical in the Nebraska records book and the second-largest from Cherry County. Unfortunately Jack passed away in 2010, leaving us guessing as to the exact location of his historic hunt.

67

Dreaming about Nebraska

The Paul Mecouch Buck, 2007

· 212⁶/₈-inch non-typical
· Sioux County

After living in a place for a while, you start taking it for granted. You begin dreaming about other places, better places, places with more interesting people, tastier food, and nicer weather. The proverbial greener grass. Nebraska hunters are no different, possibly worse, dreaming about hunting other places, other states. Land with bigger bucks and bulls, constant covey rises, and sky-darkening flocks of flushing pheasants.

Remember this, fellow Cornhuskers—as you sit daydreaming about other places, there are hunters in those other places daydreaming about Nebraska. Take New Jerseyan Paul Mecouch, for example. Paul has been fortunate enough to hunt across North America, from Canada to Texas to Alaska to Alabama, and points in between. Yet, where does he choose to spend months hunting every year? Nebraska. "My son and I consider Nebraska like a second home. We have made some great friendships and enjoy it every time we come out," shares Paul.

So how did two guys from New Jersey end up making Nebraska their second hunting home? Paul's son Brian explains, "When I was growing up, my father used to manage a big vegetable and game bird farm in southern New Jersey. The owner, an avid outdoorsman, actually attended Chadron

State College in the 1970s and recommended I take a look at it for college. Since I wanted to get away from the hustle and bustle of New Jersey, I visited the college in 2005 and decided to attend. The area grew on me so much that I stayed and got my MBA as well."

After arriving at Chadron State, Brian began exploring and bowhunting the Pine Ridge, building a network of friends and securing access to hunting properties. Hearing from his son about the great hunting, Paul decided to make a trip west to hunt the 2007 December muzzleloader season.

Nebraska welcomed him with a good old-fashioned blizzard. "When I arrived it was a snowstorm, with the forecast showing days of blizzard conditions and extremely cold temperatures," remembers Paul. Venturing out into the frigid cold on opening morning, Paul and Brian decided to start their hunt on a ranch west of Crawford, ground Brian knew well. After setting up they began rattling, hoping to draw a mature buck within range of Paul's open-sighted .50 caliber Thompson Center. Sure enough, within a matter of minutes a nice whitetail buck came within range. Although Paul wanted to shoot, Brian told him to hold off and wait for something bigger. "It was good advice, because only a short time later an older, wider five-by-five ran straight to us." With the buck at thirty yards, Paul placed the iron sights behind the shoulder and pulled the trigger. Nothing. Quickly thumbing another primer on the nipple, Paul tried again. "I had my first Nebraska buck in the pickup by mid-morning."

With snow still falling hard Paul and Brian drove back to the ranch where they were staying. After unloading the buck and relaxing for a couple hours, they decided to try to fill Paul's second buck tag. Not wanting to go far in the storm, they decided to hunt the property they were on. With deeper draws and a series of canyons and buttes, it held a mixture of whitetail and mule deer.

Pulling the truck in to start their hunt, Paul spotted a large mule deer buck standing about two hundred fifty yards away. "It was snowing so hard that it was difficult to tell how big he was," recalls Paul. While discussing what to do, Brian began videotaping the buck in the falling snow. "After a few minutes of videoing and studying the buck with binoculars, we realized he was bigger than we thought."

They decided to try a stalk. With the snow now nearly a foot deep, Paul made his way slowly toward the giant non-typical. After closing the distance considerably, the buck spooked, disappearing over a ridge with several does in tow. With Brian now joining him, they followed the tracks to the top of the ridge and peered over into the next valley. The buck was gone. Sending Brian back to the house, Paul began tracking the buck alone. "My plan was to track the buck and then just walk back to the house," explains Paul.

After following the buck's tracks in the fresh snow for a good distance, Paul realized the buck was circling, leading him across a large flat toward yet another steep hill, and farther and farther away from the ranch house. "I must have hiked for a couple miles in deep snow, and I knew it wasn't a good decision to keep following the tracks," remembers Paul.

Back at the ranch house, with the sky darkening and the temperature falling, Brian was starting to worry. Grabbing a flashlight he headed out and walked the canyon toward where Paul was hunting. "Luckily I made it back just after dark," shares Paul.

While warming up inside the ranch house, they made a plan to go after the buck the following morning. Arriving shortly after dawn near the large hill the buck was heading toward the evening before, they uncased the spotting scope and began glassing. They quickly spotted the massive buck bedded in the snow just below the crest of a flat-topped bluff. From his bed the buck had a commanding view of everything below him.

Examining the location of the buck and the surrounding terrain, Paul knew his best option was to climb the opposite side of the bluff, cross its flat top, and try to spot the buck from the edge of the ledge. After driving a mile to the backside of the hill, Brian dropped Paul off and then headed back to watch the stalk through the spotting scope. Paul meanwhile began slowly climbing the backside of the hill through the deep snow and bitter cold. "Once on top I slowly approached the ledge, hoping to mark the buck. As I worked my way along the edge, I spotted the buck staring straight at me!" remembers Paul.

With a sudden snow squall making it difficult to see, Paul slowly shouldered his muzzleloader and found the buck in the iron sights. "I aimed

FIG. 98. Paul (*right*) and Brian Mecouch with the current muzzleloader state record shot during a snowstorm in Sioux County. Photo courtesy of Paul Mecouch.

between the shoulders, hoping the gun wouldn't misfire again," recalls Paul. *Ka-boom!* Peering through the rolling smoke and snow, Paul saw the giant buck leap over the edge of a rock ledge and disappear.

Having seen the entire stalk through the spotting scope, Brian marked where the buck dove over the ledge. Making his way across the open pasture toward the base of the steep embankment, he searched for signs of a hit. Quickly finding the buck lying dead in the snow-covered sagebrush, he began counting points. After finishing he yelled up the hill toward his dad, "He's a ten-by-twelve!"

The Paul Mecouch buck is currently the Nebraska muzzleloader nontypical state record. The buck's typical frame sports nearly matching main beams of 24⅛ and 24⅞ inches and an inside spread of 23⅔ inches. The brow tines are each over four inches, while the G2 points are both over thirteen.

The typical frame grosses 181⅝ inches and nets 177⅖. With twelve abnormal points totaling 35⅖ inches, the buck nets 212⅝ inches.

After his first two days of hunting Nebraska, Paul had a trophy whitetail and a state-record mule deer. "I would say Nebraska is my lucky state. We had no clue that a state-record buck was in the area, and without that snowstorm we may have never spotted him," says Paul.

It's probably safe to say that right now there are two New Jersey hunters daydreaming about Nebraska.

68

So Much Horn

The Ken Hollopeter Buck, 1979

- 227⅝-inch non-typical
- Cherry County

Like many in the Nebraska Sandhills, Ken Hollopeter's 1979 hunt began in the hills, glassing down into the meadows. With his good friend Perry Shaul riding shotgun in his 1971 Blaser, the two drove ranch roads near the Valentine National Wildlife Refuge, checking tree groves and glassing meadows for bucks. Checking a meadow a couple miles away, they spotted three deer. Ken remembers the moment he was peering through his riflescope well: "We assumed it was a whitetail, because it had so much horn."

Ken grew up south of Wood Lake, midway between Valentine and Ainsworth. Living in the Sandhills in the 1960s, he remembers a different countryside, one with few mule deer and no whitetails. "There weren't many deer in that country back then, and certainly no whitetail. I had an uncle in Fremont who would come out grouse hunting with his friends. I would drive them around through the meadows and they would shoot right out of the bed of the pickup," remembers Ken. "I went deer hunting, with another uncle, for the first time in 1972, when I was sixteen. We went up by the Niobrara River, hunting for whitetails, and I sat on a stump and watched a couple does walk by, but I didn't shoot anything."

Ken would not go deer hunting again until 1976, when a friend took him on a hunt near Holdrege. "I shot my first deer, a fork-horned mule deer, and I was hooked," remembers Ken. His mom, Arlene, became his favored hunting partner. "I would rather hunt deer with my mom than anybody else. She would just get so excited. She would shoot a deer every year and process it herself." In 1978 Arlene shot her first buck, a three-point, which now hangs on her grandson's wall.

The following year Ken began the rifle season by first helping his mom and uncle get their deer. Later on opening day, Perry, who now owns The Gun Cabinet in Valentine, gave Ken a call. "He didn't have a deer tag that year, so he called and asked me if I was going hunting the next day. I told him I was but that I hadn't seen any good ones yet. He replies, 'Well, over by the refuge there is a really big whitetail,'" remembers Ken.

The next day, after spotting what they thought was the giant whitetail, they climbed back into the Blaser and circled back around the meadow. Parking the truck and using trees and old outbuildings as cover, they crept closer but eventually lost sight of the buck. Confident the buck was still in the meadow, they used the only cover available—haystacks. "We went from haystack to haystack, but we still couldn't find him. We duck-crawled for several hundred yards, before finally spotting the tips of his horns," says Ken.

Crawling on hands and knees, they closed the distance further. "We peeked over the hill but couldn't see him. We figured we had crawled past him, so we backtracked. We peek back over the hill, and he peeks right back at us," Ken recalls with a smile. The giant non-typical had bedded down and was staring at them from only thirty-five yards away. "He just laid there, and wouldn't stand up. Perry finally stood up behind me and waved at him."

Sitting on one knee behind Perry, Ken watched as the massive buck rose and stood facing him. Lifting his Winchester Model 70 in .243, he shot the buck dead center in the chest. The buck bolted across the meadow, with Ken finishing him off with one more shot.

"We had no idea what we had yet. When we walked up on him, we were shocked. We had never seen anything like it, or even heard about deer like that," recalls Ken. After marveling at the size and number of points on the giant buck, the two loaded him into the backseat of the Blaser. "Perry sat on

the spare tire and held that rack in his lap for five or six miles to make sure we didn't break any points off." After arriving at the house they wrapped the rack in a sleeping bag and drove to the check station in Ainsworth. "When the guy at the check station saw it, he told me I needed to go to the newspaper office. They took my picture on the end of the tailgate. There were lots of pictures and telephone calls because no one in that country had seen a non-typical mule deer like that."

The Ken Hollopeter buck definitely has a lot of horn. The buck's 159⅝-inch gross typical frame is not particularly large for a deer of this caliber, although it is very symmetrical, netting 156⅖ inches. However, the buck has seventeen abnormal points, eight on the right and nine on the left, totaling an amazing 71⅜ inches. With a final score of 227⅝ inches, it currently ranks as the thirteenth-largest firearm non-typical in the Nebraska records book, and the largest from Cherry County.

"For me, it's never about killing deer, it's always been the quality of the hunt," shares Ken. Eventually opening his own outfitting business, Niobrara Wilderness Outfitters, which he operates with his son, Tyler, and other family members, his goal is to give others a quality hunting experience. "I've only shot four deer in probably the last twenty years. I just enjoy taking my grandkids and others hunting."

His records book buck now hangs on the wall of the Purina feed store on the edge of Valentine. "Some people don't even notice it, but when a hunter walks in, they recognize right away what a special buck it is," shares Ken.

Notes

3. NEXT GENERATION

1. U.S. Fish and Wildlife Service, "National Survey—Overview," May 14, 2019, https://wsfrprograms.fws.gov/subpages/nationalsurvey/national_survey.htm.

4. PLATTE RIVER GIANT

1. Charles E. Rankin, "Bill Nye, Frontier Humorist," WyoHistory.org, March 14, 2016, https://www.wyohistory.org/encyclopedia/bill-nye-frontier-humorist.

8. FATHER AND SON

1. General Policies of the Boone and Crockett Club's Records Committee, https://www.boone-crockett.org/bgRecords/records_policies.asp?area=bgRecords, last updated 2009.

2. Joe Duggan, "Huge Buck May Not Make the Record Book," Billingsgazette.com, March 14, 2001, https://billingsgazette.com/news/features/outdoors/huge-buck-may-not-make-the-record-book/article_03062934-dc53-5367-a1db-d3ba71f4bf4e.html.

9. TRIFECTA

1. Adams County Convention and Visitors Bureau, "Site of WWII Naval Ammunition Depot" brochure, Visithastingsnebraska.com, https://www.visithastingsnebraska.com/assets/site/web/documents/Final%20NAD%20Brochure.pdf, accessed July 1, 2019.

11. PERFECT EIGHT

1. John T. Woloszyn, Gregory M. Uitvlugt, and Maurice E. Castle, "Management of Civilian Gunshot Fractures of the Extremities," *Clinical Orthopaedics and Related Research* 22 (1988): 247–51.

19. RECORDS ARE MADE TO BE BROKEN

1. RubLine, "292-Inch Nontypical Bagged in Nebraska," D+DH (Deer and Deer Hunting), April 26, 2011, https://www.deeranddeerhunting.com/articles/big -bucks/whitetail-deer-antlers/292-inch-nontypical-bagged-in-nebraska.
2. Joe Duggan, "Deer Hunters Abuzz about Possible Record Buck," *Lincoln Journal Star*, November 19, 2009, https://journalstar.com/news/state-and-regional /nebraska/deer-hunters-abuzz-about-possible-record-buck/article_7598f1a0 -d4a5-11de-babb-001cc4c03286.html.

22. 2 COUNTY

1. Nebraska Department of Motor Vehicles, "History of Nebraska Passenger Vehicle License Plates," https://dmv.nebraska.gov/dvr/history-license-plates, accessed October 21, 2018.

26. DOUBLE DROP TINE

1. History Nebraska, "Nebraska Historical Marker Program," https://history .nebraska.gov/visit/nebraska-historical-marker-program, accessed March 12, 2019; Cadrien Livingston, "First Nebraska Windbreak Gone Forever," Odyssey, May 17, 2017, https://www.theodysseyonline.com/nebraska-windbreak.

27. PUBLIC LAND

1. Tom Keith, "Scientific Sleuthing," *Nebraskaland* 64, no. 10 (December 1986): 38–41.

29. SPANKY

1. James Hilton Greenville II obituary, https://www.legacy.com/obituaries /HoustonChronicle/obituary.aspx?page=lifestory&pid=16892007, accessed December 12, 2018.

39. FIRST BULL

1. Kent A. Fricke et al., "Historic and Recent Distribution of Elk in Nebraska," *Great Plains Research* 19 (Fall 2008): 189–204.

2. Center for Digital Research in the Humanities, "Journals of the Lewis & Clark Expedition," https://lewisandclarkjournals.unl.edu/, accessed March 2, 2019.

40. PINE RIDGE

1. BHVisitor, "Paha Sapa—The Black Hills," https://blackhillsvisitor.com/learn /paha-sapa-the-black-hills/, accessed May 1, 2019.

43. DROUGHT AND FIRE

1. John W. Powell, *Report on the Lands of the Arid Region of the United States: With a More Detailed Account of the Lands of Utah*, with maps, 2nd ed. (Washington: Government Printing Office, 1879).

50. SYMMETRY

1. Boone and Crockett Club, "History of the Records Program," https://www .boone-crockett.org/bgRecords/records_history.asp?area=bgRecords, accessed January 12, 2019.
2. Boone and Crockett Club, "History of the Records Program," https://www .boone-crockett.org/bgRecords/records_history.asp?area=bgRecords, accessed January 12, 2019.

51. DEER HUNTING COMES TO FRONTIER COUNTY

1. John H. Wampole and Edson Fichter, "Management of Native Deer in Nebraska," *Wildlife Management Notes*, Game, Forestation, and Parks Commission, March 1949.

52. FORGOTTEN

1. Jon Farrar, "Deer Hunting in Nebraska," *Nebraskaland* 79, no. 10 (December 2001): 36–45.

63. WORKING CATTLE

1. Nebraska Beef Council, "Nebraska: The Beef State," https://www.nebeef.org /raising-beef/state-national-facts, accessed June 2, 2019.

64. NEBRASKA'S OLDEST TROPHY

1. United States Department of Agriculture, Nebraska National Forests and Grasslands, "History and Culture," https://www.fs.usda.gov/main/nebraska /learning/history-culture, accessed May 15, 2019.

2. Jon Farrar, "Deer Hunting in Nebraska," *Nebraskaland* 79, no. 10 (December 2001): 36–45.

3. Levi L. Mohler et al., "Mule Deer in Nebraska National Forest," *Journal of Wildlife Management* 15, no. 2 (April 1951): 129–57.

4. Jon Farrar, "Cropping the Halsey Herd," *Nebraskaland* 60, no. 16 (November 1982): 32–33, 45–46.

5. Farrar, "Cropping the Halsey Herd," 45.

6. Farrar, "Cropping the Halsey Herd," 32.

7. Levi Mohler, "Deer Hunting in Nebraska," *Outdoor Nebraska* 23, no. 4 (Spring 1946): 4–7.

65. BETTER LATE THAN NEVER

1. Joe Duggan, "Buck Fever," *Lincoln Journal Star*, November 25, 2006, https://journalstar.com/lifestyles/recreation/buck-fever/article_c16fed87-b7bd-59a6-a7e5-91603a293dd5.html.

2. Duggan, "Buck Fever."

Index

Page numbers in italics refer to illustrations.

Adams, Frosty: with buck, *38*; hunting by, 36–39
Adams, Jay, 36
Adams, Jodi, 38
Adams, Rex, *38*; hunting by, 36–39
Adams Bottles and Bows, 36
Adkins, Jeremy, 156
Ahern, AJ: with buck, *120*; hunting by, 116–21
Ainsworth NE, 318, 320
Ak-Sar-Ben Aquarium, 85
Allen, Jon: with buck, *78*; hunting by, 76–79
Allen, Leonard, 76
Alliance NE, 190, 275
Anderson, Chuck, 213, 214; with bull, *197*; hunting by, 194–97; record by, 197
Antelope County, hunting in, 3–5
antler collectors, 137–42

archery season, 32, 40, 41, 74, 98, 103, 115, 272
arrows, xvi, 31, 52, 79, 90, 91, 93, 101; Bear Razorhead, 112; blunt-tipped, 238; carbon, 179; Easton, 230; Muzzy 3 blade broadhead, 179; wooden, 7
Ashby NE, 170, 171
Ash Creek, 217
Astro Hall, 138
Austin, Del, 16; with buck, *113*; buck of, 74, 84, 103, 115; hunting by, 105–15; record by, 10, 115; scoresheet of, *114*

Babel, Charles "Chas," 138, 141, 142
Babel Island, 141
Badlands, xvi, xvii, 227
Baker, Gilbert, 191
B&C. *See* Boone and Crockett Club

Banner County, 171, 250; hunting in, 179–84, 194–97

Bass Pro Shops, 87, 206

Beaver Creek, 36

Benson, Jeff, 113

Bessey, Charles E., 302

Bessey Ranger District, 302, 305

Bhrun, Dan, 134

Bicknell, James, 52

Big Blue River, 62, 123

Big Elkhorn River, 185

Big Game Awards, 48, 59, 206

Big Game Trophy Records Program, 292–93

Black Hills, 190, 231

Blaine County, 207; hunting in, 30–35

blinds, 31, 36, 37, 70, 107, 111, 144, 145, 171, 175, 176, 217, 270, 273

BNSF Railway Company, 100

Boliver, Cody, *151*

Boliver, Dan: with buck, *151*; buck of, *150*; hunting by, 148–51

Boone and Crockett Club (B&C), xvi, 20, 28, 39, 274, 287, 306; measuring system by, 241; medals and certificates by, 48; records, 19, 48, 50, 51, 54, 59, 73, 83, 87, 116, 117, 121, 124, 130, 138, 139, 140–41, 142, 146, 162, 206, 212, 241, 256, 292; rule book, 38; scoring system by, 241, 242, 248

Bordeaux Creek, 186, 187

Bordeaux elk unit, 156, 164, 175, 208, 213

Bowhunter (magazine), 94

bowhunting, 7, 8, 36–39, 40, 41, 43, 76, 88, 95–98, 108, 174, 264, 266–67, 271, 272

bows, 36, 95, 98, 266; Bear recurve, 96; Bear Whitetail bow, 100; Bowtech Diamond, 279; compound, 7; Damon Howatt recurve, 237; Horton crossbow, 97; Mathews Q2, 266–67;

Mathews bow, 176, 230; Oneida recurve, 112; Pearson recurve, 7, 8, 10

Brashears, Hezzy, 159

Brashears, Zach, 159, 160

Broadwater RV Park, 180, 184

Broken Bow NE, 256, 257, 288, 289

Buchtel, M. R., 240

Buckley Creek, 22, 24, 25

Buffalo County, hunting in, 6–10

bullets, 12, 24, 26, 120–21, 128, 149, 169; Nosler, 53, 204, 210

Cabela's, 129, 195, 212, 213, 215, 222, 234, 278, 307, 309; arrows from, 179; display at, 307

Cambridge Lake, 294

Carnegie Museum, 59

Carpenter, Justin, 195

Casey's, 155

CCC. *See* Civilian Conservation Corps

Chadron NE, 164, 175, 187, 208, 209, 213, 276

Chadron State College, 212, 231, 313–14

Chadron State Park, 231

Chapin, Warren: with elk, *188*; hunting by, 185–89; scoresheet of, *189*

Chapin, Wauneta, 186, 187, 188

Charles E. Bessey Nursery, 302

Chase County, 274; hunting in, 261–64

Cherry County, 298; hunting in, 51–55, 310–12, 318–21

Cheyenne Tablelands, 167

Chicago and Northwestern Railroad, 231

Chimney Rock, 167, 171

Civilian Conservation Corps (CCC), 127, 304

Clark, William, 186

Clay County, hunting in, 40–44

Coffey, Glen, 155–56, *157*

Coffey, Russell: with buck, *157*; hunting by, 155–57

Columbus NE, 80, 97
Conservation Reserve Program (CRP), 159
Correll, Carter, 181
Correll, Doug: with bull, *183*; hunting by, 179–84
Correll, Marlene, 180, 181, 184
Correll Refrigeration Inc., 179
Courthouse Rock, 171
Cowan, Sam, 38, 39
Cozad NE, 186, 208, 216, 217
Crawford NE, 208, 236, 238, 279, 314
Creston Fertilizer, 61
crossbows, xii, 21, 95, 96, 97, 98
Cumwood, Bob, 311
Custer County, 207, 298; hunting in, 255–57, 288–91
Custer County Chief, 256

Dakota County, hunting in, 56–60
Dalrymple, Phil, 195
Davis, Dave: with buck, *290*; hunting by, 288–91
Davis, Ladonna, 291
Dawes County, 190, 250; hunting in, 163–65, 185–89, 207–11, 212–15, 216–19, 231–35, 236–40, 275–78
Dawson, Al: hunting by, 106, 108–9, 110, 111–12, 113
Dawson, Velma, 109
Dawson County, 207; hunting in, 26–29
Dawson NE, 69, 72
Deadwood Trail, 186
Deans, Rick, 191
DeBolt, Barbara Anne Tuller, 293, 294, 297
Devaney, Bob, 56
Dickerson, Michael: with buck, *228*; hunting by, xvi, 227–28, 230; record by, xvi, 240; scoresheet of, *229*
Dismal River, 30, 31, 32, 249, 303
Dismal River Forest Reserve, 302

DLJM Collection, 73, 74
Double Down, *120*; hunting, 117, 118, 119
Double T bar, 303
Dout, Clarence H.: buck of, *250*; hunting by, 249–51
Dout, Leona Pullen, 249
Duggan, Joe, 306
Dundy County, hunting in, 265–69
Dunning NE, 30, 304
Dwyer, Leo N.: buck of, 287, *307*; hunting by, 306–7, 309; scoresheet of, *308*

Easterwood, Jim, 69, 70
Easterwood, Joshua, 70, 71
Easterwood, Peggy: with buck, *71*; hunting by, xv–xvi, 69–72
Elk Creek, 185
Elkhorn Prairie, 185
Elkhorn River, 135, 185
Elk Lake, 185

Fahrenholz, Keith: buck of, *57*; hunting by, 56–57, 59–60; scoresheet of, *58*
Fairbury Journal-News, 281
Fairfield Flats, 310
Farm & Ranch Museum, 181
Farrar, Jon, 303
Federal Firearms License, 27
Field & Stream, 125
field dressing, 18, 54, 63, 90, 147, 160, 179, 240, 257, 281, 286
Fort Calhoun, 141
Fort Hamilton, 246
Foster, Dana: with bull, *224*; hunting by, 220–24
Foster, Trevor, 220, 221, 222, 223, 224
Foster's Taxidermy, 220
Frontier County, 99, 208; hunting in, 241–45, 246–48

Gage County, hunting in, 36–39, 88–94

Game, Forestation, and Parks Commission, 246, 302, 303, 304

Game Trophy Records Program, 292

Gangplank, 167

Garden County, 186; hunting in, 220–24

Garden County Wildlife Refuge, 221

Genoa NE, 80, 83

Gerber, Brad, 195, 196

Gering NE, 179, 187

Ghost, *157*; hunting, 156–57

Gilbert Baker Wildlife Management Area, 191

Gilsdorf, Ryan, 163, 164–65

Gipson, Jacob: with buck, *146*; hunting by, 144–47

Gipson, Julie, 144

Glenn, Bill: with buck, *281, 282*; hunting by, 279–82

Glenn, Mary, 282

Glenn, Wayne, 279, 280

Goliath, *146*; hunting, 144–47

Great Plains, 127, 185

Greenville, James "Spanky": antler collection of, 137–42

Grevson, Audrey, 134

Grevson, Brenda, 134

Grevson, Denise, 134

Grevson, Jack: buck of, *135*; hunting by, 134–36

Grevson, Julie, 134

Grevson, Tim, 134, 135–36, *135*

Grey, Prentiss M., 241

Gsell, Brad, 20

The Gun Cabinet, 319

guns: 7 mm Remington Magnum, 66, 165, 311; .22-250, 46, 47; .25-06 rifle, 26; .30-06, 12, 22, 301, 304; .30-30, 3, 46; .30-40 Krags, 304; .45-70 rifle, 250; .50 caliber Thompson Center, 314; .250-3000 Savage, 16, 17, 18; .270, 289, 291; .270 Ruger, 233; .270 Weatherby Magnum, 84; .300 Remington Ultra Magnum, 195, 213; .300 Weatherby Magnum, 191–92; .300 Winchester Magnum, 53, 160, 162, 168, 169, 210; .300 Winchester Short Magnum, 156; .308, 57; .308 Sako, 253; .410, 279, 280; BB, 46, 96; Browning, 157; Browning 7 mm Mag semiautomatic, 244; Browning .30-06, 37, 123, 159; Browning .243, xvi, 70; Marlin lever-action .30-30, 148, 149, *150*; Mauser, 257; Mauser .30-06, 277; Remington, 218; Remington 7 mm-08, 202, 203; Remington .30-06, 120, 133; Remington .280, 135; Remington 700, 12, 62, 145, 210, 222; Remington 721, 280; Remington 788, 47; Savage Model 99, 57; Weatherby, 46; Winchester .30-30, 128; Winchester Model 70, 319; Winchester Model 88, 81, 247, 248, 306. *See also* handguns

Hall County, 137; hunting in, 105–15

Halsey, Ray, 134

Halsey NE, 250, 302–3, 305

Hamik, Dave, 40–44

Hamik, James: with bucks, *43*; hunting by, 40–44

Hamik, Joseph, 40

handguns: .44 Magnum, 27, 29; .357 Magnum, 26, 27, 28, 29; S&W Model 28, 26, 27

Hansmire, Greg, *23*; hunting by, 22, 24–25

Hansmire, Mike, 23, 25; hunting by, 22, 24–25

Harrison NE, 191, 249

Harsch, Phil, 134

Harvey, Betty, 3, 4, 5
Harvey, John: with buck, 4; hunting by, 3–5; record by, 3, 4, 5, 19
Hasenauer, Alex, 162
Hastings NE, 3, 108, 112, 131, 132
Haveman, Dave, 84
Hayes County, 99, 307; hunting in, 283–87
Helmer, Hannah: with bull, 203, 204; hunting by, xv, 201–4, 206; scoresheet of, 205
Hitchcock County, hunting in, 11–14, 131–33
Hogeland, Charles, 307; with buck, 286; hunting by, 283–87; record for, 278, 287
Holcomb Drug store, 289
Hollopeter, Arlene, 319
Hollopeter, Ken: with buck, 320; hunting by, 318–21
Hollopeter, Tyler, 321
Honey Hole, 223
Houdersheldt, Christine, 61
Houdersheldt, Keith "Skip": with buck, 62; hunting by, 61–63
Houdersheldt, Marilyn Euse, 61
Houdersheldt, Roger, 61
Houdersheldt, Roy, 61, 63
Houdini, xvi, 228, 228
Hrabak's grocery store, 135, 135
hunting: big-game, 40; demise of, 11; diversity/quality of, xvi; stories, xvi, xvii

Idol, Dick, 20
Isham Ranch, 213

Jail Rock, 167, 171
James, Curtis: with bull, 164; hunting by, 163–65
Jarrett, Kenny, 53

Jefferson County, hunting in, 22–25, 279–82
Johanson, Lee, 201, 202, 203, 204
Johnson, Barry, 184, 287; buck of, 263; hunting by, 261–64
Johnson, Candice "Candy," 255, 256, 257
Johnson, Dave, 255, 256, 257
Johnson, Eric: with buck, 268; hunting by, 265–67, 269
Johnson's Taxidermy, 261, 287
Joint Expeditionary Base–Little Creek, 171
Jonas Brothers Taxidermy, 290
Jordan, James, 20

Keane, Kerry, 179, 180, 181, 182, 183, 183, 184
Kearney Locker, 7
Kearney NE, 6, 7, 99, 174
Kechely, Katherine, 116, 118
Kechely, Kurt, 116, 117, 118, 121
Kechely, Rachel: with buck, 119; buck of, 125; hunting by, 116–21
Keith County, hunting in, 298–301
Keya Paha County, 137, 139, 140, 207; hunting in, 252–54
Kimberling, Jenna, 264
Klawitter, Becky, 129
Klawitter, Bill, 138; with buck, 128; buck of, 129; hunting by, 127–30
Klawitter, Peg, 128
Klein, Brent: with buck, 243, 244; hunting by, 241–45
Klein, Jeff, 242, 243
Klein, Raymond, 242
Klein, Steve, 242, 243
Knox County, 137
Koch, Anita, 246
Koch, Eugene, 247, 248
Koch, Henry: with buck, 247; hunting by, 246–48
Koch, Kirk, 248

Korth, Tony, 85
Kreycik, David, 311
Kreycik, Jack S.: buck of, *311*; hunting by, 310–12

Lake, Alyssa, 299
Lake, Matthew: with buck, *300*; hunting by, 298–301
Lake McConaughy, 221
Lakota Sioux, 190
Lancaster County, hunting in, 76–79, 99–104, 144–47
Lauby, Heather, 28, 29
Lauby, Jerry: with buck, *29*; hunting by, 26–29
Lewis and Clark expedition, 185
Lexington NE, 26, 27
Liles, Ray, 138, *139*
Lincoln County, 137, 138, 139; hunting in, 64–66, 158–62
Lincoln Haymarket, 125
Lincoln Journal Star, 306
Lincoln NE, 5, 44, 72, 77, 80, 99, 119, 126, 255, 256, 291, 292
Loup River, 30, 80, 257
Luben, Mike, 48
Luehrs, Nate, 179, 181, 183, 184
Luehrs, Roger, 179, 180, 183, 184
Lutt, Dustin, 272, 274
Lutt, Mike: with buck, *273*; hunting by, 270–74

Madison County, 138; hunting in, 127–30
Malander, Bob: with buck, *97*; hunting by, 95–98
Marlboro pasture, 213
Marlowe, Charley, 107, 109, 112
Marsteller, Bob: with bull, *192*; hunting by, 190–93

Marsteller, Ryan, 191, *192*
McClintock, Gavin, 274
McCook NE, xvii, 99, 103, 241, 242, 246, 247, 294
Meadow Bull, 221, *224*
Mecouch, Brian, 313, 314, 315, 316, *316*
Mecouch, Paul: with buck, *316*; hunting by, 313–17
Medicine Creek Reservoir, 247
Memorial Stadium, xvi
Merrihew, Deb, 171
Merrihew, KC: with bull, *173*; hunting by, 170–73
Metcalf Wildlife Management Area, 164
Meyer, Justin, 96
Meyer, Kellen: with buck, *124*; buck of, *125*; hunting by, 122–26
Meyers, Frank: with bull, *218*; hunting by, 216–19
Miller, Howard, 311
Milligan NE, 255, 256
Misegadis, Justin: with bull, *214*; hunting by, 212–15
Missouri River, 56, 207, 208
Mitchell's Guns and Ammo, 184
Mohler, Levi, 305
Moody, Jeff: with buck, *102*; hunting by, 99–104
Moreland, Ken, 52
Mormon Trail, 186
Morrill County, 250; hunting in, 166–69, 170–73
Morse Bluff, 16, 20
Mortensen, Allen, 158, 159
Mortensen, Dillon: with buck, *160*; hunting by, 158–60, 162; scoresheet of, *161*
Mortensen, Ivan, 158, 159
Mortensen, Quenton, 159

Mosel, Jason: with bull, *168*; hunting by, 166–69
Mosel, Lindsey, 166
Muirhead, Rob, 175
Mule Deer Conservation Area, 265
Musgrave, Tom, 295
muzzleloaders, 33, 35, 40, 266, 314, 315, 316

Naithan, Duane, 134
Nance County, hunting in, 80–83, 95–98
Nason, George, 287
Navy Ammunition Depot, 41
Nebraska Big Game Trophy Records, 130, 242, 256
Nebraska Bowhunters Association, 272
Nebraska Brand Committee, 276
Nebraska counties, map of, *xviii–xix*
Nebraska Game and Parks Commission (NGPC), 5, 81, 131, 132, 133, 186, 188, 221, 249, 266, 272, 287, 292, 305: awards from, 37; Mule Deer Conservation Area and, 265; permits by, 250
Nebraskaland, 304
Nebraska National Forest, 250, 305
Nebraska Public Power, 117
Nemaha County, 186, 302
Newcomb, Kyle: with buck, *13*; hunting by, 11–12, 14
Newkirk's, 180
Newton, Russell, 65
NGPC. *See* Nebraska Game and Parks Commission
Niobrara River, 52, 190, 249, 253, 318
Niobrara Wilderness Outfitters, 321
Norfolk NE, 59, 127, 128, 134
North American Big Game, 1971 Edition (B&C), 59
North American Whitetail (magazine), 20
North Platte elk unit, 195
North Platte NE, 30, 99, 158, 261, 287
North Platte River, 15, 167, 193, 221, 223, 261, 299
Nugent, Ted, 287
Nye, Edgar Wilson "Bill," 15

Oates, Dave: with buck, *133*; hunting by, 131–33
O'Brien, Wesley, 74, 81; with buck, *85*; hunting by, 84–87; scoresheet of, 86
Ogallala aquifer, 194
Ogallala NE, 179, 220, 221
O'Hare, Steve, 132
Ohrt, Albert, 138, 141–42; with buck, *143*
Ol' Mossy Horns, 16, 84, 87, 103, *113*, *125*, 126; hunting, 108–13, 115
Olsen's, 182, 183
Omaha NE, 80, 99, 148, 150, 166
Omaha Public Power District, 148, 164
Orchard NE, 3, 127, 166
Oregon Trail, 186
Orscheln store, 12
Osbourne, Tom, 288
Outdoor Nebraska, 305
Owens, Jordan: with buck, *124*; buck of, *125*; hunting by, 122–26

Paha Sapa, 190
P&Y. *See* Pope and Young Club
Pavelka, Bernard "Bernie," 255, 256; with buck, 257
Pavelka, Deena, 256
Pavelka, James: with buck, *257*; hunting by, 255–57
Pavelka, Lillian, 255, 256
Pawnee City NE, 148, 150
Pawnee County, hunting in, 73–75, 148–51
Pawnee Prairie Wildlife Management Area, 148, 149

Pearson, Dale, 81
permits, 96, 132, 186, 250, 283, 289, 303
Peters, Kirk, 230; with buck, 239; hunting by, 236–40
Petrzilka, Dillon, 46, 47
Petrzilka, Donna, 46, 47, 48
Petrzilka, Kevin: with buck, 47; hunting by, 45–48, 50; scoresheet of, 49
Petrzilka, Mason, 46
Pinchot, Gifford, 302
Pine Ridge, 156, 164, 175, 186, 190, 201, 208, 209, 213, 217, 231, 232, 239, 249, 276, 279, 303, 314
Pine Ridge Reservation, 190
Plainview Roller Rink, 3
Platte River, xvii, 7, 10, 15, 16, 20, 26, 27, 66, 105, 111, 141, 158, 186
Pleasant Ridge, 190
poaching, 131, 303
Polk County, hunting in, 61–63
Pope and Young Club (P&Y), xvi, 242, 271, 274; records, 42, 110, 113, 115
Powell, John Wesley, 207, 208
Prairie States Forestry Project, 127
Purdum Cemetery, 305
Purina feed store, 321

Rawhide Buttes, 190
Red Rock, 96
Red Willow County, 99; hunting in, 292–97
Report on the Lands of the Arid Region of the United States (Powell), 207
Republican River, 13, 100, 104, 132
Rhodus, Brandon, 84
Richardson County, xv, 186; hunting in, 69–72, 84–87, 116–21
Rickard, John: with bull, 177; hunting by, 174–78

Rock Lake National Wildlife Refuge, 195
Rock's Bar, 83
Rogers, Will, 15
Roosevelt, Franklin D., 127, 128
Roosevelt, Theodore, 302

Sandhills, xvii, 16, 30, 33, 55, 170, 201, 253, 261, 298, 299, 310, 311, 318
Sandstrom, Terry: with buck, 232; buck of, 233; hunting by, 231–34; record by, 245, 251; scoresheet of, 235
Saunders County, hunting in, 15–21, 45–50
Scheels store, 119, 125, 126
Schleusener, John, 127
Scotts Bluff, 167, 171
Scotts Bluff County, 171, 250
Scottsbluff NE, 166, 179, 181, 186, 208
Serres, Heath, 250, 251
Seward County, 45; hunting in, 122–26
Seward NE, 123, 124, 125, 131, 133
Shaul, Perry, 318, 319
Shelby Flying Service, 61
Shelton NE, 105, 106
Sheridan County, 164, 190; hunting in, 155–57, 174–78
Simmons, Justin, 156
Sioux County, xv, xvi, xvii; hunting in, 190–93, 201–6, 227–30, 249–51, 270–74, 313–17
Skorzewski, James: with buck, 254; hunting by, 252–54
Snyder, Emily, 83
Snyder, Robert "Rick": buck of, 82; hunting by, 80–81, 83; record by, 83, 87
Snyder, Scott, 81, 83
South Platte, 15, 167, 299
Spider, 119; hunting, 117, 118, 119, 120
stands, 65, 90, 97, 145
Stanton County, hunting in, 134–36

Stanton NE, 135, 136
St. Charles, Glenn, 113
Steinmeyer, Jerry, 77, 79
Stohs, Adam, 91; with buck, 93; hunting by, 88–94
Stohs, Gary, 93; with buck, 91; hunting by, 88–94
Stohs, Kyle, 94
Strong, Adam "Alabama," 209, 210
Stutheit, Randy, 130, 256
Sugar Loaf Mountain, 289
Sup, Gale, 126
Super Slam, 271
Swanson Reservoir State Recreation Area, 132

The Table, 232
taxidermy, 129, 212, 220, 234, 250–51, 261, 262
Tenneco Automotive, 216
Thedford NE, 303, 304
Thomas, Dan, 105, 106, 108, 109–10
Thomas County, 249; hunting in, 302–5
Thompson, Bob, 27
Thomsen, Art, 287, 297; with buck, 277; hunting by, 275–78
Transcontinental Railroad, 186
Trybus, Steve, 7, 8, 10
Tuller, Delman: with bucks, 293, 295; hunting by, 292–95, 297; scoresheet of, 296
Tuller, Miriam, 294
Tuller, Stephen, 294
Twain, Mark, 15
Twisted Pine Ranch, 52, 55

University of Nebraska, 302
University of Nebraska Medical Center, 166
unknown teenager: buck of, 74; hunting by, 73–74; scoresheet of, 75

U.S. Board of Geographic Names, 141, 185
U.S. Forest Service, 127, 302, 303
U.S. National Forest, 246, 250, 303, 305

Valentine National Wildlife Refuge, 310, 318
Valentine NE, 318, 319, 321
Virka, Ed, 16, 18
Virka, Vernon: with buck, 17, 19; hunting by, 15–20; record by, 18, 48; scoresheet of, 21
Vrbsky, Bob, 16; with buck, 8; hunting by, 6–8, 10; record by, 6, 7–8, 37; scoresheet of, 9

Walker, Roy, 81
Walmart, 148, 149
Washington County, 137
Weldon, Jim, 81
Westervelt, Mike "Pellet," 52, 53
Wheeler County, hunting in, 306–9
Wiese, Brad, 184
Wild, Joe, 213
Wildcat Hills, xvii, 167, 170, 171, 303
wildlife, 11, 30, 37, 117, 159, 186, 208, 220; protecting, 131
windbreaks, 32, 107, 127, 128
Wingard, Kevin, 128, 129, 130, 138
Wirz, Bob, 303, 305
Wirz, Marie Rodocker, 303
Wirz, R. A.: with buck, 304; hunting by, 302–5
Wirz Cash Store, 303
Wolfe, Carl, 132
Woloszyn, John T., 142; with buck, 54; hunting by, 51–55
Wonders of Wildlife National Museum & Aquarium, 206
Wood, Kevin: with buck, 65; hunting by, 64–66
Wood Lake NE, 310, 318

Wood River, 141
Works Progress Administration, 127
Wullbrandt, Roy, 138, 139; buck of, *140*
Wymore NE, 36, 163

Yada, Casey: with bull, *211*; hunting by, 207–11
Yada, Lauren, 208

Yellowstone National Park, 50
Y.O. Ranch, 5

Zimmerman, Alvin, 138, 140, 141; with buck, *141*
Zutavern, Adam: with buck, *34*; hunting by, 30–35; record by, 32, 35; trophy room of, *33*